Spatial Planning and Governance

Understanding UK Planning

Mark Tewdwr-Jones

First published 2012 by
PALGRAVE MACMILLAN

Palgrave Macmillan in the UK is an imprint of Macmillan Publishers Limited, registered in England, company number 785998, of Houndmills, Basingstoke, Hampshire RG21 6XS.

Palgrave Macmillan in the US is a division of St Martin's Press LLC, 175 Fifth Avenue, New York, NY 10010.

Palgrave Macmillan is the global academic imprint of the above companies and has companies and representatives throughout the world.

Palgrave® and Macmillan® are registered trademarks in the United States, the United Kingdom, Europe and other countries.

ISBN 978-0-230-29218-5 hardback

ISBN 978-0-230-29219-2   ISBN 978-1-137-01663-8 (eBook)
DOI 10.1007/978-1-137-01663-8

This book is printed on paper suitable for recycling and made from fully managed and sustained forest sources. Logging, pulping and manufacturing processes are expected to conform to the environmental regulations of the country of origin.

A catalogue record for this book is available from the British Library.

A catalog record for this book is available from the Library of Congress.

10 9 8 7 6 5 4 3 2 1
21 20 19 18 17 16 15 14 13 12

planning • environment • cities

Series Editors: Yvonne Rydin and Andrew Thornley

The context in which planning operates has changed dramatically in recent years. Economic processes have become increasingly globalized and economic fortunes have fluctuated. Administrations in various countries have not only changed, but old ideologies have been swept away and new ones have tentatively emerged. A new environmental agenda has prioritized the goal of sustainable development, requiring continued action at international, national and local levels.

Cities are today faced with new pressures for economic competiveness, greater accountability and participation, improved quality of life for citizens, and global environmental responsibilities. These pressures are often contradictory and create difficult dilemmas for policy-makers, especially in the context of fiscal austerity.

In these changing circumstances, planners, from many backgrounds, in many different organizations, have come to re-evaluate their work. They have to engage with actors in government, the private sector and non-governmental organization in discussions over the role of planning in relation to the environment and cities. The intention of the *Planning, Environment, Cities* series is to explore the changing nature of planning and contribute to the debate about its future.

This series is primarily aimed at students and practitioners of planning and such related professions as estate management, housing and architecture as well as those in politics, public and social administration, geography and urban studies. It comprises both general texts and books designed to make a more particular contribution, in both cases characterized by: an international approach; extensive use of case studies; and emphasis on contemporary relevance and the application of theory to advance planning practice.

planning • environment • cities

Series Editors: Yvonne Rydin and Andrew Thornley

Planning, Environment, Cities
Series Standing Order
ISBN 978-0-333-71703-5 hardback
ISBN 978-0-333-69346-9 paperback
(*outside North America only*)

You can receive future titles in this series as they are published. To place a
standing order please contact your bookseller or, in the case of difficulty,
write to us at the address below with your name and address, the title of
the series and the ISBN quoted above.

Customer Services Department, Macmillan Distribution Ltd
Houndmills, Basingstoke, Hampshire RG21 6XS, England

Contents

List of Figures, Tables and Boxes

Figures

Tables

Boxes

Preface

Why write a book about planning? The short answer, in truth, is that there isn't a book I feel happy to recommend to planning students and those new to the profession to enable them to understand the central concerns of planning in the UK. Such a book would need to answer certain key questions: What is planning? How has it changed? How can it help meet the challenges of how we use the land and manage our expectations for the future? How does politics shape (or misshape) planning objectives and outcomes, and why? What is *spatial* planning, and how does it differ from traditional and historically forged forms of planning? These are the questions that I set out to answer in this book.

My starting point is what I think planning is, and here's a spoiler. My view of spatial planning is that it is, first, a useful frame within which to examine the politics of land use and the governance of change; second, a means by which to engender discussion about places, their future and territorial change; and, finally, an activity that has to be understood in the context of political economy, relational geography, and institutional restructuring. All of this means that I don't see planning as a solution *in itself*; it is better thought of as a means, a lens, through which we understand and manage spatial processes and change.

This understanding of planning is a flexible one, and one that means that the precise activities of planners will change in different times and places. In this book I present the reader with the resulting *dilemma* that is spatial planning. You are asked to look at all the issues the politicians want planning to address or manage, and to consider whether any – or all – of it is spatial planning. Labels come and go, as do paradigmatic fads, but certain features relating to land and spatial change remain ever-present. Our planning mechanisms change regularly, as do legal procedures, government structures, and rights and responsibilities, but bigger societal and structural trends are more difficult to change. This book encourages the reader to think about change, to identify the constants, the uncertainties and the vulnerabilities, and to understand the pervasive role of politics in planning.

The book is divided into ten chapters. Chapter 1 looks at the role of planning in the UK in the last hundred years and demonstrates the degree to which planning has ebbed and flowed between different, sometimes almost contradictory, expectations placed on it by different governments. It covers the history of modern planning right up to the present day, and introduces the reader to some of the key ideas and

labels that planning is associated with. Chapter 2 looks at the challenges
of the twenty-first century that have spatial and land consequences, and
makes the case for the role of planning in responding to these. Chapter
3 goes into a more critical examination of planning since the late 1990s
by assessing the rise of *spatial* planning and the influence of the European Union (EU) on domestic planning systems. It argues that three
elements gave rise to a new form of planning in the UK after 1999: the
rescaling of politics and policy between different levels of government;
growing Europeanization debates; and the need for integration between
disparate agencies and policies. These three parameters set a context for
Chapters 4–7. Chapter 4 considers the Europeanization debate, the
origins of European spatial planning, and the impact these have had on
the UK and its planning processes. Chapter 5 looks at the role of the UK
government and how it manages planning agendas originating from the
EU while setting guidelines for what planning should achieve sub-
nationally and locally. Chapter 6 examines regionalism, particularly in
England, and the form of regional governance that was attempted in the
1990s and 2000s. Chapter 7 looks at a scale below the region, the city-
region, and examines how the largest cities of the country have governed
their spaces. Chapter 8 discusses the local scale and the onset of localism
and its implications for planning. Chapters 9 and 10 conclude the book
by providing an examination of changing governance processes and
legacies, together with a discussion on the form and spirit of spatial
planning in the twenty-first century.

Acknowledgements

A number of individuals deserve special mention since my interaction and discussions with them have probably contributed in no small measure to some of the ideas developed in the book over the last ten years. These are Phil Allmendinger, Samer Bagaeen, Marco Bianconi, Ben Clifford, Allan Cochrane, Dave Counsell, Gordon Dabinett, Simin Davoudi, Marcial Echenique, Geraint Ellis, Nick Gallent, John Goddard, Peter Hall, Jim Harris, Graham Haughton, Mike Hayes, Patsy Healey, Louise Heathwaite, Greg Lloyd, Alex Lord, Philip Lowe, Gordon MacLeod, Tim Marshall, Patrick McVeigh, Janice Morphet, Joe Morris, João Mourato, David Newbery, Nicola O'Connor, Susan Owens, Nick Phelps, Chris Poulton, Mike Raco, Leonora Rozee, Alister Scott, Mark Scott, Ken Sterrett, Carys Swanwick, John Tomaney, Geoff Vigar, Cecilia Wong, and Guoyan Zhou. Those formal meetings, lunches and dinners (often animated), quick coffees, post-work drinks, speaker platform-sharing and reactions to research presentations all influenced or found their way to contributing, somehow, to this work.

I would like to thank all the students on my UCL postgraduate modules The Planning System (2001–4) and Spatial Planning (2005–11) who had to endure me testing many thoughts, ramblings, asides and brainwaves as we discussed the meaning and development of planning in often robust and thorough ways.

Some of the writings have appeared in earlier forms elsewhere and I am grateful to the editors of *European Planning Studies*, to the publishers Taylor & Francis, and to my co-authors Nick Gallent and Janice Morphet for permission to use our article in *European Planning Studies* 18(2): 239–57 (2010) as the foundation of Chapter 3, and to João Mourato for his collaboration in earlier versions of the material that forms the basis of sections of Chapter 4.

I would also like to thank the excellent staff at Palgrave Macmillan, particularly Stephen Wenham and Helen Caunce, for commissioning the book but also keeping pressure on me to ensure delivery, and to Juanita Bullough for her excellent copyediting work. I am also grateful to Yvonne Rydin and Andy Thornley, the editors of the book series, for their insightful comments. All errors, misinterpretations and blunders, if any remain, are of course my own.

Copyright Acknowledgements

The author and publishers would like to thank Taylor & Francis for permission to use material from the article 'An Anatomy of Spatial Planning', by Mark Tewdwr-Jones, Nick Gallent and Janice Morphet, in *European Planning Studies*, 18:2 (February 2010), pp. 239–57 in Chapter 3 of this book.

Figures 2.4, 3.1, 3.3, 6.1, 6.2 and 7.3 contain public sector information licensed under the Open Government Licence v1.0.

List of Acronyms

AMA   Association of Metropolitan Authorities
AONB   Area of Outstanding Natural Beauty
BAA   British Airports Authority
BANANA   build absolutely nothing anywhere near anything/anyone
BBNP   Brecon Beacons National Park
BERR   Department for Business, Enterprise and Regulatory Reform
CBI   Confederation of British Industry
CEC   Commission of the European Communities
CEMAT   Council of Europe Conferences of Ministers
CLG   Department for Communities and Local Government
CPRE   Campaign for the Protection of Rural England
CTRL   Channel Tunnel Rail Link
DCLG   Department for Communities and Local Government
DEFRA   Department for Environment, Food and Rural Affairs
DETR   Department of the Environment, Transport and the Regions
DfT   Department for Transport
DoE   Department of the Environment
DRDNI   Department for Regional Development Northern Ireland
DTI   Department of Trade and Industry
DTLR   Department of Transport, Local Government and the Regions
EC   European Community
ESDP   European Spatial Development Perspective
ESPON   European Spatial Planning Observatory Network
ESRC   Economic and Social Research Council
EU   European Union
FDI   Foreign Direct Investment
GDP   gross domestic product
GHG   greenhouse gas
GIS   Geographical Information Systems
GLA   Greater London Authority
GLC   Greater London Council
GLUD   Generalised Land Use Database
GOR   Government Office for the Region
GW   gigawatt
IdeA   Improvement and Development Agency
IPA   investment promotion agency
IPC   Infrastructure Planning Commission

LAA	Local Area Agreement
LDD	Local Development Document
LDF	Local Development Framework
LEP	Local Enterprise Partnership
LGA	Local Government Association
LSP	Local Strategic Partnership
MIPU	Major Infrastructure Planning Unit
MNE	multinational enterprise
NAW	National Assembly for Wales
NIMBY	'not in my back yard'
NPPF	National Planning Policy Framework
NPPG	National Planning Policy Guideline
OECD	Office of Economic Cooperation and Development
ODPM	Office of the Deputy Prime Minister
ONS	Office for National Statistics
PFR	planning for real
PIA	Planning Inspectorate Agency
PPG	Planning Policy Guidance Note
PPS	Planning Policy Statement
PPW	Planning Policy Wales
RDA	Regional Development Agency
RPG	Regional Planning Guidance Note
RSS	Regional Spatial Strategy
RTPI	Royal Town Planning Institute
SCS	Sustainable Community Strategy
SPD	Single Programming Document
SRB	Single Regeneration Budget
TCPA	Town and Country Planning Association
TEC	Training and Enterprise Council
TEN-T	Trans-European (Transport) Network
TIA	Territorial Impact Assessment
UDC	Urban Development Corporation
WAG	Welsh Assembly Government
WDA	Welsh Development Agency
WO	Welsh Office

Chapter 1

The Search for Spatial Planning

Why plan?

The starting point for any book devoted to spatial planning has to be the land. Planning as an activity that attempts to manage spatial change would not exist in any meaningful way if it was not for contention over the future use and development of the land. Spatial planning is owned by everyone who has a vested interest in the land and what happens to it. I am not only talking here about those fortunate enough to own land – and it is one of fortune, literally, in many cases – but those charged with coordinating and managing different uses of the land. Changes to land affect everyone, from the individual to the neighbourhood, to city-dwellers and those who live in a rural area. You do not have to be a landowner to be affected by land-use changes. In fact, just 10 per cent of the population own 90 per cent of the UK's land (Government Office for Science 2010), a startling fact in the twenty-first century when we assume that equality, rights of access, wealth redistribution and opportunity for all have come centre stage politically. Landownership in the UK remains a difficult calculation owing to the fragmented form of data available from differing sources (Home 2009). The UK is also one of the most crowded countries in Europe, with the south-east of England being the most densely populated region, and the south-west the least populated. According to the UK government departments for Environment, Fisheries and Rural Affairs (DEFRA) and of Communities and Local Government (CLG), the extent of urban land in the UK is put at 14.4 per cent of the total land mass. The land does not only enable us to have homes, shops, hospitals, schools, universities, leisure facilities, transport and places of work. It provides us with water, food, energy, recreation, biodiversity and minerals, and is a site for our waste. Whether it is urban or rural in character, or in an upland or lowland location, at the coast or in a valley, land supplies us with our essential needs and quality of life. But the amount of land we have is just about constant. There is a finite supply of it, and that means as our appetite for more essential services increases and quality of life improves, so does the problem of how to manage how our land is used, in different areas over different time periods.

Would you like to have more houses? That's desirable, but it may have to be at the expense of some fields, or woodland, or the grounds of a hospital. Fewer houses mean greater demand, which means higher house prices. Committed to protecting a species' habitat? Very admirable, but that may mean we cannot use that land for any other purpose or we are unable to extract minerals from the ground. Fewer minerals mean that the price of building materials increases or lead to a problem in constructing buildings elsewhere. Do you want to protect old buildings because of their architectural style or historical use? Fine, but that may mean we protect places and make them more expensive for owners or developers to change them into new uses. Places that start to become uneconomic to changes to modern-day requirements could lead to dereliction and decay. And so the problems tend to stack up with land use. How we use the land is rarely a discrete or isolated decision. Deciding on one course of action will probably create further problems in the long run.

When is the best time to make a crucial decision about how best to use land? Building more homes may solve a housing shortage and lead to a lowering of house prices for people looking to get their feet on the rungs of the residential property-market ladder. Demand for housing will be met, but the land used for the development could be close to a river and may be susceptible to flooding if sea levels rise at some uncertain time in the future. Should we take a decision not to build there now, because of a potential threat that may or may not happen in, perhaps, 50 years' time? Or do we press on and allow the development to go ahead, and keep our fingers crossed that a worst-case scenario will not happen? At the other end of the spectrum, more homes will require more drinking water. Where should we allocate a new reservoir to supply the water to the new homes? Water supplies to a town may be appropriate in relation to current usage, but higher usage or the need to supply water to hundreds of more homes will place pressure on that existing water supply. Should we therefore allocate some land somewhere on the edge of the town now for a possible future reservoir in the next 20 to 30 years? And what are the opportunity costs today of taking long-term outlooks?

All these contentions are difficult in themselves but are an aside from the even more tricky issue – in whose interest should we decide on the use of land? The landowner, the developer, the community, the county or even the nation? Building a new airport or railway line may be beneficial to the nation, economically or socially, but it is bound to have a detrimental effect to those individuals who live near the site of the project. What may seem like an improvement for all becomes a nightmare for some, a hotly contested battle between quality of life, rights, responsibilities, freedom and, of course, land. It is little wonder that land, and land use, tend to occupy politicians' time continuously, since they are often called on to mediate between competing uses of the land locally or become embroiled in local versus national land-use disputes. And the politicians themselves seldom like to get involved. After all, they know only too well that for every winner there is a loser in the great land-use debate. What we are talking about here, of course, is scarcity, urban–rural differences and political choice. The issue of competing uses of the land tends to exercise both landowners and non-landowners alike in the UK. There appears to be a strong sense of attachment and identity to the land and to landscape, especially in rural areas, with an almost inherent anti-development perspective (Swanwick 2009). This is not new: literary writers have bemoaned the loss of the countryside to building for well over a hundred years and have viewed the urban as threatening the rural and rural ways of life (Tewdwr-Jones 2011b).

And there is another dimension to managing land-use change and utilizing spatial planning that adds to the complexity: the territorial governing frame within which planning resides. Planning is an activity of both the public and private sectors, but the different aspects of planning occur at different geographical scales and are formulated, regulated or implemented by different governance actors. Planning has long been an activity of the state in its various guises and has been determined, for most of its life, by statute, by the conferment of legal rights and responsibilities, and by their application to defined, geographically fixed administrative or government units. This has been regarded as necessary to pin down space, to fix it, in order to understand change, but also to deal with it politically to enable intervention, a process long contested by geographers (Massey 2005). What started as an activity of the central state in the early twentieth century soon became an activity of multiple levels of government, shared between the central and local state. As the decades passed, so the governing framework of planning changed and adapted to suit political ideological preferences. The UK has flirted with these changing scales and forms of government (and therefore with planning) throughout the last hundred years, as different governments prioritized different scales of policy- and decision-making. Since 1945, Britain, like nation-states across the globe, has relied upon and sometimes experimented with centralization, localization, regionalization, city-regionalization, decentralization, Europeanization, spatialization and devolution, not in a linear way but often moving forward then doubling back to previous older forms and recognizable governing structures, depending on global economic changes, which political party was in office and the needs of nations and regions (Brenner 2004). Since the late 1990s the UK has also, to a greater extent, relied upon the market and the neo-liberalization of public services and government, with the private sector playing as dominant a role in planning as the public sector. So what sometimes might be regarded as a national planning issue or a matter of national and regional significance has been clouded by successive reforms of the governing framework around planning, with historical roles of some governing scales retaining a legacy for newly emerging forms of planning tiers. The provision of new infrastructure, such as high-speed railway lines, energy installations or airport expansion, are what might be regarded as classic examples of politically contentious land-use developments that often unleash conflicts between and across different scales of government. Since the late 1990s this picture has been clouded by the emergence of governance, alongside government, initiating policies and taking decisions on issues and in areas that perhaps had been formally occupied in some way by the state. The architecture of planning has become enmeshed in both a governmental and governance web of relations. The following questions are then often posed: Can spatial change be fixed in such a standard way? Who has the responsibility for dealing with planning matters? Who benefits from policies and decisions? Which tier of government has legitimacy to act, if at all, in matters of resolving land-use expectations and conflicts (cf. Castells 1996)?

If all these difficulties and potential uncertainties with how the land is used are causing you to think twice about land, then I am starting to engage you in the theme of this book. Spatial planning has been the process charged with managing these contentions and short- to medium-term perspectives legislatively and professionally for well over a hundred years in the UK. It has been known by many different titles over the decades, ranging from town planning, town and country planning and civic design, to urban and regional planning and urban development management. But it essentially comes down to the same thing: a professional and highly politically contentious process attempting to make sense of the drivers of change that have land-use effects geographically, against short-, medium- and long-term trends, within changing and changeable governing structures, and individual and collective expectations that have social, economic and environmental implications that change over time. It is partly a regulatory process, partly a strategic assessment, partly a governing framework, and partly a futures project. Managing land use through the planning process comprises several different forms. The regulatory element – the statutory requirement for individuals to apply for planning permission before developing land – is the part of the planning system most members of the public have come into contact with, either as an applicant or as a consultee on development proposals. But the planning system is actually much more than this, but is often working behind the scenes, strategically away from direct public gaze.

The best analogy I can use to describe what it is like to manage the land and land-use conflicts is spinning plates – a stage entertainer attempting constantly to spin a dozen or so plates as they balance precariously on top of poles. All the plates represent a different demand on the land, going at different speeds, and require you to keep an eye on each one and on the whole ensemble simultaneously. It is not so much a trick, but rather a skill.

Professional planners have been present in the UK since 1914. They are a separate professional family to architects, surveyors and civil engineers, but are closely related. The architect produces individual building designs that are intended as symbolic and iconic statements in the built environment. The surveyor measures and values the land's physical features and assets, and works on property development projects. The civil engineer designs, constructs and maintains the physical environment, including bridges, roads and other forms of infrastructure. The planner, by contrast, attempts to order and regulate the land to avoid land-use conflicts and considers alternative courses of action and short- and long-term needs in an integrated and strategic way. Frequently, land-use proposals and contentions on the ground give rise to conflicts between the different professional families who work for different clients, constituencies and interests. This is only to be expected when the future of the land and the uses to which it is put are managed by four different sets of professionals who work in both the public and private sectors. And given that land is a finite resource, and development opportunities are often limited, the rewards and penalties of different choices of action on the land and its future can be contested in a politically and economically charged atmosphere (Owens and Cowell 2010). It remains a curiosity, perhaps, to consider that landownership does not guarantee any development rights in itself. Land acquisition is a separate process to the requirement to gain planning approval prior to building. Conversely, landownership is not a prerequisite to gain planning permission; anyone can apply for planning permission for any land, even land not in the applicant's ownership. The degree to which approved schemes can be implemented will then be determined through land purchasing (see Reade 1987).

There is no greater illustration of the costs associated with this contention than to reveal the value of land itself. Land value is determined by its location and physical manifestation and by its proximity to other locations, infrastructure and services (Bateman 2009). But the value of land changes dramatically if it has been designated for development purposes or has planning permission for a particular type of land use. As a general rule of thumb, land with planning permission is worth eight to ten times the value of land for sale without planning. One-third of the value of land with a residential housing use derives from the land itself. Agricultural land may not be valued so highly, but if it is close to existing built-up areas its value may incorporate a 'hope value' – a sum over and above the basic agricultural value – in the belief that that land may be developed at some point in the future.

For decades, planning has been an enduring feature of most nations' attempts to manage land-use changes, the growth and contraction of cities, the renewal of infrastructure and the use of resources, balanced against individual and societal preferences within a democratic arena. But it has not been a static entity. It has been subject to change itself, from diverse socioeconomic and environmental conditions, the responsibilities of governments and decision makers, and from division of rights between the state, individuals and businesses. Planning is therefore an extremely fluid activity, prone to changing political preferences and structural factors, as well as the desire for physical improvement and renewal. So before we consider the nature of spatial planning, the pressures put upon it, and the form it takes territorially and governmentally, it is worth briefly stepping back in history to look at how we have planned previously and the reasons why planning has always been subject to so much alteration. We may then begin to understand the logic of planning reform, but also the expectations politically for planning to deliver quite diverse and seemingly contradictory results.

A little light history

Planning has been around for much longer than a hundred years, of course. Different civilizations over time have employed forms of ordering land in the most efficient way to solve land-use conflicts (Cherry 1974). Remains of urban planning designs in settlements have been discovered from Mesopotamian, Harrapan and Egyptian times. The Greeks and Romans also employed city planning to create street patterns of central services, rectilinear grids, squares and vistas, often close to watercourses, not only in celebration of civic pride but also for strategic and militaristic purposes. Medieval and Baroque street patterns in some towns in Europe followed these early forms, with wide avenues, grand projects and designs, and often walled for defence purposes. Some were built – the consequence of feudal lords' and landowners' desires for order and rationality in the city form – but others floundered. Christopher Wren's grand plans for a rebuilt city of London after the Great Fire of 1666 did not materialize, and the city was reconstructed using the medieval street pattern that had existed before the fire. Urban planning was also employed in the redesigns of towns and cities in Britain and Ireland in Georgian times after about 1720; Bath, Brighton, Dublin, Edinburgh, Limerick and London being some of the most well known. All these periods and styles represent a type of urban planning, but it is really from the early Victorian era that we begin to see the form of urban planning we have today start to take hold. The distinction is that in the UK from the nineteenth century, planning was no longer a militaristic exercise of the state or a vanity project of the aristocracy. Rather, planning became a broader, social and political project intended to deal with the externalities of rapid urbanization and ameliorate the social and health consequences of population overcrowding and poor public health (Hall and Tewdwr-Jones 2011). It was only in 1909 in Britain that planning was enshrined in an Act of Parliament for the first time.

The transformation of planning from a proactive defence and design activity of the elite into a reactive strategic and coordinating activity of the state was not straightforward. It came about as a reaction to the conditions of the nineteenth century not only in the UK, but also in other parts of Western Europe, the United States and Canada, Japan and Australia, countries that were all experiencing the fall-out of the industrial revolution and rapid economic growth. Urbanization and the rise of the industrial city transformed previously small towns into large metropolises, as migrants and population increases outgrew the physical extent of housing and services, creating dense living conditions, a lack of sanitation and sunlight, disease and squalor, and poorly and rapidly constructed hovels. The industrial city was largely controlled by businesses and the elite. Parliament cared little about the welfare of the citizens and working classes and was reluctant to intervene; Parliament in the UK in the shape of the House of Lords and the House of Commons comprised representatives of the elite themselves – aristocrats, landowners and successful industrialists. The Great Reform Act of 1832 had extended voting rights to adult males who rented propertied land of a certain value, but this still only represented about one in seven UK males. The 1867 Reform Act franchised all males within urban areas to vote and this was extended to rural areas in 1884. It was only in the Representation of the People Act of 1918 that women were allowed to vote for the first time, but full equality was only reached between men and women in 1928.

The point here is that the nineteenth century witnessed one of the most rapid changes to the landscape and the rise of urban populations who produced the output of Britain's industrial dominance. They lived, for the most part, in dire social circumstances and remained disenfranchised from the democratic process. What little opportunity existed for these urban dwellers to change the circumstances within which they lived rested entirely on the philanthropy and goodwill of those selective industrialists and landowners who were prepared to fund and design better-quality housing and services for their use. For most of the nineteenth century, there was no free health service, no welfare system, no subsidized housing, and no free education for children. Property development was the preserve of the landowner alone and there was no

Figure 1.1 *Westminster, where planning legislation for England is debated.*

Planning as an activity is only legitimized by the will of the state, and Parliament defines the development rights and sets parameters for possible land-use changes.

control over the wider affects of urban change or urban sprawl into the countryside, or the long-term effects of incremental change. The urban conditions were reported widely throughout the 1800s, by journalists and authors, social reformers and parliamentary campaigners, but it took the best part of 70 years for government to respond officially and recognize the need for intervention (Hall 2007). The barriers were as much ideological as moralistic. A Victorian belief that the poor should help themselves and a view that the working classes were the undeserving poor, coupled with the lack of political representation in Parliament and a voice in the democratic process, held back possible action. The land question also figured prominently in debates – the idea that the state should interfere in the liberty of individuals and their property interests on behalf of the wider citizenry was bound to agitate some. The question concerning the right for public regulation over private land interests has been an ongoing theme for well over a century. The public–private land-rights issue has served to continually question ideologically the role of a state planning process and land-use regulatory system for wider strategic purposes other than to maximize the economic potential of land and development opportunity.

The twentieth-century experience of planning

At a casual glance, it is easy to believe that 'the planning system' has been a relatively static and enduring force in the British polity and land debate for a hundred years. But the reality is far more complex, political, contradictory and less linear. It underwent change in each decade of the twentieth century and all the signs are that planning reform will be a continual process through the twenty-first century as well (see Box 1.1). Principles of planning in the early 1900s remain present in the early 2010s but they have been checked, or rather compromised, by addit-ional expectations politically in the intervening years. Those expec-tations relate directly to changing social, economic and environmental conditions and are only to be expected in a process that by its very nature is supposed to be about managing change and strategically thinking about the future of land use. But the changes are also a symptom of political preference, both ideological and institutional, concerning responsibilities allocated between and across different tiers of govern-ment, of individual politicians, and the needs of the market (Rydin 2003). We can identify different phases in the maturing of planning from the early 1900s to the present day; even within particular phases there are differences in substance, style and political commitment towards planning.

It is useful as a context to a book devoted to the changing ebbs and flows of planning to delve into a little history. This is not meant to be a rigorous historical assessment of planning or an examination of the effects and impacts of planning on land use; that can be found elsewhere. For a review of the history of twentieth-century planning, see Ashworth (1954), Keeble (1961) Bruton (1974), Thornley (1991) and Hall and Tewdwr-Jones (2011). Rather, it provides an overview of some of the changing features and phases of planning through an intensely political age. The intention here is to show how planning over time is not a linear process, but one subject to lurches between agendas and ideas, political ideologies and reactions. These shifts in planning have been discussed elsewhere in the planning literature, notably by Tewdwr-Jones and Allmendinger (2006) and Allmendinger and Haughton (2007). As time marches on, some ideas brought to bear in planning are new, whereas others have sometimes been tried before but are recycled in new times, in new guises and given new labels. The fact that 'the planning system' has endured through all these changes is a remarkable testament to its resilience. An alternative perspective is that maybe planning is a useful political tool because it has become sufficiently adaptable to take on new agendas and preferences. Let us start a hundred years ago.

By the first decade of the twentieth century, the first elements of an organized process of urban planning for improved housing and conditions had commenced. The Garden City movement and the City Beautiful movement were born, promoting a new design ethic that combined the best features of towns and countryside while promoting socially mixed communities. This was the first phase of the modern planning process in the UK. In the spirit of Greek, Roman and Georgian town planning, Garden Cities were idealized forms of the future city, with wide boulevards, tree-lined avenues, plenty of public gardens and allotments, clustered central services such as shops and amenities, and a range of housing types, ameliorating in the process those high densities, overcrowding, lack of sunlight and public open space associated with the nineteenth-century industrial city.

Some garden cities were constructed, in places like Letchworth and Welwyn, but progress was slow, notwithstanding the degree to which it is difficult for a single landowner to plan and construct a town from scratch. But even the provision of improved housing in existing towns and cities proved to be problematic. Prime Minister David Lloyd George's promise in 1918 to provide 'homes fit for heroes', hailing those soldiers fortunate enough to have returned from the trenches in World War I, was followed by a decade of divergent political views on the need for public housing, subsidized rents and finding sufficient amount of land for new house building, but new housing was developed rapidly in the interwar years. Modern planning's intention was to transform the old urban centres where the worst social problems existed. But the implementation of planning occurred as the outward expansion of urban areas through suburban growth. It was much easier to build outside the built-up area, where landownership posed less of a problem and where land was relatively cheap. Railway companies and speculative builders saw an opportunity to buy cheap land for housing adjacent to roads and railways, and so suburban housing was developed along major transport corridors into and out of cities, a practice that became known as 'ribbon development'.

From the 1920s and 1930s, planning's reputation started to become tarnished, for generating urban sprawl and for despoiling the countryside. In reality, these processes were less the result of state planning and more market and landowner opportunism. As the reaction against urban encroachment on the countryside intensified in these decades, championed by countryside groups, so parliament reacted by changing planning laws to protect amenity and agricultural land. The proactive role for planning – creating better places for people in the interests of better housing, improved public health and community well-being – was shadowed by a reactive role intended to control, stop or regulate development interests in the name of rural protection (Hall et al. 1973). Planning from the 1930s therefore had to undertake both roles simultaneously. In the UK, town planning became 'town and country planning', two processes with somewhat different rationales rolled into one legislative commitment: town planning was proactive and development-focused; country planning was reactive and amenity-focused. This was the second phase of the planning system in the UK. Although no one realized it at the time, from this moment forward, planning would become a compromised system, caught politically between several different dualisms – urban and rural, individual and collective, economic and social, developer and community. It remains at the centre of this quagmire today and is often blamed by one side or the other for its failings to deliver particular expectations. Different governments in the period since have attempted, via policy commitments, to reposition planning closer to one side or the other (pro growth/pro environment), depending on political ideology and need, but it remains the mediator in the land struggle, despite accusations from opponents that it is the force to blame.

At the same time in the 1930s, there emerged another significant issue to warrant a different type of planning: the regional dimension. As the older industrial areas of the UK declined with the loss of manufacturing in shipbuilding, iron, coal and steel, a distinctive pattern emerged between the north and the south of the country. Towns and cities in the north – in Wales, the North-West, Yorkshire, the North-East and Strathclyde – saw significant unemployment levels as whole communities, reliant on one or two types of industry, were affected by industrial closures caused by economic depression. In some places, such as in the shipbuilding area of Jarrow, male unemployment reached 80 per cent in the early 1930s. In Bishop Auckland, Country Durham, and in parts of Glamorganshire, unemployment was over 50 per cent. In the south, by contrast, those areas of the country that had not been reliant on iron, coal, steel and shipbuilding were relatively unscathed. Instead, through the 1930s, these areas saw economic growth in new industries, such as car assembly and white goods, that were not geographically fixed and were located around parts of the south-east of England, close to their targeted markets. Regional policy sought to parachute in measures to assist in employment creation in the north of the UK, but such measures were limited in their success and, even today, there remain distinctive differences in the economic profile of the North compared to the South, fuelling demands for more regional policy and planning.

World War II had a devastating effect on the UK's economy but also on the land – its housing stock, manufacturing base, railways and ports had all been targeted and bombed. And so we enter a third period of modern planning in the post-1945 era. The necessity to reconstruct the country was bound up in the socialist objective of the Attlee government to create a welfare state. In 1947, a new planning system was created allowing individual towns and cities to draw up development plans for their area (the forward-looking, proactive principle) and allowing local authorities to control new developments in the wider interest (the regulatory, reactive principle). The 1947 system founded the origins of the modern twentieth-century planning system and aspects of it remain in place today. Two issues are worth considering. The first was that to avoid central control and authoritarianism – the central state telling everyone what should be done – the new planning system delegated the functions down to the local level via local authorities. This would ensure, it was thought, democratic accountability from place to place with elected councillors held to account for their policies, plans and decisions as they affected land, land use and land development in each locality. Local authorities would draw up their own plans but each would require central government ministerial approval.

The second element of the 1947 system was the nationalization of land development rights. The Act did not legislate for the complete nationalization of land from private ownership, although that may have been a political ideological intention at some later point. Instead, the system meant that although individuals would still be allowed to own or purchase land privately, their right to develop or use the land to their own wish would be subject to state authorization. This was seen as essential in order to comprehensively redevelop and rebuild cities after wartime devastation, and bring land parcels under single landownership through the compulsory purchase of property. But it was also in keeping with a state ideology that believed in central government leading the cause of planning and the duty of the state. It was therefore one of the biggest single acts ever seen against individual liberties and the right to do with one's property whatever one wished. After this time, you could acquire property and land, but you then had to apply for planning permission to develop or change the use of the land according to your desires. That request for permission would be enacted through individual planning applications, submitted to the local authority and assessed by professional planning officers, with recommendations of refusal or approval made to the determining body – the planning committee – comprising elected councillors. The criteria for assessment would be based on a range of planning considerations alone, as defined by government and the courts, and also the contents of the locally prepared development plan. A betterment tax was levied on individual projects at 80 per cent of the uplift in land values caused by planning permission. This was controversial in itself, but the argument put forward was that it was the state that was allowing the increase in land prices by approving development schemes; individual landowners and developers would benefit in the long run, so why should not the state benefit from the resultant development value too? Once again, this was an issue that split political opinion, with the two main political parties at opposite ends of the argument.

The legacy of the 1947 Act system is still prevalent today in principle but not substance. Development plans still exist, albeit considerably amended in scope and form. Development control, now rechristened as development management, remains the process by which individuals and developers submit planning applications, and planning committees of local authorities take decisions of support or rejection. Compulsory purchase powers are still employed, less so for town-centre redevelopment or large housing schemes as they had been in the 1950 and 1960s, but mainly for infrastructure projects. The only part of the 1947 system that has been abandoned as a principle concerns the betterment tax. Over a 35-year period, betterment taxation was introduced and abandoned statutorily on no less than six occasions, depending on which political party was in office – Labour introducing and Conservative abolishing. Betterment taxation was a mixed blessing, but it did generate significant income for the state, and one may claim that it was used in part to fund public projects in the 1950s and 1960s such as the development of the motorway network, the construction of the energy and telecommunications infrastructure, airport expansion and the extension of higher education and the universities. And yet, despite the absence of the betterment tax today, the funding of infrastructure, public services and non-market goods remains a contentious issue and an ongoing financial drain on the state (Barker 2006).

The postwar period for planning and architecture created a legacy for British towns and cities that is still discussed today. From an aesthetic perspective, the postwar period is associated with the modern movement. The comprehensive redevelopment of city centres, the construction of urban motorways, the onset of high-rise tower blocks and large public housing estates, and the widespread use of exposed concrete as a building material created futuristic urban landscapes very much in the spirit of the age but which were often unpopular stylistically with the public and heritage groups. Many historic street patterns and Georgian, Victorian and Edwardian buildings were bulldozed in this period to accommodate the rise of the car, to provide new office blocks, and to provide – finally – the mass housing that was required to accommodate people. Significantly, this occurred through compulsory purchase powers by local authorities at a time when there was little in the way of formal public consultation in the planning process (that came later, after 1969).

Planners, architects, developers and politicians learned the hard way of the degree to which the public were willing to accept the depth and extent of change in the urban arena in such a short pace of time. The new developments may have been forward-looking and reflected a turning away from the industrial city of the nineteenth century and its legacy. The new city landscapes reflected the rise in personal car-ownership, the age of the computer and telecommunications, and a rational planning solution to competing demands on urban space. The planning solutions may also have been a valiant attempt to contain urban areas by increasing densities and protecting the surrounding countryside. Faced with increasing demand for land and space, cities have two options – to build up, or build out. The dominant planning paradigm of the age after 1947 but continuing all the way into the 1980s was to encourage urban containment in order to protect the surrounding rural areas from the potential of urban sprawl. It was yet again a good illustration of one of those planning dualisms – if you want to protect the countryside, you need to redevelop and create space within the city. In doing so, the planning system suppresses land and housing demand and adds to property scarcity (Cheshire 2008). Neither of the options is perfect – one group or another will lobby vociferously against the policy. History and time will judge the effectiveness of the paradigm, as history always does in relation to planning intervention.

Economists and some developers have long resented the 1947 urban containment policy. In areas of high demand for development land and where property prices are high, the economic answer of course is to meet that demand by allowing more development by, if necessary, releasing land at the urban fringe or by deregulating the green belt. That, too, is an answer, and the implication would be to allow more green fields to be built upon and to extend the footprint of the city beyond its current artificial borders. But the 1947 paradigm has created an enduring legacy for not only local planning, but also in the minds of the public and politicians. All politicians shy away from altering green-belt policy since it has become something of a political sacred cow; any discussion of deregulation produces a ferocious backlash from rural areas, countryside supporters and environmentalists. And so aspects of the 1947 urban containment policy remain evident in 2012 – green belts have become a national institution – but are probably past their sell-by date in terms of their original intention. The problem today is that solutions to the land problem require different types of policies and different types of intervention. Rather than replace the green-belt policy with an alternative to reflect current and possible future circumstances (possibly by a green-grid policy, or by selective land release, for housing and infrastructure essential for city services, for example), new policies over the decades have been merely bolted on to the green-belt policy since politicians fear the implications of changing green-belt policy per se. This, then, is a further phase and reincarnation of modern planning: a national requirement for local planners to encompass divergent issues and policies into the same decision-making process as a way to be seen to be recognizing them. In the case of urban containment, politicians really do think they can have their cake and eat it; and from a policy perspective nationally, perhaps they can. But the effects on the ground locally are somewhat different. Hard choices between development and protection still have to be made, that involve meeting national interest and reflecting local need. Planning still has to deliver practically and so the 1947 policy is placed as a consideration in development decisions alongside all the other more recent and current policy considerations locally and regionally. This is not simply local planners and local planning committees trying to avoid taking a deliberative decision; they are told by central government that they must be seen to be taking into account all relevant considerations.

For some members of the public, for some developers, and for some economists, this fact is often lost on their sensibilities. Perhaps they see the 1947 policy still in place and cannot understand why it still exists against all the evidence that planning is not delivering the essential development required in areas of high demand for land and housing. The reality is, however, that other considerations and other policies are also on the table for negotiation, including local democracy and other national policy considerations, but most of these are not necessarily on public display. They are the other relevant considerations, strategic and long-term in nature, that go in to making a planning decision. And of course they reflect the dualisms that exist in the real political world, choices of encouraging economic growth while ensuring the protection of the countryside, of meeting national interests while delivering local needs, of supporting businesses and developers while attempting to enhance local democracy and public input into planning decision taking (Murdoch and Lowe 2003). Planning is called upon by the state, legally and politically, to address all of these issues simultaneously and, naturally enough, in practice the world does not exist to deliver win–win solutions when land is finite, highly valued and sought after, and touches public nerves so prominently.

In the latter half of the twentieth century, significant increases in population, greater mobility, higher levels of car-ownership and economic growth gave the UK new prosperity. The number of cars on the roads increased from 2.25 million in 1951 to 8 million in 1964 (Starkie 1982), and homeownership rates doubled during the same period. The motorway network, planned and developed by a different government department to the ministry responsible for planning, created new conditions and contexts for development patterns that had localized effects and allowed people to live and work in different locations, thereby undermining some of the assumptions of strategic land-use planning. The expansion of airports, the increase in air travel and the demand for continental package holidays led to major patterns of new growth on the edge of towns and cities, not just for land for runways and terminal buildings, but also for airport services and logistics.

Other trends outside planning have also had significant planning and land-use implications. Two examples of these trends are worth

---

Box 1.1   The changing purpose of planning historically, 1900–80

The original purpose of planning, 1900–1920s
- Improved living conditions
- Higher environmental standards and improved health
- Improved housing standards and new housing development
- To balance high-density development with open space, "green lungs"
- The socialist objective of creating mixed communities
- To influence and control new development in the wider interest
- To end political differences over housing provision and provide subsidy for those in most need

The protectionist agenda emerges, 1920s–1930s
- Protection of the best landscapes, such as National Parks
- Protection of the coast against unsightly development
- Protection of the most historic buildings or those of architectural merit
- Control over advertisements
- Control over suburban housing development
- Emergence of regional policy to address North-South differentials

The postwar phase, 1940s–1970s
- Major infrastructure and rebuilding programme
- Necessity to rebuild houses and flats, industry, transportation links rapidly
- Protection of the Green Belt from 'the octopus' of urban growth
- Decentralization plans from inner cities to the edge of cities through a New Towns programme
- Increasing population and car-ownership create new spatial demands
- Development of the motorway network and urban motorways
- Slum-clearance programmes and comprehensive development
- Rise of council housing and high-rise flats
- Concern at the loss of heritage and historic and architecturally significant buildings, leading to heritage issues becoming a planning consideration
- Early identification of environmentalism
- Formal introduction of public consultation in the planning system
- Attempts to introduce national planning, regional planning and city-region authorities falter

---

mentioning. The motorway network enabled the development of articulated lorries, long-distance freight movements, and the transfer of goods and foodstuffs over considerable distances (McKinnon 2009). This, in turn, enabled the establishment of large superstores and hypermarkets at edge-of-town locations, threatening the urban containment policy. Just as supermarkets were able to move deliveries from central distribution depots to their stores across the country via the new road system, so consumers were able to purchase a much larger number of goods at each shop and use their cars to transfer their purchases between the superstore car parks and their homes. Planners first started to identify the implications of these changes in the 1980s – a possible long-term threat to the traditional high-street shopping environment as consumers changed their shopping habits to out-of-town locations, the rise of logistics and distribution services as a driver of land-use change, and an increase in car trips causing greater congestion on some routes and at interchanges and road junctions. Evidence highlighting these trends was provided to politicians and government at the time. But successive governments prioritized the growth of big-box retailing over other considerations, and to act in the national interest over local concerns, as they were entitled to do so politically.

The second example concerns Enterprise Zones. Enterprise Zones were first designated by the UK government in 1979 as a way of deregulating the local planning system to allow new employment-generating businesses to be carried out in locations free from normal planning controls and with low rates and taxation incentives for new business start-ups. The intention of the policy was to kick-start the economy at a time of recession and reduce the amount of unnecessary administrative burdens and costs to businesses. Evaluation of the policy by the government in 1987 indicated that between 1981 and 1986, over 2,800 firms had located to the Enterprise Zones and had employed 63,000 people (Thornley 1991). But by far the majority of the jobs created originated from non-zoned areas, i.e. the zones were successful in attracting development but at the expense of other areas, not as new business start-ups. According to the Work Foundation, 80 per cent of jobs came from other places, at the cost for the Zones of £23,000 per job.

Furthermore, the form of economic growth was not manufacturing, creative industries or business services that perhaps the government had been hoping for, but rather short-term in nature or out-of-town retailing developments. Box-goods shopping stores, such as hypermarkets and do-it-yourself outlets, flocked to the zones in the 1980s, enticed by cheap taxation and little planning control compared to that for towns. These projects, although objected to by local planning authorities in order to protect the vibrancy of high streets, still met the employment-generating requirements of central government's policies. These projects then caused problems for town centres commercially and the life of towns, that needed addressing eventually in the 1990s through a change in planning policy away from out-of-town stores in favour of town centres.

Planning changes since the 1980s have been just as marked (see Box 1.2). The 1980s was a low point for UK public-sector planning compared to previous decades. The government deregulated vast swathes of the planning system by either removing planning agencies, such as metropolitan counties that had been responsible for strategic planning, or by creating Enterprise Zones, simplified planning zones and Urban Development Corporations (UDCs). These reforms introduced a market orientation to planning, under a neo-liberal agenda, by prioritizing job creation and economic growth as dominant considerations over and above social and environmental concerns, but also shifting the power towards central government – and therefore national – interests over local interests. Enterprise Zones and UDCs were, in effect, nationally imposed territorial islands of enterprise standing outside local authority control, breaking the postwar link between planning and local authorities but also, in most areas, at the expense of direct democratic accountability. Planning survived the period and was strengthened to some extent as it became an activity of both the public sector and of private-sector consultancies. Market considerations now played a more prominent role in policy making and in decisions on individual planning applications. But the 1980s did change the pattern of land use in Britain, with more edge-of-town development, out-of-town shopping stores, housing estates in the countryside, and the demise of council housing with the end of state-housing construction and the introduction of the Right-to-Buy legislation. By the end of the decade, planning had undergone an immense change and entered another new phase of its history. Although local authorities' development plans and decision-making powers were returned in the following years, the effect of the policies from these years is still being felt.

Urban policy became private-sector property-led and so the role of local authorities in urban planning became less prominent and certainly less strategic. The focus was more on speedy responsiveness to market needs, site by site, with priority to commercial and recreational developments. That shift probably did mean that town and city centres regenerated more quickly and more successfully than perhaps would have been the case had they occurred through the planning system and statutory development plans. The only credit that public-sector planning could perhaps take from some of these concerns is its ability to coordinate and align the different actors necessary to a project's implementation. But the evidence is difficult to ascertain.

The environment became a matter of greater public concern from the early 1970s, as the signs of our industrial past made themselves evident, with polluted landscapes and watercourses, a concern about waste and emissions, the effect of development on the natural world, the dramatic impact of mining and quarrying, and a feeling that we had exploited the earth for far too long. Government policy on environmental issues began in the 1970s but there was a mismatch between environmental policy and the planning process. In fact, it took until the late 1980s for the UK planning system to start to embrace environmental considerations (McCormick 1991). This was partly because it was viewed as more desirable to establish a separate legislative system to deal with the environment and with environmental protection than reform the legislative planning process to address the environment in an integrated way alongside land-use and development matters. The result was that planning has had to take account of environmental issues as planning considerations in policy development and decision making, but alongside economic, social and other considerations.

With hindsight, it may have made more sense to take the environment and the earth as a starting point, to take account of the earth's limits to growth and change, and its ability to adapt and recover from past environmental intrusions, before thinking of land-use change and development and assessing potential environmental impacts. But this has never happened, although why this is the case is an interesting issue. Could it simply have been because legislatively it was too problematic to realize? Or was it because it would have meant that the dominant neo-liberal economic growth paradigm would have been replaced by an alternative agenda? Whatever the reasons, the result gave rise to the policy agenda of 'sustainable development'. Sustainability had been debated academically and in political circles for some time, but its imposition into the UK planning system was unique, suggesting – quite conveniently politically – that you could have the three tenets of sustainable development – economic growth, environmental protection and social inclusion – simultaneously through planning. As a policy commitment, this was both practical and desirable. But as with previous incarnations of the planning system, the effect was quite different on the ground when applied to various contentious land uses in competition for each other in specific locations (Owens and Cowell 2010). In some respects, the three elements of the sustainable development agenda tended to cancel each other out when it came to taking difficult decisions over particular development projects. There were forces pulling for and against each of the three issues in almost every single case. Much was sought after and promised in the sustainable development debate, but in the planning system it simply could not be delivered as things stood. As time passed, sustainable development morphed into policy as a sort of *uber*-planning agenda.

After 1997, aspects of the 1980s style of the non-planning and pro-development agenda continued but within a much more positive political stance towards the public sector, the role of local authorities, and sustainability. In fact, strategic long-term planning was reintroduced in the planning system by the government's commitment towards devolution to Scotland, Wales and Northern Ireland, and to London (Tewdwr-Jones 2002). Sub-national agendas of growth and contraction were covered through the designation of Sustainable Community Growth Areas in the south-east of England and through an equivalent in the north of England, 'the Northern Way'. As these territories embarked on introducing their new assemblies, so strategic planning – in the form of

---

Box 1.2   The changes in planning since 1980

- Urban planning achieved through private-sector property development
- Bypassing local authority development plans and decision making
- Introduction of public-sector planning-free areas through Enterprise Zones, Simplified Planning Zones and UDCs
- Job creation and economic development the principal policy agenda
- Development of out-of-town retailing and edge-of-centre business parks and housing
- End of council-house building and reliance on private residential development
- Planning agendas shaped by stronger central policies

The sustainable development phase, 1990s
- Refocus on balance of public-sector and private-sector interests in planning
- Planning to tackle economic growth, environmental protection and social inclusion
- Focus on town centres and urban regeneration
- Environmental protection and environmental considerations brought into planning
- Growing influence of the EU on some planning issues
- Heightened interest in community involvement in planning and alternative approaches to participation

Planning's renaissance, 2000s
- Commitments to spatial planning and sustainable development
- Implementation of stronger national decision making for infrastructure projects   →

'spatial planning' – began to be placed centrally in their activities. The government also attempted to introduce regional government in England and new institutions of planning emerged at this level, Regional Spatial Strategies (RSSs), to coordinate long-term trends and think about issues and land-use changes beyond smaller municipality borders. Planning bounced back from its 1980s low point into a more proactive and coordinating activity in the 2000s than previously. Local development plans were strengthened, new forms of national planning decision-making for major projects were introduced, sustainability appraisals of plans and policies became a central consideration, and professionally and politically planning appeared to embrace land, space and place contentions in a way not witnessed for decades. All of these proactive agendas for the planning process of the 2000s were placed, rightly or wrongly, under a 'spatial planning' label, partly to reflect a new spirit and age but partly to symbolize a change in direction for planning compared to the previous two decades. But while this new phase of planning was being intro-

$\rightarrow$

- New regional tier of planning introduced in England
- Devolution to Scotland, Wales, Northern Ireland and London allows start of distinct planning arrangements
- Sub-national planning models devised in the South and North in England, and eco-towns
- Faltering attempts to integrate planning, environment and transport issues
- Stronger local development planning introduced and attempts made to resolve planning and local government service and delivery arrangements
- Urban renaissance agenda and commitments to brownfield development
- Questioning of planning's role in enabling economic growth

Planning's fragmentation, 2010s
- Sustainable development defined politically as job creation
- Changed agendas for major national development projects
- Abandonment of regional tier of planning in England
- Planning systems and differentiation in Scotland and Wales increasing
- Abandonment of sub-national planning models but introduction of Local Enterprise Partnerships
- Reintroduction of Enterprise Zones and abandonment of brownfield development targets
- Local authorities retain development plan and integration powers
- Ideological commitment towards Localism, Big Society and collaborative planning
- Introduction of neighbourhood planning and neighbourhood forums to determine local planning matters
- Businesses allowed to prepare local neighbourhood plans

duced, it was being overshadowed by a second agenda within government that sought politically to extend the neo-liberal approach of deregulating planning further and prioritizing economic interests.

As this more proactive planning approach was rolled out across the UK's territories in the mid-2000s – with varied degrees of success, it has to be said – so further changes were on the horizon politically. After the 2010 general election and the establishment of the coalition government, a very different agenda for planning quickly emerged, reflecting the ideological shift between different governments and their policy preferences. In England, the regional level of planning RSSs – and other aspects of the institutional framework – were abolished, together with the newly introduced national decision-making structure for major development projects. The emphasis was now on 'localism', but this was not about simply removing the middle tier of planning between central government and local authorities and focusing attention on local development plans and local authority decision-making. The new agenda involved transferring some policy and decision-making powers away from the local authorities directly to local neighbourhoods in a democratic shift. New neighbourhood plans would be established with neighbourhood forums, increased use of referendums to determine projects, and the use of incentives and other fiscal instruments to enable proposals to be realized. This was hailed as a fundamental change to planning (Conservative Party 2010), yet another phase of planning's evolving journey, and one still being embarked upon.

As planners and elected local politicians started to weigh up the implications of the change, practically and academically, in 2011 the coalition announced further reforms as the localism changes were being debated in parliament, and these tended to focus less on local democracy and neighbourhoods and more on economic growth and job creation. With the UK still emerging slowly from recession after the global downturn in the late 2000s, so the government decided that a stimulus was required in the form of planning deregulation. Enterprise Zones returned to the national policy agenda after a 25-year gap and a policy 'presumption in favour of sustainable development' was announced within a new pro-economic growth National Planning Policy Framework (NPPF) where sustainable development was viewed as job creation and economic growth, a somewhat different interpretation than those of previous governments or even academic ideas about its definition. Businesses were given the powers to prepare their own local and neighbourhood plans for the first time (as opposed to local authorities and local people), a complete contrast to the 1947 planning system ethos of ensuring democratic accountability through representative planning decision-making. And finally, the government announced the establishment of Local Enterprise Partnerships in some areas of the country, covering amalgams of local authority areas but of a lesser size and powers than the regional structure they replaced. In Scotland, Wales and Northern Ireland, planning processes are being amended with a distinct separation of policies and agendas in those territories and a different ethos towards land-use planning to that in England.

The form of planning operating in England after 2012 and the key agendas for it to deal with (see Box 1.3) is a curious mix of the more participative alongside the more deregulatory but with varied forms and approaches, almost like a patchwork quilt, across the country. With two seemingly opposing concepts being implemented in planning, one favouring neighbourhoods, localism and the 'Big Society', the other being business-led and economic growth-oriented, it will be interesting to see how planning practices develop on the ground in distinct areas of the country, site by site, over the next 5–10 years. So long as government alters the institutional and legislative forms of the planning system continuously, there is a danger that the real issues that planning should

> **Box 1.3   Planning today**
>
> *The form of planning*
> - Regulated and framed by the state, central government and local government
> - Private landownership, but regulated publicly
> - Planners devise master plans and control development in the wider interest
> - Implemented by developers and private consultancies
> - Planning an activity of public and private sectors, working in partnership to design, develop and deliver tomorrow's places
> - Increasing powers of communities and neighbourhoods to shape local areas
>
> *Key agendas for planning to deal with*
> - Meeting national and sub-national needs against a global backdrop
> - Balancing local and community desires with wider concerns
> - Balancing environmental costs with economic gains
> - Ensuring transport infrastructure is tied to development phasing
> - Provision of strategic visioning, master planning and fast decision making
> - Mediating between conflicting users and allow more people a voice within the development process
> - Reconciling conflicts and disputes
> - Protecting the past, planning the future
> - Delivering through policy, negotiation and implementation

be addressing – the provision of decent homes for all; employment; essential energy and infrastructure; a choice of retail, recreation and leisure developments; improved health facilities; the protection of our best landscapes and architecture and a democratic voice for all communities – will remain ever-elusive and frustratingly mired in procedural and political contestation between different parts of the state.

Chapter 2

Spatial Challenges of the Twenty-first Century

We saw in Chapter 1 how the planning system lurched from one set of political objectives to another all the way through the twentieth century in response to changing socio-economic and environmental conditions, and as a political tool of governments. Some of those conditions remain issues of concern today, even if there have been subtle variations in their form and governments and ideology have changed significantly over that time. We remain concerned about the provision of new housing, there are consequences of possible increases in population numbers for the provision of essential services such as health and education, but also of water and fuel provision, and there is growing anxiety at the impact of extreme weather conditions on both the land and the activities that occur on it. And of course there are geographical or spatial differences in these activities across the UK. Later in the book we will look at the different political and governmental ways that have been used to deal with these changing conditions and drivers of change, and who has taken responsibility for reacting to the change. But before doing so, it is necessary to consider in detail how the UK is expected to change in the twenty-first century. Only in this way can we then recognize a role for planning in analysing and addressing spatial change.

Nearly every activity UK citizens engage in are in some way connected to land. Our everyday experience of travelling to work, the quality of our surroundings, the quality of the water we drink and our ability to enjoy outdoor space are all affected by land-use decisions. Land-use decisions not only significantly affect the well-being of individuals, but the way land is used and managed has consequences for issues of national importance: the long-term stability of ecosystems, social justice, food and energy security, long-term economic competitiveness and the mitigation of and adaptation to climate change. Land is finite, but it is also a national asset and its use is therefore a critical consideration in the long-term future of a nation. How land is used and managed, and the processes and mechanisms through which land-use conflicts are determined, are core matters for planners at all spatial scales. But the means by which these contentions are recognized and possibly even resolved through planning are not straightforward when landownership is the preserve of the privileged few, and when planning itself is stretched across and between public and private actors and several tiers of policy making. Like land, the process of land-use management and planning is contested continuously. That political context creates uncertainty for any form of state intervention, leaving aside for the moment debate about the merits of whether or not to intervene in the first place to resolve land-use problems. When some of these interventions can only be addressed through market investment, the form and nature of land-use planning is also at the mercy of, first and foremost, neo-liberal thinking. And against the backdrop of all this uncertainty, change in and on the land continues unabated.

Debates about the land, its use and its future have long occupied the writings of scientists and social scientists. At certain moments in history, such debates have intensified, for example in wartime or in extreme environmental circumstances. And how we define land use remains problematic – land use is not the same as land cover (Comber 2008). We can recognize the physical surface characteristics of land, whereas the use of land may be for social or economic functions. The two are linked, but the linkages can be complex and sometimes unobservable. The historic perspective of land has centred around the dominant functions of land, such as agriculture and forestry (Stamp 1948) and the main activity taking place on land (Best 1981). But this suggests that it is possible to separate out different land uses in neat divisions, when clearly a single plot of land may have multiple uses associated with it and might be affected by activity as well as land cover, and the spatial scale. In 2005, the government's Generalised Land Use Database (GLUD) for England revealed that only 9.95 per cent of the land area is regarded as developed, while the Department for Environment, Food and Rural Affairs (DEFRA)'s figures suggest that over 70 per cent of land is in agricultural use (CLG 2007b; see Figure 2.1). By far the biggest change in land use over the course of the twentieth century was not due to development, but actually relates to forestry and woodland cover (some 8.6 per cent of England's land area in 2005), a doubling of coverage since the 1920s.

The 9.95 per cent developed land figure may seem surprising, even more so when one considers that half of that figure actually comprises householders' back gardens. Perhaps this is the consequence of the UK being so densely crowded into its urban areas, leaving the impression that we are surrounded by development or that we are crowded too heavily in particular areas of the country (Evans 1991). Ninety per cent of the UK population resides on just 10 per cent of the land, and it gives rise to what Murdoch and Lowe (2003) term 'the preservationist paradox', the gap between the actual percentage of developed land and the public perceptions of an over-built England, while simultaneously desiring low-density living. The Barker Report on land use planning

Figure 2.1   *Estimated breakdown of land use in England, 2005*

Agricultural uses account for the majority of land-use cover, with developed land only comprising less than 10 per cent.

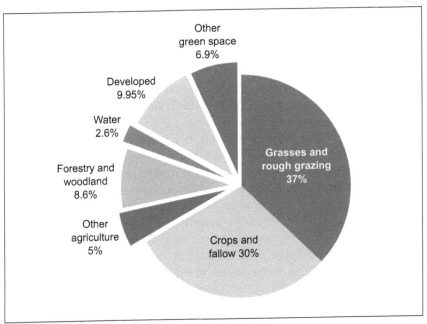

Sources: DEFRA; CLG; Forestry Commission, Environment Agency.

(Barker 2006) reported that, when surveyed, the public's perception of Britain being considerably urbanized is completely at variance to the actual statistics. The Ipsos Mori poll indicated that when asked the question, 'What proportion of the land in England do you think is developed?' over 50 per cent of respondents believed the figure to be at least half of the land, with one-third believing the proportion to be three-quarters developed (see Figure 2.2). This is an astonishing misconception, and the reasons are difficult to ascertain – perhaps it relates to the urban location of the vast majority of the population, or a belief that enough of the country is already built upon to an undesirable level (Upham et al. 2009). Whatever the exact reasons, the implications are clear from a land-use planning perspective – the misconception could well drive public and political attitudes to both development and to the planning system itself, leading to public resistance to new development projects, and a difficult climate within which governments, businesses and householders can progress planning projects successfully through a democratically debated and mediated decision-making process.

In summary, decisions about UK land use are therefore taken within an uncertain global economic and geopolitical context; a governmental

Figure 2.2   *Perceptions of the proportion of developed land in England, 2007*

In an Ipsos Mori poll conducted for the *Barker Review of Land-use Planning* (2006), over half of those surveyed thought that 50 per cent or more of the land in England is developed, compared to an actual figure of 10 per cent.

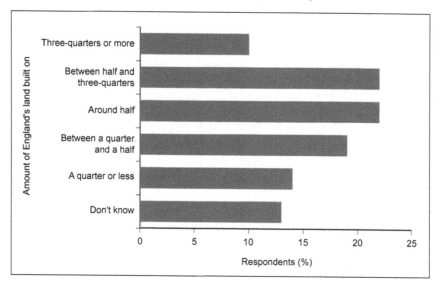

structure which is fluid and susceptible to change; a fragmented agency and institutional process shared between the public and private sectors, resting on democratic decision making, while mediating predominantly between private landownership and the public interest, and where the public have an overwhelming perception that that the UK has accommodated more than a sufficient amount of development already. In this context, the equally startling revelation that in 2010 over 87 per cent of all planning applications in the UK were approved suggests that land use and spatial planning deliver on the development proposals put forward by the private sector and individuals against all the odds, and certainly against occasional ministerial and economists' views that the planning system is a barrier to enterprise and growth (Cameron 2011).

Land, planning and the future

Juggling all the different requirements in managing land use in coming to decisions for today's needs is one skill, but ensuring that future concerns can be addressed in an era of uncertainty is even more challenging. The UK's Chief Scientist, Sir John Beddington, has talked of the possibility of a 'perfect storm' occurring around 2030 with water, food and energy shortages as the global population rises and climate change takes hold (Beddington 2009). The link between how present and future drivers of change play out at the global and UK levels will not always be straightforward. But what is clear is that the UK's response to changing global circumstances will have land-use implications. Within the UK, the uncertainty relates to key long-term drivers of land-use change:

- *Population levels* – the total UK population is currently 62.3 million (2010) and any population increases would almost certainly create additional demand for resources and land. The Office for National Statistics (ONS) projections of 2011 suggest that the total UK population could increase to 67.2 million by 2020, 73.2 million by 2035 and to over 75 million by 2050 (ONS 2011). Twenty-five per cent of the UK's current population reside within the south-east of England, so this region may be demonstrably affected by any growth but also will have to find ways to deliver essential new development against a backdrop of intense resistance to change; population and migration change will also see differences in the number of new households being formed, with consequences for housing demand and land supply (see Table 2.1).
- *Changing economic conditions* – Levels of economic growth and affluence, for example, affect consumption patterns, such as creating changing demand for housing and leisure time. The UK has seen high levels of growth and prosperity, but as the 2008–10 recession demonstrated, global shocks can trigger rapid change and leave a long-term legacy to deal with. In recent economic recession terms, there are also considerable differentials in unemployment between the north and the south of the UK and the reliance on public-sector jobs over private-sector employment. Between June 2010 and June 2011, the North-East lost 8.2 per cent of its public-sector jobs, whereas the South-East saw an increase of 2.2 per cent (NOMIS 2011). The economically active workforce is also set to fall to 61.7 per cent by 2020, which will have implications for taxation revenue and, in turn, investment into infrastructure and other public services (Stern 2006; Deloitte MSC 2008).
- *Changing environmental conditions* – how individuals, businesses, civil society and policy makers adapt to climate change and find ways to live more sustainably will clearly have a significant impact on land use. The UK currently imports 0.78m tonnes of fresh fruit and vegetables from Africa each year. Currently, 95 per cent of fruit and 50 per cent of vegetables are imported into the UK (Cabinet Office 2008). Changes to the global climate will affect crop production and availability, the price of foodstuffs and the ease with which they can be transported elsewhere. Plans to cut emissions from the UK's agricul-

ture sector may also affect the availability and range of food we currently take for granted (Audsley et al. 2009). Flood risks from rising sea levels may also affect low-lying farming areas in the UK, especially in East Anglia and bordering the east coast (Chatterton et al. 2009; Environment Agency 2008).

- *Transport and infrastructure requirements* – meeting the needs of an increasingly mobile society, the number of cars on Britain's roads has increased from 2 million in 1950 to 31 million in 2010. Congestion costs the UK economy £17.5 billion annually (British Chambers of Commerce 2007). The number of passengers using the rail system grew by 27 per cent between 2003 and 2009 and is expected to increase significantly up to 2020 (Eddington 2006; Office of Rail Regulation 2009), while the number of people using the UK's airports rose sixfold between 1970 and 2002 to nearly 200 million, a figure forecast to double by 2020 (DfT 2003; Commission for Integrated Transport 2009). As densely crowded cities struggle to cope with increases in the population, commuting between home and places of employment may become much more difficult without significant forms of investment and viable alternatives; almost 4 million people use the London Underground system daily.
- *Energy provision* – possible shortages of gas, oil and water in future decades, with concern about rising energy prices, a reliance on imports and regional disparities. Already some parts of the south-east of England lack sufficient water needs, and by 2020 our consumption of water will have increased to an extra 800 million litres per day, with spatial implications for the need for reservoir and water piping and transfers between regions (Chilton et al. 2004; Enviros 2005; DTI 2006; DEFRA 2008).

These issues represent some of the major themes the UK needs to address over the next few decades, but there are other matters that are just as relevant, including the future of agriculture, waste management, retailing and the high street, protected landscapes, the built heritage and the provision of sport, recreation and culture. All these sectors and their trends make for difficult reading, not only because they immediately put a question mark over our current land uses and future demands on the land, but also because they comprise a mix of fact and projection. It also becomes apparent that in considering the role of planning as a mediation process by which competing land uses are assessed and contested, significant challenges lie ahead. These relate to the added value of retaining a planning process during an era when strategic and synoptic thinking in planning has become much more difficult, but more generally how all these trends will be recognized, dealt with and acted upon by any government.

Table 2.1 *Projected household growth in England by region, 2003–26*

Region	No. of households 2003	No. of households 2021	No. of households 2026	Average annual change 2003–36
North-East	1,088,000	1,194,000	1,211,000	5,300
North-West	2,847,000	3,290,000	3,378,000	21,900
Yorkshire and Humberside	2,104,000	2,437,000	2,511,000	17,700
East Midlands	1,782,000	2,146,000	2,230,000	19,500
West Midlands	2,193,000	2,526,000	2,602,000	17,800
East	2,286,000	2,797,000	2,926,000	27,800
London	3,093,000	3,756,000	3,926,000	36,200
South-East	3,348,000	4,013,000	4,184,000	36,300
South-West	2,137,000	2,622,000	2,745,000	26,400
England	20,904,000	24,781,000	25,713,000	209,000

Source: ODPM (2006).

Perhaps the bottom line is that we have had it good for too long. We have embraced notions of sustainable development in the belief and policy convenience that we can achieve economic growth, environmental protection and social inclusion – win–win–win scenarios – all the time, irrespective of their practical consequence on the land, on land supply, on biodiversity or equity between different places and for different people. The Copenhagen Earth Summit 2010 indicated that the world cannot go on consuming the equivalent of three planets in resources; there is a myth circulating in Whitehall that if you read through successive governments' policies that have a land take, the government has always believed the UK to be three times bigger than it actually is. Government policy has covered so many different areas that, on paper, we can appear to be accommodating all our diverse needs and changes. But away from Whitehall, on the ground, town by town, land parcel by land parcel, there is a realization that the policy statements are rather more rhetorical, since difficult choices between different needs, drivers of change and demands will have to be made politically. Land is finite. And this is where the planning system comes into play, looking across the sectors, gathering intelligence and data, analysing trends and formulating options. Ultimately, it will be the politicians who take the final decisions, based, one hopes, on vision and principles, rather than through what Charles Lindblom referred to as

Figure 2.3 *The rise of car ownership and the impact on urban patterns: Birmingham*

One of the biggest drivers of change to land-use patterns and the form of planning has been the car and the need to accommodate it into the urban realm. In 2007 there were 33.9 million vehicles on UK roads.

'muddling through' (Lindblom 1959) and a series of incremental ad hoc responses.

The planning idea of analysing land-use change and considering alternative futures has always been conceptualized around the idea that human use and the management of land interact with natural processes and environments. These biophysical, social and economic processes come together to form a 'land system'. Having a systemic perspective should, in theory, help us to gain a better understanding of where interventions in the system may cause unforeseen problems and exacerbate vulnerabilities and explore the future of land use in an integrated way. It is a system of forces creating pressures and land-use change on the ground – whether urban, rural or peri-urban. Space and natural resources are not, of course, in endless supply, and decisions taken now about how land is used and managed can have long-term consequences for the health of the land system. For some, however, these trends are politically uncomfortable, either because they constrain the supply of goods or services we take for granted or threaten existing liberties and ways of behaving, or else because the planning system, often unpopular and criticized, is the process charged with monitoring and assessing these trends into an uncertain future.

General land-use trends

Historical priorities for land have largely been successful, if highly contested. Some dominant principles have been in existence for decades, prioritizing agricultural production, for example, or achieving urban containment by designating green belts and not usually permitting development in the countryside away from existing settlements (Elson 1986). Postwar priorities to prevent urban sprawl, raise agricultural productivity and increase the quality of life in cities have largely been successful, but probably at the expense of housing supply and other distortions in land values (Cheshire and Sheppard 2003). Over 80 per cent of the population live in urban areas and greenfield development has been extremely low; if anything, since the 1940s there has been a nibbling away of the countryside at the urban fringe by selective land releases for new development, but not on a scale noticeable to the public, perhaps, and certainly not to meet market demand. Given the sort of trends outlined earlier that comprise the drivers of land-use change, there is now a question mark over whether existing patterns of land use and the way land use is conceptualized, allocated and managed can stay the same in the light of twenty-first-century challenges.

Land is a critical national asset but its use and value is not always fully reflected in decision making. Together with our human capital, land is possibly the UK's greatest asset. It provides the basic services society needs to prosper and flourish, the environment which supports us, and the historical and cultural bedrock of the country. But in recent decades land, as a basic factor of production, has often been ignored or undervalued. The government is only just starting to look at this issue, although it has been evident in academic debates for decades. In 2011, the government announced the application of valuation to the natural environment and ecosystem services in the natural environment white paper (HM Government 2011). We should expect more of this type of assessment in the years ahead of other aspects of land-use management and planning. Macro patterns of land use have not changed significantly since the 1940s but the intensity of use has increased. Land for agriculture remains dominant at over 70 per cent – a fact only really noticeable when viewing the UK from the air – forestry accounts for approximately 12 per cent and urban areas approximately 10 per cent (but uncertainty in the statistics is high). These patterns have not changed substantially over time but the density of housing, crop yields and forest cover has increased. There are, however, natural limits –

intensity cannot increase indefinitely or without severe social and environmental costs.

In order to address all these different trends, which will probably occur differentially in different places, there has to be a common understanding of the issues, their effects, the cumulative impact of change across policy sectors, and greater harmony in the governance arrangements with integration of land-use policies to ensure increased benefits from the land (Government Office for Science 2010). Complexity in the governance arrangements – who is responsible for what and through which mechanisms – together with a lack of integrated science create confusion among landowners and managers but also the politicians and the public, with the danger of unsustainable decisions being made without a significant assessment of the likely impacts of those decisions in the long term. Policies which significantly affect how land is used are often even now made by different government departments with different priorities, which are sometimes in conflict or even indirectly cancel each other out. The cumulative effects of the policies themselves and on the land system are unknown until well after the decisions have been made.

We can expect the planning system, in whatever guise it adopts politically, to be called upon to manage rising tensions and conflicts over land use in the future. Land is set to come under increasing pressure as the twenty-first century unfolds. The population is expected to grow by 15 million by 2048 (though this remains uncertain), and whilst this growth is generally good for the economy and for prosperity, it creates demand for space and resources. Growth will not be uniform – certain areas of the UK will feel pressures more acutely, for example the Greater South-East of England, in an arc stretching from Norfolk and Cambridgeshire, through Northamptonshire to Oxford, Berkshire, Hampshire and Sussex (ONS 2008). Increased conflict creates difficulties in implementing land-use change for the wider public good and for future generations. Therefore balancing competing pressures and demands on and for the land is a major challenge for the coming century, and one that is all the more pressing due to the time that may be needed to roll out new land use policies. Factors such as climate change, demographic shifts and changing patterns of work and habitation will all create major challenges. As these pressures intensify, so will the demands on land.

Individual preferences and attitudes towards land often conflict, creating irreconcilable demands – for example, 85 per cent of people surveyed support the existence of the green belt to achieve urban containment but also dislike living at the higher density necessary to prevent sprawl (Barker 2006). This is not an easy paradox to resolve through any management process, and it may be that the planning system alone is unable to address the dilemma. New approaches to using land, the availability of incentives, changes in urban forms, and new technologies may help accommodate most preferences but without tough decisions being taken by government, social inequities could worsen. The UK is not 'space poor', and all land is being 'used'. For many years, planners have described undeveloped land in terms of absence – 'there is nothing there' – but this ignores the importance and role of biodiversity, agriculture, recreation and water in supporting land and, most likely, urban services. The UK is also not an overcrowded island; society has chosen to contain urban development, which can create the perception of crowding as the majority of the population live at high densities. However, all land is being used in one respect or another and provides services to society (whether they are ecological, cultural or aesthetic in character). While this space creates opportunities to use land differently in the future, decisions may need to be taken with full cognizance of the ecological, social and economic costs and benefits – something that has been absent in the planning system to date. Often the true value of land is only partially reflected in decision making – a wider range of values need to be attributed to land to ensure optimal use of land and maximize the benefits.

Land-use challenges to address basic needs

Already we can see that, globally, the challenges of securing food, water and energy will intensify. For example, it is estimated that global food production will need to rise by 50 per cent by 2030 to meet demand (Food and Agriculture Organisation 2005; Government Office for Science 2011). Total world water demand is predicted to rise by 50 per cent by 2030 (DEFRA 2008), and in 2008 demand for energy from non-OECD (Office of Economic Cooperation and Development) countries outstripped demand in OECD countries for the first time (HM Government 2009). While demand for food, energy and water are expected to continue to rise, unlike in many parts of the globe, the UK is less likely to face a situation where society's basic needs cannot be met in the short to medium terms. However, security of supply of energy, water and food in the UK will continue to be high priorities for government. The UK is committed to producing a greater proportion of the country's energy requirements from renewable sources by 2020 (HM Government 2009). In addition to this, a programme of new nuclear power stations has already been announced, together with their specific locations, a decision ratified in October 2011 despite uncertainty following the Fukushima nuclear plant meltdown following the Japanese earthquake in March 2011, and Germany's announcement that it was abandoning its nuclear programme and shutting down its nuclear power stations by 2022. The implications for land use both above and below ground are both immediate and long-term.

An increase in winter rainfall, rising sea levels and more frequent storm surges may increase flood risk. The average winter rainfall is projected to increase by 14 per in the north-east of England in the 2080s and the sea level is projected to rise by 18cm in London by 2040 (HM Government 2009). The three regions of England that are potentially at most risk by the number of people resident are Greater London, Yorkshire and Humberside, and south-east England. Cardiff and Newport are the two local authorities in Wales by population most at risk from rising sea levels and flooding (Environment Agency 2009). Flooding and coastal erosion will impact on the amount of land resource available and influence short- and long-term land-use decisions, particularly if the flooding affects existing locations of essential infrastructure. Electricity infrastructure, major roads and railways, water-pumping stations and treatment works and gas infrastructure are all located in flood-risk areas in the UK and may affect supply to unaffected locations.

The Leitch Review (2006) recognized that the global economy is being restructured and the success of the developed countries will depend on a flexible economy with a highly skilled workforce which can respond quickly to change. In a similar vein, the UK must consider the ways it can develop a resilient land system which can respond quickly to changes in global circumstances and markets. Governance structures and planning mechanisms for allocating land use and incentivizing certain practices have to be aligned to ensure basic needs continue to be met in a volatile and uncertain global context. It is therefore important that scientists and policy makers in future consider a full analysis of land's contribution to help address some significant future problems but also recognize the potential of the planning system in providing the evidence base to inform critical choices and assist in the delivery and implementation of decisions. These issues include:

- *Increasing demand for water* as a result of continuing population growth and urbanization will exceed water availability, while pollution will require increasing expenditure on water treatment. Unavoidable climate change will see significant reductions in river flows and groundwater recharge, amid rising demand through to 2050. The balance of supply and demand is therefore likely to worsen unless further measures are taken. The upward trend in the volume of groundwater requiring treatment will continue.
- *The vulnerability of farming communities in upland areas* could result in a serious loss of the goods and services provided by agricultural land where the land has been managed for landscape quality, water resources and recreation, as well as food production.

- *Food security* – the possibility of land being brought into food production quickly if needed. Where will the UK's best and most versatile arable land be? Will new technologies and management practices mean that more food can be produced on less land? What are the environment and social consequences of this?
- *Energy security* – the global demand for energy is projected to be 53 per cent higher in 2030 than in 2004 (based on current energy policies; HM Government 2009). In Britain, as indigenous energy resources decline, dependence on imported fuels will rise to meet energy demand. The UK will face costs associated with dealing with global emissions, greater exposure to developments in the energy-supply systems, volatile energy prices, vulnerability and risk to overseas disruptions to energy supplies. Well-functioning markets, stable supply routes and diverse sources of energy will be needed. A policy of diversity and targets for renewables would have land-take consequences.
- *Dealing with increased flood risk* – an assessment of where the greatest flood risk may be (urban and rural) and the likely associated costs. How can land-use planning help to reduce the cost of flood risk, and which land-use changes could increase flood risk? The role of natural flood-alleviation schemes may offset some of the risks of flooding in some areas but at the expense of some agricultural land or low-lying areas on the coast. Above all, how could incentives encourage such schemes and what might be the impact on the value of the land? – issues that individual landowners are bound to consider as paramount.

The spatial impacts of these trends and drivers vary region to region in the UK. Some of these problems are related more to the physical landscape (coastal or upland areas), whereas others stem from economic and market demand. What is clear is that the problems of each region will be quite unique and, as trends continue, the problems experienced in one region may be in contrast to the problems occurring in a neighbouring region. The Greater South-East of England, for example, is likely to experience a number of problems, resulting from pressure for land development and existing as well as future growth. But it is also the region that could suffer from water shortages, rising floodwaters and the loss of the best agricultural landscapes to a greater extent than regions to the west and north of the country. It is for analysts and policy makers in each region to identify the assets and capacity of their areas. The northern region, conversely, may not suffer these problems so distinctly and may, by implication, offer a much better quality of life in the long-term future. The region, by capitalizing on its assets which may be absent elsewhere, could consider its environmental and ecosystem profile and start to assess the economic potential of its land and functions that would assist with furthering the quality of life in the North. At the present time, there is a significant amount of work to be done in looking at places and regions in this territorially distinctive way, and a gulf currently exists between the place-based evidence and the form of land use and spatial planning existing across the country. The coalition government's determination to dismantle large swathes of the national and regional planning framework in England since 2010 only serves to miss the opportunities, environmentally, economically and synoptically, to capitalize on place assets and understand the links, and sometimes tensions between different drivers of change as they affect the land. It is a woeful abdication of responsibility.

Land management to address needs

How we use land to manage water resources in the future will be severely affected by factors such as population growth, climate change and changes in urban and peri-urban areas and agricultural practices. Climate change will alter precipitation patterns, which affects river flows and groundwater recharge. Managing land use to protect the future quality of both surface and groundwater will increasingly come into conflict with other land uses. Sustaining a larger population will require a combination of increasing water supply, which would be expensive (desalination, pipelines, reservoirs), and managing demand (perhaps through pricing or metering). The land's capacity to regulate water supply and quality will become more important. Technological solutions such as re-use and recycling of water are likely to become more important by treatment on site and direct reuse, or by indirect reuse. These may impact on the efficacy of water-related ecosystem services.

In the UK, as elsewhere, few landscapes remain natural. Nevertheless, many of our distinctive range of semi-natural habitats and cultural landscapes are valued by society, both in their own right and for the contribution that they make to people's well-being and prosperity (Selman 2006). The effect of human-led land-use change combined with changing climatic conditions will be significant. Wildlife is already responding to climate change through changes to seasonal events such as flowering, species distribution and species abundance. These issues are already being identified on the ground by local authorities, land managers and environmentalists even if they are not prevalent in current national planning statements. Importantly, changes in land use mean that some habitats have become fragmented. As climate change begins to affect land cover, some species may not be able to move to adapt to these changing habitats. Biodiversity and ecosystems are starting to be assessed by and through the local planning system, even though the legal and professional relationship between land-use planning and ecosystem services remains relatively under-assessed and undefined (Harris and Tewdwr-Jones 2010). Agriculture is probably the single most dominant influence on the landscape, of course, currently occupying over 75 per cent of the UK land surface. It underpins food security and contributes to the economy and wider environmental agendas. However, current estimates suggest that agriculture would account for nearly 30 per cent of the target for total greenhouse gas (GHG) emissions in 2050 (MacMillan 2009). The two main drivers of agricultural land use in the future will be agricultural policy and conditions in international markets for agricultural commodities. It will be necessary to recognize and reward the multiple roles of agriculture, as a producer of food, and a provider of ecosystem services such as climate change mitigation through carbon sequestration, flood-risk management, biodiversity and recreation.

Forests and woodland provide diverse benefits and services, including commercial timber production and non-marketed services including biodiversity, flood protection, climate change mitigation, recreation and amenity. Woodland now covers nearly 12 per of the UK land area, although this remains low compared to the EU average of 37 per cent. The commercial value of forests, and the incentives provided to the new planting of forests and woodlands, are in most cases much less than the value of the benefits provided (Bateman 2009). Forests and woodlands involve long-term investments, for the most part on marginal land. Investment in forestry is sensitive to incentives given to other land uses, such as livestock production, and requires long-term policy commitment. The location of forests relative to centres of population can be a critical determinant of value.

Land use is intimately connected with flood risk. Where we build and how we manage land can affect the likelihood of flooding and where the flooding occurs. There is broad experience in the UK in flood-risk management, but given the prospects of increased pressure on land use and environmental change, there will be much greater need in future for a better understanding of the relationship between land use and flood-risk management. The extent to which changes in land management can 'mitigate' flooding at the catchment scale for extreme rainfall events remains unclear, although it is likely that rural land can contribute to flood alleviation by retaining and storing floodwaters in vulnerable catchments.

In response to the Stern report, the government set out its *UK Low Carbon Transition Plan* to reduce greenhouse gas emissions by 80 per cent by 2050, compared with 1990 levels (HM Government 2009). Part of this will come from lower energy use, but there is also a need to displace other fossil fuels with zero-carbon electricity. Overall electricity demand could be 17–65 per cent higher than in 2005 and the plan gives various scenarios for the level and sources of electricity supply in 2050. Wind is the most mature renewable electricity technology and, in the 2050 scenarios, might provide from 90 TWh (23 per cent of a low total) to 260 TWh (46 per cent of a higher total), requiring between 40 and 120 GW of wind turbines. However, it has substantial implications for land use. In particular, siting wind turbines onshore has been difficult, as has securing planning permission for new transmission lines. To give an indication of the tradeoffs involved, a wind farm to replace Drax Power Station would take up an area of 1,750 sq km, although the land underneath would still be available for agriculture (not forestry). In addition, wind-farm development, particularly in upland locations where wind resources are available, may be more feasible but may be held up by planning delays. If half the 2050 scenarios' wind power were onshore, the land-take would range between 1.5 per cent and 4 per cent of the Britain's total.

Energy crops offer another option for decarbonizing. However, they have significant implications for land use because of their low-energy density in Britain. Changing land use to energy crops might release carbon from the soil, and the low-energy density of the crops would either require considerable transport infrastructure or very dispersed energy use. Unlike wind, energy crops necessarily displace other land uses. At the high end, the Royal Commission for Environmental Pollution calculated that to respond to the earlier 2003 energy White Paper and deliver 16GW of energy from biomass (8–12 per cent of the 2050 energy demand), 5.5 million ha (22 per cent of Britain's land area, 125 per cent of cropped area) might be needed to reach our renewables target, competing with food production.

Land-use challenges to address well-being

Quality of life is also concerned with improving societal well-being. Domestic changes, rather than those related to the physical and natural world, are more likely to be easily influenced by early intervention. They are all topics which affect quality of life, though they also go to the heart of some of the conflicts and tensions in the land-use arena. It is therefore imperative that policy makers in future consider a full analysis of land use and quality-of-life issues in respect of:

- Looking at the challenges of meeting development needs, including housing demand and delivering quality homes in the context of changing life/work patterns, internal and global migration patterns, changing demographics, the systemic-level implications and different means of increasing and paying for increasing supply.

- Explore what science is telling us about how access to and enjoyment of green space and scenic landscapes improve our health and well-being, how our green spaces and green belts are used and the significance of the location and quality of green space relative to populations.
- The cutting-edge thinking on creating thriving and sustainable cities, who might live in cities in the future, questions around different densities and critical densities, providing the necessary infrastructure and renewing ageing infrastructure, dealing with recognized market failures such as congestion and generating necessary funding streams.
- The latest interdisciplinary research on the future of rural communities, upland areas, managing land for ecosystem services, livelihoods and the impact of tourism.
- Links between land use and health and well-being (for example, research on obesogenic environments and the impact on changing diets on agriculture).

Future demands on the land

Trends

- To meet steadily increasing demand for housing – by 2031 there could be 29 per cent more households than in 2006 – more greenfield land for development is likely to be needed (Gallent 2009). The amount of greenfield land needed for housing growth will be more significant if suitable brownfield land cannot be identified and preferences of an ageing and more prosperous population (which presently prefer less dense living) continue. The government will need to prepare to accommodate additional growth (e.g. whether to continue with existing policies, adopt high-density or sanction land release) and on what basis (combining economic, planning and environmental considerations).
- In order to create more high-quality green spaces for recreation near and within population concentrations – the frequency of visits to green spaces are increasing, with an average of 60–70 per person per year. At the same time, there will be a continuous requirement to enhance our best landscapes and heritage sites. Landscapes have great value for amenity, but as connected habitats and spaces for wildlife delivering a range of services for tourism, recreation, health and well-being. Urban areas are also landscapes. Making the best use of these assets and recognizing their value is important for local economies as well as national interests.
- To store carbon for climate-change mitigation, land will increasingly need to be valued for its capacity to store and sequester carbon.

- To store floodwaters as flood risk increases – climate change will mean an increased flood risk. Some land has excellent capacity to store flood waters naturally and to regulate and slow the flow of storm waters.
- To provide the food and agricultural products needed in a globalized world – including energy crops and the deliver of vital ecosystem services; to support low-carbon energy production – in order to meet targets of an 80 per cent cut in GHG emissions by 2050 on 1990 levels.

Key implications

A perspective on land is needed whereby policy makers are able to serve better the interests of future generations as well as the present. This may mean that new approaches to using and managing land, and, by implication, new planning processes will be needed. Politicians and policy makers will need to find mechanisms to balance and, where possible, to overcome rising spatial tensions, for example the balance between urban and rural needs and between national and local interests. Targeted measures will be needed to tackle 'pressure points', especially in the greater south-east of England, for example on housing and land for further house building, water supply and quality, congestion and the local environment, and the wider implications for the rest of the UK.

Land-use policy and science will be needed to effectively link to climate-change mitigation and adaptation policies, and support the transition to a low-carbon economy. Government will need to take action to ensure the continued delivery of vital public goods and services, including countryside amenity and ecosystem services, in a land system increasingly influenced by global and domestic market pressures but increasingly regulated through the planning system at the neighbourhood level.

Critical issues for strategic choice

Having considered the present and emerging drivers of change, the land-use challenges to the quality of life and to well-being, and highlighting future trends and implications, we can move forward to consider some critical issues for practice and to possible challenges for policy responses over the medium to long terms. These issues are not exhaustive across the subject of land use, but are considered some of the most pertinent, and place planning within its wider context. At whatever spatial scales planning and other land-use management processes operate, these land-use drivers and trends will need to be addressed in a synoptic and strategic way.

Pressures on land in the south of England may continue to increase. Population projections indicate that the most significant growth will be in areas on the edge of the South-East, and comprise an arc stretching from East Anglia and the Fens, through Northamptonshire to Oxfordshire and Hampshire. The South-East's sphere of influence is therefore likely to increase over the next 50 years, all things considered. This is likely to place some of these areas under intense development and infrastructure pressure, even more so when it is considered some of these areas coincide with the food-production areas that may also be vulnerable to rising sea levels. Furthermore, the areas also house airports or airports with the potential to expand, adjacent to the motorway network and the location of logistics and distribution services. The North, by contrast, may well enjoy a gentle urban to rural migration as new settlements grow around the cities and where market pressures for development land is less intense.

Quality-of-life issues may be affected in the greater South-East as development pressure mounts and stresses are placed on the existing, perhaps inadequate, infrastructure. In addition to congested road and rail routes, there is some indication that the availability of drinking water may reach critical capacity in some, but not all, places in the region. This is a subject currently contested by different experts. Whereas the North may not be subject to the same sorts of tensions in land-use stresses, it may be affected by changes occurring in other regions. The development of further high-speed rail routes, particularly High Speed 2, and technological advances would benefit northern cities economically, but might also promote a shift in the population to the North from London and the South-East. This could be permanent in nature, for quality-of-life purposes, and the North could potentially use this to its advantage. Or rather it could be because commuting times to London will be reduced. Does the North have the capacity and ability to accommodate a migration from the south of England without sacrificing its current quality of life and, if so, should society invest now in the assets and infrastructure of the North despite continuing migration to the South? The push-and-pull factors associated with 'southerners' being prepared to move northwards are extremely difficult to quantify or assess with any degree of certainty, as so much will depend on prevailing social, economic, environmental and climatic conditions in the South as well as the perceived attractiveness and conditions in the North.

A key issue will be how to ensure that growth of cities, towns (such as market towns) and villages does not reduce the quality of life for those already resident there, for example through loss of tranquillity, increased light pollution and increased congestion. As the demand for limited resources increases, access to sustainable ecosystem services, affordable housing and green space may become problematic. Social cohesion and greater inequalities could be created.

A significant investment in renewable energy will require space as well as funding and may create unwanted visual effects, for example from renewable energy developments in upland and coastal or offshore areas. A growing population and subsequent demand for housing will also compete for this land and energy needs will continue to grow. Adaptation to climate change as well as the global quest of long-term mitigation will have implications for land use.

Car usage will remain high over the next 20 years and a significant shift in human behaviour and/or technology will be required to reduce carbon emissions in the transport sector. Assuming investment in the public transport network and interventions to change behaviour occur, there will be land-take implications with a possible change to life/work patterns that will also mean a change for the future of cities, rural communities and the distinction between the two. There is a danger that ribbon development may reoccur along main transport routes where land prices are cheaper but also take the form of the further extension of retail and logistic distribution points.

Rural villages may benefit from investment in technology and information technology which will impact on life/work patterns, but the benefits may not be felt across all sections of society. Rural areas will continue to contain both wealthy individuals and those at or below poverty levels. As society ages, so access to services and facilities will become a key issue. If economic conditions force the amalgamation and centralization of services into urban areas, particularly in the health sector, access to services, especially for the elderly, may become more difficult and may affect life chances.

Policies across all land-use sectors should recognize the value of biodiversity which resides in everyday surroundings. This means, for example, recognizing the important role that gardens and green spaces in urban areas can play, and protecting them from over-development. Local development schemes could maximize environmental benefits, for example, by incorporating green roofs as well as areas of new habitats and landscape networks. Such measures would help compensate for historical environmental losses.

In the context of global economic restructuring, there may be wider impacts of restrictions on land use and land release which affect the price of land in some regions of the UK. Different regions possessing geographically distinct land and land features and assets may be in a position to utilize the values of the land in ways unique to the regions. As climatic zones shift, so the North could be in a beneficial position with respect to agricultural production, fish farming and job creation, and further serve or trade with other UK regions. This would be dependent on the North receiving the true benefit from production and developing agribusiness opportunities.

Dealing with uncertainty and fragmentation of governance

Addressing the current issues and possible future trends in land use and managing the drivers of change that have land and spatial implications is an extremely difficult task, compounded by the current governmental, administrative and planning processes and the availability of data and intelligence on the issues. Historically, land-use management concern focused on continuing processes of urbanization, suburbanization and urban sprawl and how this could be contained. More recently, new patterns of urbanization since the 1980s (that have often been located at the urban edge, in peri-urban or fringe locations), mean that land use management is also now concerned with externalities arising from 'polycentricity' (Hall and Pain 2006), as each urban location (whether it is a city, town or even motorway intersection) all compete for development, services and infrastructure and cater for externalities caused by changing living, commuting and migrating patterns, technological change and new faster transport links.

The UK has largely been successful in containing urban development, but as market pressures and changing socio-economic conditions are beginning to outmanoeuvre the principles and practices concerned with historical perspectives of managing development. The processes, divided between various governance agents and strategies, have difficulty in anticipating change and the consequence of change over shorter time periods, causing perceptions that the processes themselves are inadequate, slow and bureaucratic or fail to respond to market drivers. As Table 2.2 shows, the state has been in transition from a Weberian bureaucratic state to a postmodern state, where government has been replaced by governance (Richards and Smith 2002), allowing different forms of collaboration and corporatism between separate arms of the state, those of business, and other vested interests. Planning, as predominantly a function of the state at least historically, has been directly affected by this transition.

Even if individual land parcels are under single landownership, the responsibility for managing change over and on the land may reside with a number of different agencies. Since the late 1990s, much urban land is now managed by a range of quasi-public, private or market-led management and delivery mechanisms, such as development corporations, enterprise zones and business improvement districts, and these sit alongside the local authority planning mechanisms, which mean that attitudes towards how urban land should be managed and developed or protected strategically cannot be coordinated with ease because of conflicting interests.

Table 2.2   *The transition from government to governance*

Weberian bureaucratic state	Postmodern state
Government	Governance
Hierarchy	Heterarchy
Power (1) Zero-sum game	Power (1) Positive sum game
Power (2) Concentrated	Power (2) Diffuse
Elitist	Pluralist
Unitary, centralized, monolithic state	Decentralized, fragmented, hollowed state
Strong, central executive	Segmented executive
Clear lines of accountability	Blurred/fuzzy lines of accountability
State central control	State central steering
Single homogenous public service ethos	Heterogeneous service culture

Source: Richards and Smith (2002, Table 2.2, p. 36).

Processes of governing land use and spatial change

The planning system provides valuable democratic forums for the public to express a voice in change in their surroundings. But since the late 1990s society has become increasingly pluralist, with a concomitant shift from representative government to participatory governance, enhanced public participation and involvement mechanisms in policy development, and enhanced vocal rights within decision-making structures. There have also been increasing opportunities within government and governance to challenge, protest legitimately, appeal and seek legal redress within the formal decision-taking processes.

As land-use management and decision making within planning has become more flexible, arguably fragmented, participatory and less regulatory, the formal agents of decision taking have in turn sought more certainty and legitimacy from the state in their actions against possible future challenges. Coupled with the existing law and policy framework, this has often led to decisions favouring the lowest-common-denominator solutions, with decision makers and indeed government attempting to placate simultaneously all the various interest groups that have an interest in land. It symbolizes a shift to more pragmatic ways of dealing with matters rather than on the basis of defined political principles. And against this backdrop in the twenty-first century, the case for and role of planning become much more difficult to argue, since planning itself is founded on the basis of historically set principles and also now is expected to mediate between the different actors and their vested interests.

How the pressures on land are managed is also affected by uncertainty on who has responsibility for decisions and at what scale. Land-use management is increasingly complex and there are key distinctions and tensions now between land-use planning operating as a governmental, public, private and participatory set of processes. There is also a distinction to be made between land-use planning policy, planning regulation and spatial planning. And there are overlapping relationships, interlocking and co-dependencies between land-use commitments at European, UK, national (four countries), regional, sub/city-regional, local and neighbourhood levels of government and policy making, each with its own planning level and degree of discretionary judgement.

For example, land-use planning after 1997 was broadened in scope beyond its regulatory role, into three tasks:

- a facilitator and regulator on a host of measures;
- a coordinating or choreographic tool for regional and local public bodies; and
- an access point for wider stakeholders to get involved not only in planning but local and regional governance and strategy making.

These three planning tasks are still evident across the UK in 2012, albeit in different guises. Managing land-use change in England appears to be splitting up in many ways that suggests both continuity with the past (dealing with planning applications through development control, for example) and the changed requirements of the twenty-first century (spatial planning that emphasizes public participation, place shaping and well-being agendas). The problems around these emerging forms of managing land-use change and their interrelationships rest on a number of core issues, the most prominent of which are the rights and responsibilities of national governments to respond to nationally important matters and to shape and determine nationally significant issues. Within a changed government structure that emphasizes decentralized, local and neighbourhood governance, how can the UK government lead the management process(es) to assist in action on national land-use priorities? The provision of national infrastructure issues or housing are good examples here of finding new management processes to deal with what can be called 'wicked problems' (Rittel and Webber 1973), but the principle applies equally well on questions of national policy for a range of land-use issues and how this filters down to other layers of policy and decision making that are based on enhanced local participation, neighbourhood discretion and subsidiarity.

Coping with disjointed governance

A further problem concerns the relationship between statutory planning and environmental protection. Planning, the environment and climate change are three separate legal disciplines in the UK and each is governed by unique legislation. On questions of sustainable development and climate change, these tend to fall between stools at the present time because of the legislative separation. The government provides a broad national planning framework on issues such as flood risk and climate change but these are policy tools, and have taken their place historically alongside a range of other policy advice issued by the government on such matters as infrastructure provision, housing development, retail change and economic development. In many ways, this is the crux of the problem: over decades local-level decisions needed to take account of a range of national policy statements in formulating strategies but with little guidance on which issues take priority. Similarly, imposing a direction in a particular substantive policy could be seen as riding roughshod over other democratically elected tiers, an issue made even sharper as land-use change mechanisms have embraced stakeholder participation at the grassroots level and, politically, the planning process is coping with localism and neighbourhood-level decision making.

A final tension concerns the relationship between the formal land-use planning system (government policy making at all tiers and their associated plans and strategies) and shadow or ad hoc strategy and delivery bodies. This is especially so in urban areas or where governments have created new delivery mechanisms in specifically targeted areas that stand outside the formal land-use planning tools in order to provide expedited arrangements for change. The New Towns are an example, but so too were the urban development corporations, enterprise zones, urban regeneration companies, business improvement districts and Local Enterprise Partnerships. As a consequence, since they are outside the formal statutory planning system, there is a danger that these governance bodies fail to address the broader suite of land-use policy issues in the synoptic way that would be required of planning authorities (e.g. climate change).

There is also the danger that they create different types of land-use management processes, a patchwork of governance systems that are confusing and with which citizens and businesses may not be able to identify. Some of these processes are shaped and led locally, but others are established nationally and, historically, regionally or sub-regionally. The result of this patchwork system is a multitude of governance mechanisms that frequently lead to contentions locally over who should set visions and directions for change and which set of political priorities should prevail. To manage this fragmentation and disjointed set of

Figure 2.4 London's fragmented governmental structure

The key statutory bodies, excluding partnership, voluntary and community bodies.

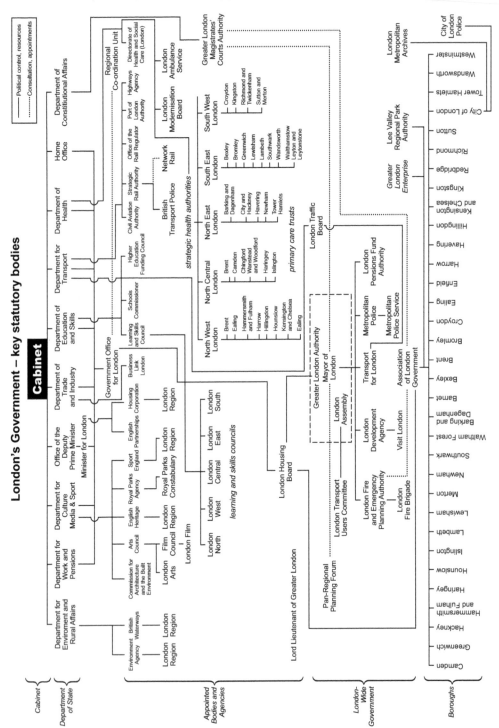

arrangements, and as Chapter 3 goes on to explain, the term 'spatial planning' emerged in the late 1990s to describe the process of the agents of change attempting to balance and integrate the various competing agendas and policy.

Significantly large solution interventions in land-use problems were introduced historically throughout the twentieth century, for example motorways, nuclear power stations and high-rise housing. However, land-use change since the beginning of the twenty-first century can be characterized more as 'incremental' and increasingly participatory. As with most attempts to broaden governance processes into more participatory modes, this presents governance challenges in terms of societal constraints on implementation, resistance to change, and conflicting policies that seek to achieve consensus across and between tiers of governance (Tewdwr-Jones and Allmendinger 1998). As governance has promoted and introduced new forms of locally based participation mechanisms, policy forums and spatial planning, the tension between privatized and decentralized decision making with the promotion of collective action and need has risen sharply.

The system for determining how we wish to manage the land depends in part on how we want to use it to address existing problems and emerging issues. In part, of course, managing land-use trends is also one of political choice and the prevailing governmental arrangements. The analysis of the long-term drivers of land-use change as set out in this chapter begins to make a compelling case to try to build an emphatic moral approach to consider future land use that moves beyond short-term and narrow political vested interests. Without a synoptic perspective on land use, issues such as climate change, food security, energy availability and access to services and homes could make UK populations more divided and more unequal in the future.

Chapter 3

Spatialization: Coming to Terms with Spatial Planning

We saw earlier in the book that the land-use conflicts that emerge in nations have a peculiarly complex effect on sub-national territories as they are addressed by politicians, developers, planners and the public, and discussed and acted upon through a fragmented governmental structure and a highly contentious land-use and spatial planning process. We also saw that the UK, like other countries around the globe, is facing a number of critical challenges ahead in respect of economic growth and competition, population and demographic changes, a shortage of homes, uncertain impacts on the land of climate change and extreme weather conditions, and shortfalls in the provision of infrastructure. This chapter goes on to discuss the ways in which these issues and tensions are, first, recognized and assessed by planners, and secondly, dealt with through land use and spatial planning.

'Spatial planning' is a phrase that continues to resonate throughout many planning systems across the globe (Friedmann 2004). It is being used as a label to describe pan-national, regional, strategic and even aspects of local planning processes. It may be found in Europe, where attempts have been made to formulate perspectives on the European territory (Faludi and Waterhout 2002); in China, where city-regions are devising new ways to deal with competitiveness and economic growth (Xu and Yeh (2005); in South Africa, where the government has published a national spatial development perspective (South African Presidency 2006); and in the United States (Lincoln Institute (2004), Carbonell and Yaro (2005)). Within the UK, spatial planning has been used alongside, or even in place of, more traditional phraseology associated with planning, such as 'town and country planning' and 'land-use planning'. It is being used by a range of institutions of the state, professional groups and academic commentators to describe the processes of planning reform, modernization, policy integration and strategic governance that politically are now required to make planning fit for purpose to address the challenges that, as we saw in Chapter 2, are likely to create problems in the twenty-first century. And like all ideas and concepts, it is also highly contested academically (Allmendinger and Haughton 2009, 2011).

The precise meaning and definition of spatial planning remains difficult to pin down, as does its origins within the UK. Certainly planning
has been around in the UK and in other Western nations for more than
a hundred years. But spatial planning is a particular type of planning
activity and is a more recent phenomenon. European planning ministers
and the EU, deriving its work from the European Spatial Development
Perspective (ESDP) of 1999, one of the first published documents to
refer to spatial planning, viewed the role of 'spatial development policies' to work 'towards a balanced and sustainable development of the
territory of the European Union', through the adoption of member
states' planning policies promoting polycentric development, balanced
competitiveness, economic and social cohesion and the management of
the natural environment and cultural assets (CEC 1999: 3). But the
European origin of the phrase originates from a much earlier period
than this. The UK government has referred to spatial planning as something that 'goes beyond traditional land use planning to bring together
and integrate policies for the development and use of land with other
policies and programmes which influence the nature of places and how
they function' (ODPM 2005: para. 30). The professional planning body,
the Royal Town Planning Institute (RTPI), meanwhile, has defined
spatial planning more broadly as the 'critical thinking about space and
place as the basis for action or intervention' (RTPI 2003).

Academic definitions of spatial planning are characterized by their
diversity. According to Faludi (2002: 4), the term is 'ambiguous' and an
alien concept to North American and British planners steeped in town
and country planning, particularly as it originated within German and
Dutch planning ideologies. Williams (1996: 57) and Kunzmann (2006:
43) both consider spatial planning to be 'Euro-English', a non-US/UK
concept but conveyed in English, and not easily transferable, stemming
from the German *Raumplanung*. It has been described as 'an ongoing,
enduring process of managing change, by a range of actors, in the interests of sustainable development' (Tewdwr-Jones 2004: 591) and as the
'coordination or integration of the spatial dimension of sectoral policies
through a territorial based strategy' (Cullingworth and Nadin 2006:
91). The academic view of spatial planning is that it is situated at the
juncture of the integration of official state policy-making and a requirement for joined-up government (Healey 2007), characterized by a
'fluidity, openness and multiple time-space relations of "relational
complexity" ideas' (Healey 2006: 535). It expresses 'a shift beyond a
traditional idea of land-use planning to describe many aspects of planning practices that provide proactive possibilities for the management of
change, involving policy-making, policy integration, community participation, agency stakeholding, and development management' (Tewdwr-
Jones 2004: 593). And it makes a commitment to embed strategy making

within specific distinctive territories that can be sponsored or owned by government or governance actors (Albrechts 2006).

These definitions stem from varied sources, disciplines, political and professional expectations of a reformed planning process, and the changing form and function of the state. As such, it can often seem bewildering to analysts and practitioners to dissect spatial planning's true meaning and role (Tewdwr-Jones 2008; Taylor 2010). Is spatial planning something radically different from what we have been used to in planning on times in the past? Is it anything new substantively, a new label for existing practices, or merely an ordering of ideas from planning theory that have been in circulation for many years (Needham 2000)? What is the relationship between spatial planning and traditional forms of land-use planning (Cowell and Owens 2006)? Does spatial planning exist at a particular politico-geographical scale, or comprise a rescaling of planning processes from one tier of the state to another (Vigar et al. 2000)? And if spatial planning involves more integration and less prediction, does this mark the end of the use of traditional land-use modelling in practice (Couclelis 2005; Wong, Baker and Kidd 2006)?

We need to be concerned about what form spatial planning is taking and its conceptual origins, since the varied ebbs and flows in policy making within a fluid state, together with unequal territorial claims on spatial agendas, result potentially in spatial planning becoming deeply implicated in the emergence of meta-governance (Jessop 2004) and the re-territorialization of the state (Brenner 1999). Although some commentators argue that decentralization and devolution are part of a move towards a greater centralization of power, the majority view is that such changes are part of what Deas (2006: 83) refers to as the 'internationalisation of capital, the re-expressed pattern of state territoriality and in some accounts, the changing centrality of the nation state'. As such, the re-territorialization of the state is driven by a policy reaction to a mix of global economic logic and reinvigorated sub-national territorial identities; if spatial planning is viewed as a process of shaping and delivering more place-based strategies and investment to deal with the challenges and conditions of the twenty-first century, there are clear implications of it being appropriated for both territorialization and centralization claims – how is it designed and implemented, who has the power, who has the control, and what shape does this take?

This chapter goes on to consider these issues. Its intention is to attempt to dissect the various components of the term 'spatial planning' and set out its meaning and origins in the UK context. It provides a conceptual, rather than practical, debate on the anatomy of spatial planning, situated within ongoing processes of institutional transformation, through the lens of governance and distinctiveness in state policy development. This is undertaken by an analysis of three origins (illustrated in Table 3.1) that

Table 3.1 *Three theoretical and political origins of UK spatial planning*

- Re-territorialization – the re-territorialization and rescaling of policy making
- Europeanization – the European origin and development of spatial development
- Integration – the push towards sub-national agency and institutional integration

Source: Tewdwr-Jones, Gallent and Morphet (2010).

together, it is contested, form an influence on the emergence, shape and development of spatial planning, in an attempt to question and theorize how UK planning has embraced the phraseology.

Later in the book, these three elements serve to provide a more in-depth discussion that seeks to position the spatial planning label within a broader, more social-science perspective of the subject matter, and within the political emphasis on place shaping and territorial governance. This chapter does not go on to consider how spatial planning has occurred on the ground with planning practitioners. Several research studies have been completed recently that analyse these processes practically, including an Economic and Social Research Council (ESRC) project undertaken by Hull, Newcastle and Reading universities (Haughton et al. 2010), an effective spatial planning-in-practice project undertaken by University College London and Deloitte (Morphet 2010) and a UK government-sponsored study, 'Spatial Planning in Practice', undertaken by Manchester and Liverpool universities. This chapter considers the academic, professional and political interpretations of the phraseology. And it is precisely the diversity of studies and reinterpretations of the spatial planning phrase now under way that prompted this book to be developed in the first place.

Re-territorialization: Adapting the fixed static state to state fluidity and rescaling processes

A territory is a given area of land under the jurisdiction of the state, or an organized division of a country that has a particular set of powers and jurisdiction. The word territory is one of the themes of spatial governance and reflects its close relationship to the role of planning strategy-making which, in itself, is a function of government and governance within defined boundaries. We are more concerned here with the territory as a geographical and political form/vessel, rather than with the processes of 'territorialization', 'de-territorialization' and 're-territorialization', concepts that have been permeating academic debate in political and economic geography since the early 2000s (Brenner 2004). Planning, traditionally, has been a process or tool of defined and boundaried states and geographies, associated with administrative and political functions, namely central or local government. But increasingly, new 'spaces of flows' (Castells 1996) are occurring through global processes of capital between sub-national territories which do not necessarily reflect the boundaried administrative entities of the state or match the pre-existing planning framework. These new spaces focus on learning regions, global cities, industrial districts and new economic spaces (Scott 1996), which in themselves are part of the rescaling of activities from the national to multiple spatial scales (Boyer and Hollingsworth 1997). These processes continue to fascinate geographers and planners since they transcend the very study of geography and territory as we have traditionally seen them, those 'static entitles frozen permanently into geographical space' (Brenner 2004: 7). Smith sums up these changes succinctly:

> Geographical scale is traditionally treated as a neutral metric of physical space: specific scales of social activity are assumed to be largely given as in the distinction between urban, regional, national and global events and processes ... There is now, however, a considerable literature arguing that the geographical scales of human activity are not neutral 'givens', not fixed universals of social experience ... geographical scales are the product of economic, political and social activities and relationships; as such they are as changeable as those relationships themselves. (Smith 1995: 60–1)

Scale may be defined as 'the level of geographical resolution at which a given phenomenon is thought of, acted on or studied' (Agnew 1997: 100). There are various ways of studying scales, including the scaling and rescaling of processes; the relationality of scales between geographical scales upwards and downwards; the amalgam of various scalar organizations creating a vast institutional landscape; scalar fixes, involving the shifting sands of institutions and organizations that are fixed temporarily and that create benefits for modern capitalism; and scalar transformations, where one scale transcends into new scales and creates its own legacies and forms (Brenner 2004).

Within the literature, geographers, planners, political scientists and others are using many of these concepts to describe the changing economic, political, social and institutional events unfolding across the UK and other capitalist countries. Massey, for example, discusses the importance of 'the places in between' rather than with embedded practices (2005: 119) and of avoiding 'a billiard-ball view of place' (2005: 68) that sees space as static rather than unbounded. Similarly, Allmendinger and Haughton (2007) discuss the new generation of 'soft spaces' and ' fuzzy boundaries' that characterize emerging political objectives within new state relations, all of which are causing a changed agenda for planners and others charged with formulating territorial-based strategies. Perhaps there has been a somewhat belated acknowledgement within planning academe that the traditional approach of planners to problemize, plan and strategize geographies within bounded entities has never really worked, nor is such an approach suitable for a twenty-first century characterized by re-territorialization and state fluidity. As Sandercock (2003: 2–3) makes clear with reference to 'the places in between': 'In the postwar rush to turn planning into an applied science much was ignored – the city of memory, of desire, of spirit; the importance of place and the art of place-making; the local knowledges written into stones and memories of communities.' Within the planning literature, these concepts have taken some time to take hold, principally because planners have been overtly concerned with strategies, their politics, power, coercion, implementation and delivery, within fixed territorial limits. Planning – as a political creation and function of the state – is legitimized, operationalized and realized by the will of the state and, of course, its relationship to increasingly global economic forces – a point that has long been a criticism of planning over many decades (see Cooke 1983; Reade 1987, for example).

The focus here on territory is relevant since it relates directly to the geographically organized jurisdiction of the state and, therefore, analytically, can encompass planning as a strategy-making, integrating and participatory activity that is worthy of study, with all its associated political, economic and social externalities. That is not to say that planners can defend planning within its current state manifestation with any form of alacrity; rather, it has been argued over many years that planning as a state function is constantly misused politically and economically, to the detriment – socially and environmentally – of non-national and multinational interests (see, for example, Allmendinger 2001; Tewdwr-Jones 2002). But we live in new times politically, economically and socially, and the fact that planning has survived as a state activity in the UK and continues to swing between use and abandonment politically as a key agency of land-use management and public policy delivery (depending on which political party is in office) indicates the political, economic and social potential that is inherent within the subject.

As different scales of the state continue to demand and strategize political visions within territorial scales, balancing these visions against forces that actively push against static, bounded and fixed geographical universals, so planning can be seen to be morphed from its postwar

welfare-state determinist mould into a more open, multiple and relational activity that can adjust to the fluidity of the state, albeit one still
delivering some of those postwar objectives. These are the trends distin-
guishing UK planning in the twenty-first century, as it undergoes a meta-
morphosis through stretching, tugging, expanding and loading,
associated with increasing expectations of it delivering at various spatial
scales, within and outside existing territories, that suggest both forces of
continuity with and radical breaks from the past (Tewdwr-Jones and
Allmendinger 2006; Allmendinger and Haughton 2007). The political
and economic geography literature has served a useful purpose within
planning in assisting in the analysis of this multifarious change within
territories, an attempt – in essence – to 'make sense' of it all (Healey
2007). But in doing so, there is a realization that the land-use planning
process will not, in itself, be able to respond to these demands.

Europeanization: The ESDP, re-territorialization and UK planning

Any process of change requires, to varying degrees, a catalyst environment: single or multiple agents, or specific circumstances, that provoke
or speed up such processes. Such an environment can well be argued to
exist so far as changes in EU member states activities are concerned.
Indeed, one might say that the whole European regionalization, integration and terrirorialization processes helped provide a riverbed for these
changes in spatial planning to occur (Faludi and Waterhout 2002). In
this sense we can highlight as formative catalysts the creation of the
single market, a concern with lagging regions, the development of a
multi-level governance framework, specific sectoral legislation and policies (Trans-European (Transport) Networks (TEN-T), the Community
Environmental Directives, the Community Regional and Cohesion
Policy, the ESDP and the Community Initiative INTERREG, for
example) and the enlargement process. There is a danger that these may
seem another world away from the land-use changes and trends identified in Chapter 2, or else a new form of 'Euro-speak', but the reality is
they are connected indecorously. On the other hand, it is nonetheless
difficult to determine the nature and degree of influence each of these
has had both in shaping both the overarching European spatial planning
agenda and domestic land-use planning systems and practices.

Kunzmann (2006) argues that the origin of spatial planning in European terms can be traced back to Christaller's central place theory of
1950 and his hierarchy of European cities and central places to illustrate the spatial dimensions of Europe (see also Dickinson 1967). These
ideas took hold within the new Council of Europe from the 1960s

onwards, when the Parliamentary Assembly passed a resolution (289 of 1964) calling for an initiative to explore the prospects of regional planning. This, in turn, led to attempts to conceptualize principles for the guiding of spatial development in Europe and led to the foundation of the European Regional Development Fund in the 1970s (Kunzmann et al. 1977). But it was not until the Torremolinos CEMAT conference of 1983 that the term was first used, in the European Charter of Regional and Spatial Planning (CEC 1984) adopted by European ministers. The Charter states:

> Regional/spatial planning seeks at one and the same time to achieve, balanced socio-economic development of the regions, improvement of the quality of life, responsible management of natural resources and protection of the environment, and rational use of land ... the achievement of regional/spatial planning objectives is essentially a political matter. (n.p.)

It was from this Charter that research work began to embark on the concept of European regional and spatial development in the late 1980s (Cheshire and Hay 1989) and into the 1990s through documents such as *Europe 2000* and *Europe 2000+* (CEC 1994). By this time, European ministers were already embarking on the ten-year initiative that eventually led to the publication of the ESDP in 1999. To some, like Kunzmann (2006), spatial planning derived within certain member states of the EU as an umbrella term, 'a relatively neutral and inclusive term for all the various styles and concepts of planning found in the EU, and to encompass all spatial scales from the local to the whole of Europe' (Williams 1996: vii). To others, spatial planning refers more to the political objective towards realizing enhanced European integration: the growing dynamic of change hinted at upcoming national transformations as a result of the emerging European spatial planning field's 'recourse to new policy processes, instruments and techniques' (Giannakourou 1996: 608).

European spatial planning could not be perceived as a federal-like reproduction of national practices at the European level, nor as a simple exercise of intergovernmental bargaining that would leave national spatial planning policies, where they existed, untouched (Giannakourou 1998: 27). But it was the ESDP in particular, the product of EU member states' cooperation over a ten-year period to consider the future of the European territory, that precipitated greater awareness of spatial planning, spatial development and territorial development in individual countries. Although there was no possibility for the ESDP to become a legally binding force over individual states or their planning systems, there was a clear expectation that something was 'going to have to give' with domestic planning systems if the concept of spatial planning was to take hold. As the ESDP stipulated on its publication in 1999:

> The Member States ... take into consideration the European dimension of spatial planning in adjusting national spatial development policies, plans and reports. Here, the requirement for a 'Europeanisation of state, regional, and urban planning' is increasingly evident. In their spatially relevant planning, local and regional government and administrative agencies should, therefore, overcome any insular way of looking at their territory and take into consideration European aspects and interdependencies right from the outset. (CEC 1999: 45)

The emphasis here was the necessity for different territories to see beyond their own borders and respond to existing interdependencies between them and Europe when setting their planning agendas. The links between the 1999 ESDP's sentiments and the writings of geographers and planning in the following few years about the need for states and planning to respond to soft spaces, new relational dynamics and new patterns of growth are immediately apparent, although attributing a degree of causality here is problematic. Nevertheless, there are several developments that occurred in the 1997–2000 period that enabled the UK to start reforming the planning system and to embrace 'more European' notions of spatial planning. Some of these are accidents of history, others relate to the presence of personalities, and others stem from institutional change. Together, they form a unique set of circumstances that enabled a greater degree of Europeanization in UK planning than was previously possible (Zetter 2001).

The first issue was changing governments. As soon as the Labour party was elected in May 1997, attitudes towards Europe and the EU changed markedly within government (Bache and Nugent 2007). Prior to this, it would be fair to say that the Conservative government promoted a somewhat Eurosceptic attitude towards anything European (Tewdwr-Jones, Bishop and Wilkinson 2000). Negotiations on the ESDP were continuing, of course, while all this happened, and it apparently came as something of a surprise that, on taking office in June 1997, the new UK planning minister Richard Caborn did not hesitate to sign the UK up to the principles of the ESDP.

A second influence on this process of Europeanization concerns re-territorialization and, more specifically, the UK process of devolution. As greater European integration occurred on the part of the UK government, devolution to Scotland, Wales, Northern Ireland and London – a central plank of the incoming government's agenda – resulted in those territories looking towards the ESDP and its style of planning for motivation, inspiration and distinctiveness (Tewdwr-Jones 2002). The distinctiveness agenda was partly to do with distancing the form of planning in these EU regions from their UK roots and the overly regulatory type of activity planning had become under the Conservatives (Thornley 1991). But it was also intended to demonstrate unequivocally that the territories were politically now in new times, were taking a pro-European stance, and were looking strategically at the post-2000 EU Structural Fund programme and their own ability to capitalize as peripheral locations by attracting significant EU investment. The transition in both Scotland and Wales was assisted by the fact that the first ministerial holders of the planning portfolio in the Scottish Executive and the Welsh Assembly Government (WAG), Sarah Boyack and Sue Essex, respectively, were not only professional planners, but also planning academics, well versed in ongoing debates relating to European spatial planning and influenced by academic colleagues researching and teaching aspects of the emerging European spatial planning.

Since 2000, the Celtic countries of the UK have embraced a European-influenced form of spatial planning, through the adoption of the Wales Spatial Plan (WAG 2005) (see Figure 3.1), the Regional Development Strategy for Northern Ireland (DRDNI 2001) and the Scottish national spatial planning framework (Scottish Executive 2004), together with the adoption of the UK's first spatial plan, the Mayor of London's Spatial Development Strategy, or London Plan (Mayor of London and GLA 2004; see Figure 3.2). The establishment of these spatial strategies within each jurisdiction did not occur in isolation, and there was a degree of reproduction of styles between the various forums as expertise began to be drawn from each country's experience.

These processes were mirrored in the following years by an ongoing process of enhancing regional governance and strategy making within the English regions after 2001. In fact, it was the Minister for Planning for England in 1998 who first gave a signal that styles of planning might change. In Richard Caborn's *Modernising Planning* statement of 1998, he stated: 'there needs to be a significant European dimension to our planning system ... spatial development issues do not respect national boundaries' (DETR 1998b: 6). At the time, commentators suggested that this referred to the need to bring together the land-use function with the funding allocation, particularly that available through EU Structural Fund programmes (Tewdwr-Jones and Williams 2001). But with hindsight, the statement may have marked the start of more spatial planning thinking in government, even if it was not stated explicitly at the time. The Europeanization of UK planning, along with the re-territorialization issue for the devolved areas, unleashed spatial thinking that began to be transposed across the UK. One might even suggest that this degree of policy entrepreneurship occurred as different English regions increasingly glanced over their shoulders at what their neighbouring

Celtic regions were promoting. They attempted to adopt similar approaches for fear of losing out economically or strategically, or potentially losing some competitive advantage because of weaker institutional arrangements. In fact, once these processes of spatial strategy making were put into place, the key diagrams and illustrations of the new spatial strategies began to include some familiar EU ESDP terminology, with phrases such as 'polycentric development', 'major economic growth zones', 'transport corridors' and 'gateways' littered throughout the documents. In other words, officials and planners within these territories intentionally utilized the discourse of the ESDP as a source of ideas for the development of their own strategies, a process in itself that extended not only the ideas of spatial planning and development, but also the Europeanization of UK planning (Dühr 2007).

Figure 3.1   *The Wales Spatial Plan, 2004*

The diagram provides a spatial and strategic overview of opportunities across Wales based on assets, constraints and flows.

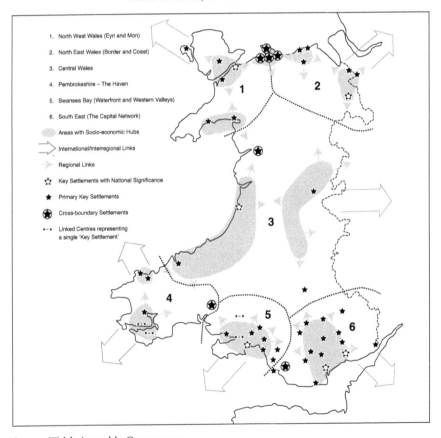

Source: Welsh Assembly Government.

Figure 3.2 *The UK embarks on strategic spatial planning:*
The London Plan

One of the first spatial plans in the UK, the London Plan attempted to look at
spaces of flows and drivers of change across the London region, by
balancing the economic growth westwards to Heathrow and along the M4
corridor, with a policy focus eastwards along the Thames estuary. Many of
the flows originate from administrative outside the control of the Mayor
and the Plan.

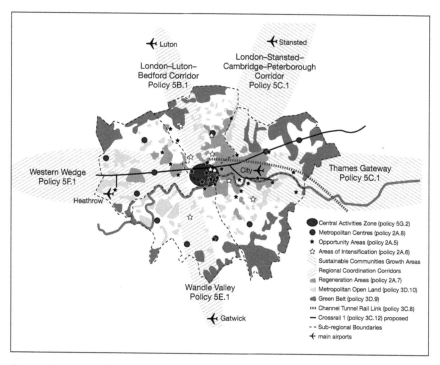

Source: Greater London Authority.

Integration: The sub-national state and the integration imperative within UK planning reform

The Planning Green Paper of 2001 'Delivering a Fundamental Change'
(DTLR 2001), that triggered the process of UK planning reform
throughout the 2000s, made no mention of spatial planning or of developing a European dimension of British planning, and rather employed
familiar ministerial rhetoric about planning concerning overtly inflexible, bureaucratic and legalistic responses and a fixation on planning as

a land-use and regulatory – business-delaying – vehicle. This change may have reflected the fact that by 2001 different ministers – Stephen Byers and Charles Falconer – were now in charge of planning, and were given the task of planning reform with greater attention from the Treasury about planning's perceived impact on economic growth.

The resulting legislative change stemming from the Green Paper occurred through the Planning and Compulsory Purchase Act 2004. Although there was little debate on spatial planning during the passing of the planning Bill in Parliament in the 2001–4 period, some of the spatial planning syntax did find its way into related policy documents. The publication of the national planning policy statement PPG11 on Regional Planning in England in October 2000 was significant as one of the first UK governmental planning documents to recognize the importance of the ESDP. Polycentric development of the EU territory, a principle of the ESDP, had started to be a required principle of English Regional Planning Guidance (Note)s (RPGs); after 2004 and until their abandonment politically in 2011 these documents were replaced with Regional Spatial Strategies (RSSs) that, as their name implies, rested on the same expectations of working within the concept of spatial thinking. Additionally, the introduction of 'Sub-Regional Strategies' (SRSs) potentially addressed economic growth and contributed towards the improved economic performance of all regions beyond traditional local government boundaries. At the local level, the government was committed to introducing a more flexible spatial planning process with strong community involvement, and new 'Local Development Frameworks'(LDFs) (replacing structure, unitary and local development plans) have been intended to address social inclusion, economic and environmental issues and their spatial implications and interrelationships (Tewdwr-Jones, Morphet and Allmendinger 2006).

Alongside the legislative reforms of the planning policy documents, the government first provided its own definition of spatial planning in national planning policy note PPS1 Delivering Sustainable Development of 2005:

> The new system of regional spatial strategies and local development documents should take a spatial approach. Spatial planning goes beyond traditional land use planning to bring together and integrate policies for the use and development of land with other policies and programmes which influence the nature of places and how they function. (ODPM 2005: para. 30)

The statement went on to state that a spatial planning approach involves local and regional authorities setting a clear vision for places, by considering problems of places and their potential solutions, and to integrate a range of activities relating to development and regeneration.

This version of spatial planning is somewhat different from its European origin, and takes a more British land-use perspective and an integrative requirement, which may reflect the complexity in UK planning of the private sector negotiating a public sector-led or partnership planning process within an increasingly fragmented state. In the period since the planning Act of 2004, some planners have remained confused as to the purpose and direction of planning in the UK even prior to the following wave of planning reform in 2011; does spatial planning rest on its traditional focus of land use and development since the statutory definition of planning remains unaltered, or does it comprise a more spatial planning focus that extends beyond the land use? And if it is the latter, where does the statutory legitimacy emanate from to operationalize planning in this way?

The parallel direction of planning, as both a land-use regulatory process and a spatial planning process, appears to be the way UK planning is heading at the moment, with concomitant debate on the differences (Allmendinger 2006), in changes pre- and post-2010 (Tewdwr-Jones 2010) and between different parts of the UK. The distinction between land-use planning and spatial planning is important because it illustrates two apparent tensions within English government ministries concerning planning's role and purpose; the ODPM (Office of the Deputy Prime Minister; after 2006, the Department for Communities and Local Government, CLG) stressed the spatial approach until 2010, while Treasury perspectives (epitomized through publications such as the Barker Reviews of Housing and Planning (2004, 2007) and later the Localism Bill (2010)) stressed the land-use regulatory process, with seemingly little harmony or direct reference to each other. Somewhat tellingly, at a ministerial launch of a planning report in 2007, the junior Minister for Planning at the CLG, Baroness Andrews, remarked that the 2004 Act:

> establishes a process it [the government] calls 'Spatial Planning' … It facilitates and promotes sustainable and inclusive patterns of urban and rural development. Rather than operating through a narrow technical perspective, spatial planning should actively involve all members of society because everyone has a stake in the places in which they live, work and play. (cited in Morphet et al. 2007: 6)

Whether this was post-hoc labelling or not, it is clear what the CLG's perspective was; it was partly to legitimize a role for planning in the twenty-first century and partly an attempt to deal with the costs associated with a fragmented state. But equally, there was a conscious recognition within government about the economic changes occurring below the level of the region, and finding appropriate sub-national government frameworks and tools to deal with them (CLG/BERR 2007). The government's sub-national review of economic development, published in 2007, proposed a strengthening of the role of local authorities in economic development, by establishing a new statutory economic assessment duty, and promoting collaboration across local authority boundaries through Multi-Area Agreements (CLG/BERR 2007: 3). Since 2010, these reforms have been replaced by a new agenda imposed by the coalition government and contained within the Localism Act, which removes the regional and strategic element and focuses attention on planning deregulation and neighbourhood planning, but retains a statutory duty for local authorities to cooperate with each other. Whereas some commentators suggest this marks the death of spatial planning (Allmendinger and Haughton 2009, 2010, 2011), the reality is that spatial planning as an evidence base and as a way of mediating between different actors territorially is still required, even if politically at the national level in England it is not being discussed. The abolition of documents called RSSs does not remove spatial planning, and to do so suggests a total naivety about the form and role of land-use planning in understanding and contributing to the resolving of land tensions. Taking one spatial scale out of the picture also neglects the fact that spatial planning has no boundaries: it continues in other parts of the UK, in the UK's relationship to the rest of the European territory, and globally in city-to-city relationships and investment competition. The planning reforms after 2011 simply make the governing of places as they are affected by external forces much more difficult to deal with.

In contemporary discussions in the UK on the purpose and organization of the planning system and the practices surrounding it, Healey (2006) identifies a recurring theme as the role of the system in 'integrating' disparate agendas, activities and actors. She sees this as an 'integrated' approach that links diverse policy objectives as a way of connecting issues as they play out, as a way of linking different types of government intervention, overcoming the fragmentation of area- and development-based policy initiatives and the competition between individual projects, and linking policy with delivery. These discussions have focused on 'joining up' or 'holistic' government (Wilkinson and Applebee 1999; 6 et al. 2002), at a sub-national level of government – regions, local authorities, or town, parish and neighbourhood administrative units. The objective here is to connect different governance initiatives focused in the arena of the planning system, through the system's concern with the use and development of land, with spatial organization and the qualities of places. The intention has been to join up economic, social and environmental policy contentions, and address conflicts over the qualities of places and the impacts of development proposals. With the Coalition government's policies now being rolled out, it seems clear that the administration has a fundamental misunderstanding about how governance works. Perhaps this has been fuelled by economists' failure to see this wider role of planning in governance arrangements within a fragmented state and to see planning negatively as an overtly regulated, state-led, 1947-style planning system. Do economists really not recognize that governance, delivery bodies and participatory priorities have not only changed the planning system in the last 40 years, but they have also changed the context within which change and debate about change occurs?

Until 2011, the responsibility of the (spatial) planning system was to work out how policies interlink at the local level, through development investment and land-use regulation. Planning in the twenty-first century is not a Soviet-style centralized monster as the Conservatives, the Treasury and some economists suggest. Planning is a key governance, integrative and delivery mechanism – it enables the market to take investment decisions. Of course planning is still present, but it is faced with an ambiguous challenge: as spatial planning, it is no longer in 'the lead' but it is a key component and facilitator of delivery. So if the Treasury and economists do want to do something about planning, they really need to start focusing on the real issues that affect land: governance, the fragmentation of delivery bodies, the relationship between landownership and development rights, and opportunities for democratic involvement in land-use change. Only when they start to systematically address these wider matters will they finally be able to claim that they are doing something about planning. In the meantime, the coalition government, like most of its predecessors, plays around with the planning mechanisms in the optimistic and ultimately shallow belief that they truly understand the land system and the role of planning in managing land-use conflicts.

It will not be surprising to learn, then, that the practices of the traditional land-use planning system have always been deeply embedded in an increasingly legalized conflict-resolution process. The reforms to planning after 2001 were set within this wider remit and perspective of the system, to take on an integrative and delivery role in territorial development, on a regional, sub-regional, urban and neighbourhood scale. This was referred to by government as a spatial planning movement, pushed by forces both within local government via the local government legislation, rather than with planning laws per se, and the planning profession (RTPI 2003). The challenge for those planning reforms and for the adoption of spatial planning is that they assumed a new governance institutional framework that did not arrive in England. This is partly because of the continuous turmoil created by regional and local government modernization in England and the interference of the UK government to continually reform sub-national policy arrangements; there has been no time to embed new processes to deal with some of the

sub-national and local land-use issues before another wave of governance reform has been parachuted in by Whitehall. The contribution of
the spatial planning movement and the planning policy community has
not been, as imagined in the past according to Healey (2006), to produce
a comprehensive, all-encompassing strategy for the evolution of a place
or territory. The efforts in producing RSSs regionally 2000–10 and LDFs
locally indicated what this would have involved. It was political mobilization with place visioning, and not planning technique, that had the
potential to carry the place-focused movement into the remoulding of
the landscape of urban and regional governance:

> A New Vision of Planning is required which seeks to build the
> capacity within society and its institutions to take effective and rele-
> vant decisions. This challenges us to think beyond the scope of statu-
> tory systems and to take a broader view of what society needs
> through planning. It also challenges us to see planning as an activity
> which professional planners facilitate, but do not own or monopo-
> lise. (RTPI 2003: 2)

The Local Government Association (LGA), RTPI and others have
appeared to have been successful initially at pushing this agenda politically at the right time. The RTPI had adopted a new vision for planning
in 2003, committing the profession to the idea of spatial planning,
defining it as 'the critical thinking about space and place as the basis for
action or intervention'. This was dissected into a series of themes by the
RTPI, notably that a spatial planning approach is one that is 'broad-
ranging, visionary, integrating, deliverable, and participative' (RTPI
2003). The intention here was to broaden the activity of professional
planning in the UK beyond its regulatory core and adopt a much wider
concept of planning, one that returns a more strategic role for planning
and simultaneously positions planning at the heart of public-sector
service coordination. These strategic and corporate roles bore all the
hallmarks of aspects of the UK planning system that were endemic in the
period 1945–79, prior to the deregulation of planning by the Thatcher
government but within a new context and a new role for the state,
private sector and citizenry.

The twenty-first-century emphasis on spatial planning as place
management and policy delivery, as the means of providing infrastructure, and as sub-national integration, found favour at the heart of
government at the right time. The government commissioned Sir Michael
Lyons to undertake an inquiry into local government financing and services. His report, the Lyons Report (2006), stated little on planning per se
but stipulated that a key role for local government in the future would
be as agents of 'place-shaping'. This was defined as an emphasis on

building and shaping local identity, representing the community, maintaining the cohesiveness of the community, working to make the economy more successful, understanding local needs and preferences, making sure the right services are delivered to local people and working with other bodies to respond to complex challenges. A subsequent research report on effective spatial planning in practice, commissioned by the Department of Communities and Local Government (CLG) and RTPI, made the link between the place-shaping agenda of local-government service delivery, the emerging spatial planning reforms of the 2004 planning Act, and the RTPI's new vision agenda (Morphet et al. 2007). The report redefined spatial planning as 'the practice of place shaping and delivery at all spatial scales' that aimed

> To enable a vision for the future of regions and places that is based on evidence, local distinctiveness, and community defined objectives;
> To translate this vision into a set of policies, priorities, programmes and land allocations together with the public sector resources to deliver them;
> To create a framework for private sector investment and regeneration that promotes economic, environmental and social wellbeing for the area; and
> To coordinate and deliver the public sector components of this vision with other agencies and processes.

What we were witnessing here was yet another transformation and re-politicization of planning through the governmental, institutional, professional and legal frameworks of planning in the UK. This evolution is, perhaps, unique to the UK, and just one interpretation and reinterpretation of how the EU origin of spatial planning – something different to the existing ways of thinking and operating – has unleashed different ways of thinking and working in different member states.

Having reviewed the three ongoing processes of reform and their conceptual underpinnings, we now go on to provide a critique of how spatial planning is attempting to find a practice base in the UK.

A critique of spatial planning in practice: Emerging processes and realities

The current forms of government and institutional restructuring, and the emergence of new governance and partnership forms at formal administrative government levels and within the spaces between, has occurred in existing formalized geographical territories and transcending state and spatial boundaries. These processes are juxtaposed next to an intense bout of debate on the ongoing modernization of government and the state, the broadening out and overhaul of planning as an integrating and as a regulatory tool, and the state's rather sudden conversion to attempt to address the meaning of, and activity within, places. All this is providing a vast canvas for academic interpretation, political analysis and professional introspection.

This suggests ongoing uncertainties with the form of government–governance and with the state at various levels, a process that Healey (2006) refers to as 'jerky', but also with the ability of spatial planning to embrace integration and become more than, to use Healey's description, a legalized conflict-resolution process. For far too long planning has been concerned with official spaces and fixated with (perhaps archaic) established boundaries but, echoing the work of both Massey (2005) and Sandercock (2003), this tends to miss most of what is going on in places, the interactions between citizens, the relationship between policy intention and delivery, and with an associated failure to concentrate on space–place tensions.

The last 13 years or so within the UK have witnessed increasing attempts of existing and new forms of government to adopt new broader and participatory forms of spatial visioning that transcend, overlap or even replace established boundaries and silo mentalities. It is, as Deas (2006) rightly observes, a faltering process of governance that is as much about overcoming barriers, perceptions and traditional institutional cultures, as it is about creating new sub-national agendas that relate to distinctive problems and distinctive places. This fluidity and duality in purpose suggests the existence of multiple identities within territories that need to be recognized and legitimated in the first instance. But for such identities and territories to form a bedrock upon which successful spatial strategy-making can occur, there needs to be a distinction made between the forms of identities, strategy ownership and place-meanings that may lead to alternative ways of conceptualizing problems. Like land, even the governance arrangements to deal with places can be contested matters.

Harris, Hooper and Bishop (2002) have referred to this tendency in their discussion of the Wales Spatial Plan that offers much in its style of planning, but since the strategy also performs the role of corporate document for the Welsh government, its actual function rests somewhere between the political and the functional, where the role of spatial planning is to perform the role of a policy-integration tool. With this evidence, one can question whether this style of spatial strategy-making and planning is starting to address the real space–place tensions that spatial planning as a concept was meant to address. Graham and Marvin 2001: 115) question, pertinently, the leverage that these strategic planning exercises will have over time. They are, in effect, mobilization exercises to articulate new policy frames and new policy relations. They tend to be associated with centre-left governments which give more emphasis to strategy and to social objectives ... do they have the persuasive power to shift territorial development trajectories, or, as some argue, are they little more than a cosmetic covering that hides the growing disparities evolving within Europe?

We may therefore question whether these new forms of spatial planning actually lead to an ability on the part of government to provide strategic policy without central direction, and thereby allow sub-national and local distinctiveness to emerge within the new processes. Since strategists spend an inordinate amount of time striving for consistency and compatibility, and want to ensure progress in strategy formulation over time, the resulting strategies are themselves in danger of becoming overtly timid since they avoid tackling problems boldly. Furthermore, there is a prospect of new forms of spatial planning and governance remaining set within what MacGinty (2006) refers to as 'decidedly old notions of territory'. Lloyd and Peel (2006) also discuss this latter point in their discussion of city-regionalism, and refer to what they call a 'new mercantilism of spatiality', where ideas of spatial strategy-making and the use of spatial language and labels are traded across territories, places and governments. In the case of city-regionalism, this is leading to the celebration of diversity and identity within metropolitan areas but is nevertheless firmly articulated through broader spatial contexts and international flows and competitiveness.

Raco (2006), in his discussion of identity, devolution and governance, suggests that there is now a hybridism of differing ideas and practices emerging in different parts of the UK. He maintains that the state is fixed with the necessity to draw boundaries and set parameters, or limits, to governing, which is convenient and assists in attempting to embed new processes within particular scales. This also benefits a concern to fix identities for the purpose of governing and to seek a consensus to enable the electorate to interact with their political institutions, but it does little to resolve place–space tensions. Similarly, MacLeod and Jones (2006) draw out differences in conceptualizing spaces and territories, and how an overt concentration on the politics of scalar structuration potentially misses the attributes and substance of places and their significance. They argue for a topological approach to find conceptual footing alongside rescaling debates in order to capture, or at least appreciate, the looseness of exchanges, the way people occupy and use space, so as to transcend rigid and archaic boundaries, and various territories. What would be more suitable than utilizing the land and the uniqueness of land as a starting point for this process?

Conclusions

There are bound to be difficulties with planning within all territories in the next decade. Spatial changes and spatial differences between places are expected to become dominant themes for public services and market investors and for policy development, alongside planning's tradition role as a land-use regulatory activity, while being stretched across several tiers of government and owned across state and non-state agents of governance. A number of significant issues and areas of interest arise from these difficulties, including treating spatial planning simultaneously in diverse ways

A key issue here, and one contested by academic authors, is that these components of spatial planning coexist. They are present in policy and professional intentions for spatial planning as a frame of thinking and occur in various practices that have distinctive territorial and practical characteristics. In some cases, they may even not be present in local or regional practices. But given the form of the components and the intentions behind the spatial planning label, it is appropriate for us to think of spatial planning in diverse ways and not confine it to particular ideas or practices. After all, this – by its very nature – is what prompted spatial planning as a phrase and way of thinking to be coined in the first place; something that would not sit in one particular silo and also be immune from ownership by one actor or dismantled easily by another.

As authors point out, spatial planning is a contributor to and a reflection of a more fundamental reform of territorial management that aims to, *inter alia*, improve integration of different forms of spatial development activity, not least economic development. So, at one level, devolution, decentralization and localism and their implications for spatial planning must be analysed in respect of other aspects of the changing state, not least a preoccupation on the part of governments with state competitiveness. At another level, reforms that privilege specific-scale policy interventions will inevitably require changes in the divisions of powers and responsibilities at other levels (Tewdwr-Jones and Allmendinger 2006). Spatial planning has always been viewed as both a tool of re-territorialization and as a coordinating mechanism between government and governance actors that is unfolding differentially in different regions and locales.

So compared to older types of planning, as discussed in Chapter 1, is spatial planning something radically different from what we have been used to in planning in the past? To some extent, the answer has to be yes, but only in relation to recent history. The regulatory focus of UK planning through the 1980s and most of the 1990s makes spatial planning quite radical in comparison. And yet there are also similarities between spatial planning and the type of planning that was practised in the UK in the 1950s and 1960s, particularly a concern with more corporate agendas, a focus on the sub-national economic state such as city-regions, and ensuring strategies are aligned to service and resources and can be delivered. The change relates to the role of the state; in the 1950s these types of planning were devised and enacted by the state, whereas today the state and spatial planning provide a supportive and facilitation or choreographic role to a range of public and private bodies. We may therefore conclude that the spatial planning term has been appropriated politically and professionally to describe a broader role for planning that, a generation ago, had become deeply unpopular and questioned. That role is essentially one of strategic planning. From this perspective also, we may remark that spatial planning is only partly new substantively, and a revised label for pre-existing practices, involving the reintroduction of ideas (partly from planning, partly from geography) that have been in circulation for many years. As Nadin (2007: 57) states: 'The spur for changes comes from awareness of the need for a spatial dimension in the task of joining-up government in order to achieve critical economic and social outcomes.'

Chapter 4 will now go on to consider some of these issues further by examining the European origin of spatial planning, and the way it was formulated and had an impact on different planning systems across Europe, and the increasing Europeanization of the UK's planning system.

Europeanization, Spatial Planning and Competitiveness

In the first three chapters of this book, we set out the contested nature of both land and the spatial planning and land-use management processes charged with gathering intelligence on spatial change and mediating conflicting claims on territory. Chapter 3 highlighted one of the origins of spatial planning since the mid-1980s, compared to older or more traditional forms of planning that were devised in the first half of the twentieth century. This origin was explicitly Europe and emerging debates and ideas within the EU and in European member states. This included an attempt through the 1990s to develop an overview of spatial development, of territory and change across the European continent. This atlas of change, known as the European Spatial Development Perspective (ESDP), and published in 1999, was a catalyst to both pan-European assessments of territorial change and also unleashed new attempts to consider land use and spatial change, at present and in the future, within individual nations and regions but in a fairly incremental way. In Chapter 4, we examine the ways in which evolving academic and governmental debates within the EU have contributed, in part, to ideas of spatial development and spatial thinking. These ideas have centred on the need to achieve balanced development and growth in different parts of Europe, within each member state, and between different cities and regions within nations, and to the achievement of sustainable development. They have also related quite strongly to the belief that spatial planning and land-use management processes have been designed, to some extent, to provide the intelligence and evidence base about spatial change, consider the medium- and long-term trends economically, environmentally and socially, and an integrative means to deal with policy complexity and agency fragmentation.

Debates on European spatial planning literature have illustrated, in essence, different dimensions of an existing dynamic of change; a change in the way we perceive and inquire into the multitude of aspects that spatial development and growth within the EU entails (Jensen and Richardson 2004; Duhr, Colomb and Nadin 2010). In this context, it can be agreed that the idea of European spatial planning is a unique catalyst of change (Williams 1996; Tewdwr-Jones and Williams 2001), and one that has had an impact on emerging forms of planning in the UK. And the question one might ask from the outset is the extent to which the 'heroic efforts of an epistemic community [push] forward the sound concept of European spatial planning' (Gualini 2005: 1) have actually kick-started a process of change across the Continent that we can unpick analytically. This chapter addresses this question by focusing specifically on the meaning of Europeanization and the impact of European spatial planning on domestic planning systems and spatial planning strategy-making of the EU member states, with specific reference to the UK.

In the opinion of Featherstone:

> Europeanisation is, to put it somehow crudely, a matter of degree. It also has a dynamic quality: its structural effects are not necessarily permanent or irreversible ... The impact of Europeanisation is typically incremental, irregular, and uneven over time and between locations, national and subnational. Profound disparities of impact remain – it is inherently an asymmetric process – and the attraction for researchers is to account for them. (2003: 4)

Making sense of Europeanization is not a task without obstacles. The fact is that there are many ways to approach Europeanization, depending on the academic discipline or specific line of inquiry adopted, or the direction towards one of 'the many faces of Europeanisation' (Olsen 2002: 921). The research focus of Europeanization can vary between its relationship to government structure and policy making (Ladrech 1994; Ioakimidis 1996; Majone 1997; Featherstone 1998; Lawton 1999; Cole and Drake 2000; Cope 2001), administrative structure (Spanou 1998), spatial planning traditions (Faludi 2004), economic policy (Dyson 2000), political parties (Ray 1999) and culture and identity (Hedetoft 1995). In short, 'there is no single grand theory of Europeanisation that can help us understand how institutions co-evolve through processes of mutual adaptation. Nor is there a single set of simplifying assumptions about change, institutions and actors that will capture the complexity of European transformations' (Olsen 2002: 944).

This chapter's structure is fourfold. First, we briefly introduce the theoretical framework supporting our analysis by debating the concept of Europeanization and its possible systematization and operationalization as a feasible research framework for the sort of changes under inquiry. Secondly, we introduce empirical examples of these changes throughout the EU member states in general and in the UK in particular. Thirdly, we address the relationship between European spatial planning and cohesion and competitiveness with specific reference to the idea of 'balanced competitiveness' and forms of regional economic development. This is intended to illustrate the problems of addressing Europeanization concerns spatially and its potential within different territories. Fourthly, we conclude by interpreting to what extent there is an ongoing Europeanization process occurring and how we can expect it to evolve in the future.

Europeanization: Systematizing the concept

There is a strong claim to be made to equate emerging forms of spatial planning in the UK with growing Europeanization. If we accept that elements of spatial planning, stylistically, owe their origin to both the ESDP and more continental forms of planning, it is reasonable to consider what Europeanization could be in order to unpick the meaning and form of planning in the UK. There have been some attempts to unravel Europeanization in planning and in public policy debates as part of a systematization process (Adcock and Collier 2001; Featherstone 2003, 6:12; Radaelli 2004: 6). For example, Featherstone carried out a review of the most common trends in the usage of the concept (2003: 6). He identified the dominant usage to date to be that related to institutional adaptation and the adaptation of policy and policy processes. The first addresses the 'domestic adaptation to the pressures emanating directly or indirectly from EU membership' (7); the latter pertains to the specific impacts of EU membership on public policy inclusive of a series of different approaches, such as constraints due to EU regulation or the indirect effects of the EU's role on national policy (10). Additional input can be found nested in the work of Adcock and Collier (in Radaelli 2004: 2). These authors make a conceptual differentiation between Europeanization as either a background concept or a systematized concept. As a background concept investigation takes an encyclopaedic approach, 'reporting on all major meanings associated with a concept' (Radaelli 2004: 2). However, if it is impossible to exhaustively review all studies on Europeanization (e.g. domestic changes in the EU member states' planning systems), a way to proceed is to identify the key enquiry themes within the process systematizing the analysis. Radaelli (2004: 6) exemplifies this by outlining three themes: governance, institutionalization and discourse. In order to debate how to better evidence Europeanization, we return to these themes later in the chapter.

Systematizing Europeanization can be achieved through focusing on what it is. Alternatively this can be attempted by focusing on how it works. In the latter case there are two schools of thought in the literature. The first, mainly developed in the 1970s and 1980s but ongoing, adopts a top-down approach, investigating 'the pressures from the EU on member states, and by considering intervening variables targeting the identification of reactions and change at the domestic level' (Radaelli 2004: 4). This approach was primarily dedicated to 'tracking down the implementation of European policies', or alternatively, aiming to 'understand how member states organized their European business' (ibid.).

The second school of thought, commonly addressed as the second generation of Europeanization studies (Featherstone 2003; Gualini 2004; Radaelli 2004), is predicated on a totally different bottom-up research design. The starting point in this case is the system of interaction of actors and institutions at the domestic level. The research aim is, by seeking to identify 'time and temporal causal sequences' (Radaelli 2004: 4), to clarify when, how – and, critically, if at all – the EU provokes change in any of the components of the domestic interaction system. A critical line of inquiry here is how do we know if observed domestic patterns of change are really generated by Europe instead of by some other form of pressure? It may be that the endogenous logic of domestic interaction between actors and institutions holds an independent dynamic of change, even if the implementation of EU directives occurs.

Furthermore, initial considerations of Europeanization as an end state have in later studies been replaced by the notion of Europeanization as a process (Goetz 2002; cf. Radaelli 2004: 5). Hence, instead of aiming to determine if a member state has been Europeanized or not, the purpose becomes to investigate what actually goes on within the process of Europeanization in its own right. Finally, this new generation of studies draws a careful line between the definition of processes of Europeanization and their potential outcomes in terms of convergence or divergence. This means that Europeanization is not automatically conceived of as a homogenizing process. The second part of this chapter, which will draw on empirical examples of domestic changes in spatial planning, will help illustrate this point.

According to Hine, a top-down research framework fails to take into account the indirect influences operating at member-state level that emanate from elements exogenous to EU policies or regulations. These indirect influences account for those changes where there was no formal requirement for member states to conform (Spanou 1998). A bottom-up line of inquiry within the Europeanization field based on a research design pitched at the level of domestic politics and policy making is, then, better suited to factoring in such indirect influences and to looking for the 'missing link between (EU level) pressures for change and the perceived (domestic) substantive adaptations (Goetz and Hix 2000: 222). In other words, this research design places the investigator in a 'favourable position to observe when major alterations of the logic (of interaction of domestic actors and institutions) are produced endogenously at the domestic level or by more global pressures' (Radaelli 2004: 5).

This chapter has so far provided a succinct introduction to the concept of Europeanization in which we cover the thematic typologies of the concept, its defining characteristics, and different research design approaches (top-down and bottom-up). Understandings of Europeanization as a concept can be characterized by a multiplicity of approaches, depending on the different disciplinary contexts in which it is used as an inquiry framework. Hence, pinning down a specific definition of Europeanization per se becomes problematic. Indeed, if one agrees with the view that 'the conceptual challenge is not primarily that of inventing definitions' (Olsen 2002: 944) but to explore 'the relevance of the concept for inquiring into change' (Gualini 2004: 4) within a specific policy field, one may conclude that setting a deterministic definition is counterproductive. In reality Europeanization's greater potential is to be understood as a multi-faceted phenomenon 'in search of explanation, not the explanation itself' (Radaelli 2004: 2).

The themes of Europeanization

The dilemma is how to evidence that such a process of change is actually occurring and, if it is, whether we can determine a causal link between observed changes and Europeanization. This may become more elusive where at the domestic level, political actors camouflage local politics under the cover of Europeanization, either by constructing 'blame-shifting' strategies or by retrieving from Europe extra legitimacy for domestic decisions. So the key question is: 'How do I know it when I see it?' (Markusen 2003: 702). One way to try to minimize uncertainty is to run a series of inquiry lines to track down adaptational pressures and the presence of change, or the lack thereof, as indicated by Radaelli (2004):

- There is Europeanization when the logic of domestic political actors changes. This happens when elements of EU policy-making become a cognitive and normative 'frame of reference' and both the logic of action and the logic of meaning are guided by Europe. Think of Europe as the 'grammar' of domestic political action.
- 'Europeanisation is change both in the sense of responses to EU pressures and in the sense of other usages of Europe which do not presuppose pressure.'
- 'Europeanisation is a process consisting of complex sequences and time patterns.' Only the analysis of time patterns in processes of change can help determine causality.
- 'The presence of fully fledged European policies in a certain domain is not a pre-condition for Europeanisation. Europeanisation does not require the formulation of EU policies.'

- 'Clarify the role of socialisation processes. It is only when socialisation to Europe is followed by domestic change that one can speak of Europeanisation. Socialisation is neither a sufficient nor necessary condition for Europeanisation.'

In addition to the above-mentioned inquiry guidelines, there are additional tools to help systematize research on Europeanization. We want to highlight a series of frameworks, non-mutually exclusive, within which one can explore the process of Europeanization: governance, institutionalization and discourse (Radaelli 2004: 6).

The initial paradigm to have in mind here is that Europeanization is 'eminently about governance' (Radaelli 2004: 6). Indeed, there are several interpretations of Europeanization as a process of governance (e.g. Kohler-Koch and Eising 1999; Scharpf 1999; Gualini 2004). Europeanization has modified shared notions of governance in EU member states (Kohler-Koch and Eising 1999) and has further included regions into a complex multi-level matrix of governance (e.g. Goldsmith 1993; Gualini 2004). However, if one takes for granted that Europeanization is in fact producing qualitatively new governance (as opposed to just reshaping already existing forms), then one must tackle the normative dilemma: 'is Europeanisation producing good and legitimate governance in Europe?' (Radaelli 2004: 6).

The second paradigm relates to the emphasis placed by some authors on Europeanization as institutionalization (Cowles, Caporaso and Risse 2001; Olsen, 2002; Radaelli 2003, Börzel 2004). This approach envisages that

> Europeanisation consists of processes of a) construction, b) diffusion, and c) institutionalisation of formal and informal rules, procedures, policy paradigms, styles, 'ways of doing things' and shared beliefs and norms which are first defined and consolidated in the EU policy process and then incorporated in the logic of domestic (national and subnational) discourse, political structures and public policies. (Radaelli 2003: 30).

In other words, what is first experienced at the EU level is later on institutionalized 'inside the logic of behaviour of domestic actors' (Radaelli 2004: 6). Concurrently the role of domestic actors and agency is also under the spotlight. Some authors highlight the fact that 'institutional design and change do not take place in an institutional void, or only through the sway of actors' preferences and material resources (Caporaso and Stone Sweet, 2001: 225). Yet, 'institutions do not change institutions, actors do' (Cowles et al. 2001: 229).

The third and last research framework here associated with Europeanization is discourse (Radaelli 2004: 8). Here the paradigm is that language and discourse are the tools used by policy makers and other actors to construct Europe. Schmidt (2002) and Radaelli (2004) have looked into discourse at the institutional level, developing the notion of discursive institutionalism. The principle is that discourse has a transformative power in EU policy and politics, but if one wishes to understand if and when Europeanization actually produces change, one must situate discourse in its institutional riverbeds (Radaelli 2004: 8).

Europeanization is far from a self-explanatory concept, the research framework of which is still undergoing construction. Currently the main focus is on the development of systematized knowledge about the mechanisms of Europeanization. This chapter has sought to avoid oversimplified use of the term to safeguard it from the conceptual generalization through which its research value can be undermined. Summarily, Europeanization is about change, governance and processes. Europeanization is not a spatially or temporally even phenomenon, and some domestic policies are more permeable to it than others. It can have both vertical and horizontal dimensions and it can be manifest independent of EU policies. Linkages between policy and politics dimensions are leading to a growing intermeshing of the European, national and regional levels. At this point one must highlight the position that Europeanization is not synonymous with convergence. Nonetheless it is possible to a certain extent to discuss convergence clusters (Börzel 2002; Goetz 2002), groups of member states that present similar converging Europeanization processes.

From the outset one can assume that processes of change require to a large extent a catalyst environment. By this, we suggest that a series of agents or specific circumstances assist in provoking or speeding up such processes. So far as changes in spatial planning are concerned, these have been ripe. The whole European integration process helped to provide a riverbed for these changes to occur. As we saw in Chapter 3, we can highlight the creation of the single market, the development of a multi-level governance framework, specific sectoral legislation and policies (e.g. TEN-T and the Community Regional and Cohesion Policy, the Community Initiative INTERREG), the enlargement process, and the emerging European spatial planning agenda. Although difficult to determine the degree and type of influence each of these has had, it can be hypothesized that a key catalyst in changing the spatial planning scenario at multiple levels and scales within Europe has been the ESDP process (see Box 4.1).

The following aims to bridge the theoretical debate addressed earlier in the chapter with the changing empirical reality of spatial planning both at the European and domestic levels. To that effect, the chapter will contextualize this change, illustrate it and explain how it can be – to a certain extent – systematized.

Box 4.1 The European Spatial Development Perspective

The European Spatial Development Perspective (ESDP) is a document approved by the Informal Council of Ministers of Spatial Planning of the EU in 1999. It was the product of ten years of negotiation and is officially a non-binding non-statutory document that acts as a policy framework to be considered by all tiers of government and administration across the EU territory. It acts as a spatial development strategy for Europe with the goal of creating a balanced and sustainable Europe.

They key elements of the document that relate to its spatial component are that it attempts to provide an integrated, multi-sectoral and indicative strategy for spatial development. These features have, to some extent, become the hallmark of a spatial planning approach and have been copied by nations and regions across Europe and elsewhere methodologically in the devising of new spatial plans for territories.

The ESDP is centred around three objectives:

1. The development of a polycentric and balanced urban system to form a new relationship between urban and rural areas.
2. The promotion of an integrated transport and communication concept supporting polycentric development across the EU with parity of access to infrastructure and knowledge.
3. The management of Europe's natural and cultural heritage to support and enhance regional identity and cultural diversity in the face of globalization.

Since its publication, the degree to which member states and regions have taken up the ESDP's objectives and challenges and transferred them to their own territories has been dependent on sovereign planning systems; political attitudes towards Europe and Europeanization; and attitudes towards core vs. periphery debates, particularly in relation to economic growth. Those countries that have embraced elements of the ESDP within their own sovereign planning systems have tended to be pro-European and pro-spatial planning, but have nevertheless had to match up their pre-existing styles of planning with the newer European objectives. For most member states, this has not been an easy process.

European spatial planning: Riverbed for Europeanization?

A systematic in-depth assessment of the impacts of the ESDP has only been shaping up over the last few years (ESPON 2006; Faludi 2009; Duhr et al. 2010). Contrastingly, the search for possible frameworks of analysis to better understand the multidimensional implications of the emerging European spatial planning concept is all but new. This search has in fact run parallel to the making of the ESDP and to the emergence of European spatial planning. In the early 1990s the development of a European Spatial Planning agenda was far from certain. Even so, in 1994 Davies envisaged that 'the future for planning in Europe ... lies in the growth of mutual learning and cooperation at the regional and local levels of government out of which will come a gradual convergence of planning policies and practices' (Davies 1994: 69 in Rivolin and Faludi 2005: 196). This view was not widespread at that time, but it marked a turning point towards what would later be echoed in Williams's seminal book *European Union Spatial Policy and Planning* (1996). The growing dynamic of change hinted at upcoming national transformations as a result of the emerging European spatial planning field's 'recourse to new policy processes, instruments and techniques' (Giannakourou 1996: 608). This author later advised that European spatial planning could not be perceived as a federal-like reproduction of national practices at the European level nor as a simple exercise of intergovernmental bargaining that would leave national spatial planning policies, where they existed, untouched (Giannakourou 1998: 27). Furthermore, while addressing the 'Europeanisation of national spatial planning practices', this author highlighted the 'need to consider other conceptual possibilities which match the nature of the European integration process in the field of spatial planning' (Giannakourou 1998: 27). Later in the ESDP meaning of Europeanization seemed prima facie straightforward:

> The member states ... take into consideration the European dimension of spatial planning in adjusting national spatial development policies, plans and reports. Here, the requirement for a 'Europeanisation of state, regional, and urban planning' is increasingly evident. In their spatially relevant planning, local and regional government and administrative agencies should, therefore, overcome any insular way of looking at their territory and take into consideration European aspects and interdependencies right from the outset. (CEC 1999: 45)

Here, the way Europeanization is portrayed reflects the imperative within the EU for different territories to see beyond their own borders and respond to existing interdependencies between them and Europe when developing their planning agendas. Some authors have reflected that 'making and applying the European Spatial Development Perspective (ESDP) is part of the wider process of Europeanisation' (Börzel 2002a). This view is not without its' challengers: some have criticized the perceived hegemonic nature of the process of change under analysis, evoking 'the silent development of a discourse of monotopia across the new multi-level field of spatial policy' (Graute 2000 in Jensen and Richardson 2004: 179), and suggesting weak or uncritical adaptational dynamics at the domestic level. The latter perspective is undoubtedly ground for further research. The suggestion of homogenization, however, has not gone unchallenged: 'The Europeanisation of spatial planning in the Mediterranean countries neither follows uniform mechanisms nor produces homogenous domestic structures and spatial planning identities' (Giannakourou 2005: 229).

However, returning to the issue under analysis here, our focus is not on the content per se of the ESDP- and EU-led planning policies but how these have directly or indirectly influenced change in member states' planning systems, practices and perception of their individual territories within the wider EU context. Change often generates scepticism, so it may not be surprising that 'academics still appear to consider European spatial planning as a separate field of analysis and discussion within planning studies, as if it was of interest only to a restricted circle of eccentric amateurs' (Rivolin and Faludi 2005: 196). Yet there is general agreement in the literature that the European spatial planning agenda is having some type of impact. The determination of what it consists of exactly, and especially how uniform it is throughout member states, lies at the heart of this chapter.

The making of the ESDP brought together at a common table a wide range of different planning cultures. It was hypothesized that 'like in the European Monetary Union, in planning, too, we perhaps need to accept a Europe of variable speeds' (Zonneveld and Faludi 1996: 59). Fully understanding such differences and how they would all interact resulted in a need for further systematization. In this context the European Commission designed the EU Compendium of spatial planning systems and policies (CEC 1997). This helped create the basis to better understand not only planning traditions individually but also the existence of potential regional clusters based on cultural similarities. But, to avoid blinding generalizations, one must appreciate that 'European planning traditions do not of course correspond automatically to identical perspectives on European spatial planning' (ESPON 2005). It is therefore necessary to strike a balance between recognizing the specificities of each member state and coming up with typologies of responses to European spatial planning.

From the outset the existing literature points out that European spatial planning symbolizes mainly a North-Western European perspective (Faludi and Waterhout 2002). However further developments have helped outline four distinctive regional clusters of change or 'macro-regional perspectives' (ESPON 2006) and adaptation within European spatial planning: the North-Western, British/Irish, Nordic, Mediterranean and Eastern perspectives (Rivolin and Faludi 2005). These four clusters have been described as follows (ESPON 2006: 68):

The North-Western perspective is that European spatial planning may have an institutional future, based on progressive cooperation among the EU Member States and between them and the European Commission.

The British/Irish perspective has cast light on the crucial and complex link between spatial planning and land use planning. Consequently, it has paved the way for a conception of European spatial planning as embedded in a multi-level governance system that could reach from the supra-national to the local level.

The Nordic perspective highlights the discursive nature of European spatial planning. This may explain how such a multi-level governance system acts in practice, showing that the performing capacities of European spatial planning depend in a crucial way on the quality of interactions established between decision-makers and territorial policies, operating at the Community and at the national levels.

The Mediterranean perspective suggests that, ultimately, European spatial planning takes shape by passing through the prism of progressive and complex changes in planning practices. Even if EU-led, this is an eminently local and diversified process and therefore less visible at the continental scale.

Many of the Eastern European countries have encountered the ESDP discussion and contents. The ESDP did have an influence on the creation of new planning systems and institutions around the turn of the century. It should be seen however as providing more of a 'helping hand' within the context of the process of EU accession rather than a clear guidance document.

It must be highlighted that even within each 'cluster' there are different degrees of domestic change. Furthermore, some countries (e.g. France), due to their geography, end up displaying characteristics of more than one 'cluster'. The necessity is therefore to 'further research in order to explain in depth the extent and the direction of change in each domestic system and refine actual comparative observations' (Giannakourou 2005: 329).

Within the UK, as was discussed in Chapter 3, the adoption of the ESDP was paralleled by the process of devolution and regionalisation in the period 1997–2001. It was no accident that the parts of the UK governance structure that embraced the syntax and style of the ESDP were the devolved authorities in Scotland, Wales and, eventually, Northern Ireland, as those countries progressed their own territorial spatial planning strategies for the first time. Those Celtic spatial strategies used terms such as polycentricity, growth points, core and periphery, balanced economic growth and transport corridors in their development of spatial plans for their country. This terminology was as much related to lifting elements of the ESDP into their domestic settings as it was about establishing a clear separation of planning styles from England and the previous one-size-fits-all planning system. The ESDP was the catalyst of this differentiation, but built upon a different approach to planning that had long been emerging in the Celtic, and more particularly peripheral, parts of the UK over the previous 20 years.

Previous studies (DETR 1998; see also Tewdwr-Jones, Bishop and Wilkinson 2000; Tewdwr-Jones and Williams 2001) indicated that there was a growing relationship in planning between the periphery of the UK and Brussels, thanks to the availability and allocation of regional development funds, the designation of and support to new transport networks, and other Community policies in support of lagging regions economically. So although there were relatively minor formal and statutory links in planning terms between the UK government and the European Commission before 1999, parts of the UK had embraced elements of Europeanization in their acceptance of European funding to support regional development and rural development and transportation networks. Those parts corresponded to UK peripheral, as opposed to core (i.e. south-east England) perspectives of planning and reflected warmer attitudes towards Brussels as well. So whether it was intentional or not, devolution allowed the development of alternative styles of planning to that already existing in England, and the pro-European political stance in those countries enabled a more European style of spatial planning not seen previously in the UK.

The only other part of the UK to adopt a more European style of spatial planning at this time was, interestingly enough, London, where devolution had enabled the creation of the Greater London Assembly and a mayoral system and a new spatial development plan (later known as the London Plan) was also initiated. It was perhaps no accident that the Mayor of London's planning adviser was Robin Thompson, a former Kent County Council Chief Planner, who was in office while the Channel Tunnel was being constructed and who built up a strong dialogue with his French counterparts on territorial and planning borders. He was also a former President of both the RTPI and European Council of Town Planners. Again, an accident of history, perhaps, but Thompson may well have been at the right place at the right time to push more European spatial planning terminology into the developing London Plan.

After Scotland, Wales, Northern Ireland and London commenced their own spatial development strategies, the rest of England soon followed, and the new regional governance and planning level established after 2001 also adopted a style of spatial planning that owed its origin to the ESDP but fused into a UK style. RSSs in England in the period 2001–10 adopted similar syntax and served as the more obvious illustration of European spatial planning thinking brought into the UK to address strategic issues.

Cohesion and competitiveness: The evolving context

As forms of European spatial planning emerged in the UK and indeed across the European territory after 1999, the Europeanization debate continued and itself morphed into different forms. Adding to the previous notions of economic and social cohesion identified in Articles 3 and 158 of the European Community (EC) treaty, the text of the Constitution for Europe, and of its natural follow-up – the Lisbon Treaty – has embodied the territorial dimension of European development policies with greater political significance than ever before. With the ESDP now over 12 years old, the spatial development debate within Brussels and the member states has switched to discussion of 'territorial cohesion'. Territorial cohesion has the aim of combating territorial disparities to achieve a more spatially balanced pattern of economic development by securing the coordination and coherence of development policies (CEC 2004: 28). The main concern with this objective relates to the unevenness and, by implication, the concentration of economic activity within particular territories of the EU and its implications. The message outlined by the Commission of the European Communities (CEC) is clear: market forces alone will not result in balanced economic development across the Union as a whole and Eastern Enlargement only has served to double existing regional disparities.

The remainder of this chapter will discuss the concept of cohesion as one element of spatial planning and the paradox associated with the notion of 'balanced economic competitiveness' stemming from the ESDP and the subsequent Commission policies associated with planned economic growth (Davoudi 2003). It is possible to suggest that the ongoing emphasis on polycentric development in spatial strategies across the EU, in the aftermath of the ESDP's publication in 1999, might have informed a shift towards spatial planning as a vehicle for the generation of economic growth in regions away from concerns to redistribute or compensate such regions (Ezcurra, Pascual and Rapún 2007). But, in practice, 'polycentricity' and 'balanced competitiveness' remain somewhat abstract phrases (Dühr 2007). This is largely a consequence of the lack of an evidence base behind the terminology of the ESDP as it was developed in the 1990s (Meijers, Waterhout and Zonnenveld 2007). These abstract phrases allowed for different interpretations across member states and the resultant planning policy nomenclature within nations and regions have had uncertain but variable impacts on urban form, development patterns and mobility. Furthermore, the economic performance of member states was in a different situation in 1999 compared to the present, and the disparities between them were far less dramatic than they have been in the current post-Enlargement scenario. In light of the recent global economic recession in 2008, the importance of stimulating economic growth within European cities and regions is likely to find stronger political footing as a pan-European agenda within the EU, and thereby challenge aspects of both the ESDP's agenda and to the spatial planning concepts within territorial cohesion.

The ESDP, economic growth and 'balanced competitiveness'

One of the key objectives of this chapter is to try and inform the development of a spatial implementation strategy contained within the 'territorial cohesion' concept (Faludi 2005). This is in the spirit of the recently published Commission Green Book on Territorial Cohesion (CEC 2008), which aims to constitute the basis of a discussion platform for different stakeholders in order to define the operational outlines of 'territorial cohesion'. Notwithstanding uncertainty concerning its existing political validation, as one of the main principles in the Lisbon Treaty, it remains to be seen how this reshuffle of competences concerning cohesion policies will actually translate into a territorial dimension (Doucet 2006; Evers 2008). As other commentators have suggested (e.g. Faludi 2006, 2007), the concept of 'territorial cohesion' has been seen as a suitable conceptual follow-up to the ESDP process. According to the Commission of the European Communities, the rationale behind the formulation of the ESDP in 1999 involved strengthening economic and social cohesion and achieving the sustainable development of the EU territory as a whole. But the EU goals of competitiveness on the one hand and economic and social cohesion on the other are ultimately different and possibly contradictory (Lawton-Smith, Tracey and Clark 2003: 865). Whilst the management of EU economic competition-related tensions is clearly embedded in the ESDP, it nonetheless failed to address the competitiveness concept. The ESDP flagship objective of a shared vision of the European territory (CEC 1999: 3) was structured on a development model of competition between regions and cities in order to secure a better balance between competition and cooperation (Jensen and Richardson 2004: 21). This objective, which was eventually included in the final document, envisaged the preservation of an "optimum level of competitiveness" (CEC 1999: 2).

The ESDP outlined a new vision for European space, introducing a new scale of spatial planning in order to pursue polycentric urban systems – that of transnational infrastructure networks and growth-zone development. Growth-zone development, in particular, has underlined the importance of promoting complementary relations between cities and regions through simultaneously building on the advantages and overcoming the disadvantages of economic competition between them. Nonetheless, the ESDP also advocated that this complementarity should not be focused solely on economic competition. Rather it also should be expanded to all urban functions such as culture, education and knowledge, and social infrastructure (CEC 1999: s.74). In reality, the ESDP developed and shared a coexistence with the interventionist policies intended to overcome the problems of the lagging regions (i.e. cohesion policies) and those of anti-interventionist character (i.e. competition policy) that are designed to remove existing barriers to full market integration (Lawton-Smith et al. 2003: 859). It is interesting to note the inclusion of both competitiveness and cohesion objectives within the document, reflecting perhaps differing attitudes within those member states participating in the drafting of the document (see Faludi and Waterhout 2002; Waterhout 2008).

Critical insights may be introduced as the ESDP championed – among other objectives – a vital goal of EU spatial policy: 'the need to proactively counterbalance the negative effects of increased inter-European competitiveness brought about by the single market and globalisation' (Peters 2003: 322). Breaking down this objective raises interesting debates that underline, for instance, the lack of absolute reasoning on the impacts of globalization. As has been debated at length (see, for example, Cooke and Morgan 1998; Swyngedouw and Baeten 2001), the uniform and constraints-free single-market Europe, upheld by some EU policy-makers, has failed to materialize. From another angle, the noticeable market and competition-orientated spatial development content of the ESDP (Jensen and Richardson 2004: 21) raises the issue of how coherent and effective this strategic spatial document has been in advancing the EU ideals of equity, justice and political legitimacy (Getimis 2003: 85) – if it does not directly address the management of its conflicting interests. Faludi's (2009) recent reflection on the making of the Territorial Agenda highlights the dual elements of 'territorial cohesion' and 'territorial capital'; both of these notions continue to be emphasized in the Territorial Agenda in much the same way that 'cohesion' and 'competition' featured within the development of the ESDP. In this regard, it is useful to recall Evers's (2008) assertion that European spatial planning can, at times, prove to be somewhat 'elusive'.

Another significant issue in this discussion concerns EU regional policy and its important contribution towards convergent economic development (e.g. Rodriguez-Pose and Fratesi 2004). As intense agglomeration of corporate and research and development (R&D) activity has developed in key areas of Europe that privilege distinct geographies within the EU, a great increase in regional disparities has not been witnessed. However, Rodriguez-Pose and Fratesi (2004) have concluded that economic cohesion and convergence targets show low levels of compatibility and that there remain doubts about the capacity of development funds to actually foster a further higher degree of 'territorial cohesion' (a point previously pre-empted by Morgan and Nauwelaers 1999: 16). They have produced a set of recommendations for future use that emphasize the risks of disproportionately focusing on a certain development axes as a disrupting strategy for establishing long-term sustainable growth patterns. They suggest a regionally tailored development strategy, taking into consideration factors as diverse as premature exposure to the market, 'brain-drain', or subsidization of non-competitive local firms, and it would not seem too far-fetched to extend this suggestion into notions of 'territorial capital'. The subsidization argument reverts to the discussion on competition policy and its direct impact on achieving economic and social cohesion, as well as the reduction in inter- and intra-regional disparities as targeted in article 158 of the Treaty of Rome. Indeed, article 92(1) of the Treaty provided a general ban on so-called state aids for economic development (Lawton-Smith et al. 2003: 867); state aid would be possible, but under the ruling regulatory role of the European Commission. This mechanism, known as Regional Selective Assistance (RSA), is then regulated by determining the type of assistance allowed and by examining how assisted area maps are determined (Armstrong 2001: 252).

Therefore, the current EU economic development approach is argued to have had, to some extent, a positive impact in lagging regions via a set of policies that places competitiveness in a central position in determining objectives, and in designing measures (Hall and Soskice 2001). In this context, some authors state that the systemic choices underlying EU development policy are adequate, considering the uncertain challenges that lie ahead (e.g. Molle 2002); a reconsideration of the fundamentals of this approach is not, consequently, a priority. Molle (2002) identifies two crucial tasks for sustainable evolution: first, to reintroduce knowledge accumulated into the policy-making system in order to optimize the effectiveness and efficiency of these policies; and secondly, to distinguish between problems resulting from adaptation processes and systemic faults. However, regardless of the placement of structural and cohesion funds under different objectives, the real coordination mechanisms behind these development policies remain unclear. Faludi (2004) has discussed these issues extensively in the context of the 'territorial cohesion' concept. The rationale behind this concept, originally outlined in the third cohesion report (CEC 2004), encompassed, among other objectives, the promotion of greater coherence and coordination between regional and sectoral policies with a spatial impact. Before going on to look at these implications further, it is necessary to outline trends of regional economic development in the EU and the spatial implications of the impacts of globalization.

Trends in regional economic development in the EU

As global economic integration continues to create interdependencies among nations and localities, competition for inward investment has intensified in the last ten years (see Phelps and Raines 2003). The economic geography literature reminds us that internationally mobile investors nevertheless remain, to a greater or lesser extent, embedded in particular places (Yeung 1998), while the political geography literature points to the contribution of local politics to processes of economic globalization (Jessop 1999). Under conditions of rapid international economic integration, the quality and efficiency of markets for the factors of production – such as labour, land and property – become, if anything, more important to economic competitiveness. Most academic and policy concern has, to date, focused on debates surrounding the significance of labour skills and flexibility in economic performance. However, MacLennan pointed out that where international competition is speeding up, 'competitive responses need not be limited to making labour markets more flexible. The role of housing, land and planning policies may play a critical role in shaping which places, even nations, adjust successfully to the new international economic order' (1995: 397).

Land use and spatial planning practices are an important and neglected element of such national and local modes of social regulation (Berry and McGreal 1995: 8). An exploration of how planning systems contribute to the competition for FDI has been lacking, but it could provide an invaluable window onto the articulation of global and local economic and political processes (cf. Caprik 2010).

On the one hand, the recent history of inward investment attraction in the EU suggests that planning systems have been largely bypassed as a result of promotional bodies wishing to minimize disruption to prospective investors (Tewdwr-Jones and Phelps 2000; Phelps and Tewdwr-Jones 2001). A planned approach evident in the 1960s and 1970s gave way to an approach customized to the needs of inward investors. Arguably, planning systems have played their role in ensuring that inward investors have rarely been integrated into existing clusters of economic activity. This might be viewed as almost globalization from below in that agents of local governance are helping to reinforce the mobility of these companies. This is also reconfiguring the planning system from a purely regulatory mechanism into a supporting, enabling and collaborating spatial process, with a renewed emphasis on policy and agency integration, regional and spatial differentiation, and development management.

On the other hand, more recent EU and regional interest in issues of sustainability, territorial-based interventions and clusters implies a return to potentially more plan-led approaches to economic development and to the steering of inward investment in particular. Here, robust local responses and the development of spatial plans might offer more progressive attempts to embed otherwise mobile companies. Devolution and the incorporation of these new concerns with clusters and sustainability (along with the increasing potential influence of new spatial development perspectives) are likely to be geographically uneven, not least because of the variable development pressures faced across different territories within the EU, but also as a consequence of the high political support within devolution.

Underlying the developments of the past 25 years or so has been a political agenda to open up the EU regions (space economy) as a viable and efficient location within the international market for mobile investment. As part of a much broader agenda of regulatory reform, the planning systems of some EU countries have undergone immense structural and policy changes over the past two decades and successive governments have reoriented the system to ease the externality costs facing businesses and investors. This has affected planning within Central and Eastern European states in particular, but it has also started to occur within older member states as well, eager to modernize their planning systems to address twenty-first-century problems while also taking into account new planning regimes in the East that may, potentially, create better conditions and provide a competitive advantage for investment and growth. This process may not solely relate to further deregulation of planning regimes, but rather may concern the redesigning of internal administrative borders to reflect spaces of flows, and reconfigure responsibilities between tiers of governance to embed EU funding and inward investment more smoothly within spatial governance arrangements (see Dabrowski (2010) on Poland and Marot (2010) on Slovenia).

These political agendas and regulatory reforms have been evident in the UK (see Chapters 1 and 3), but have also been apparent in planning within other EU member states – where competing models of social welfare and national economic management have persisted (Rhodes and van Appeldoorn 1998). These reforms affect planning systems but, more pertinently, they may also affect planning cultures (Nadin and Stead 2008). To an extent, these have touched upon planning systems that are very different in organization and practice to the UK system (Newman and Thornley 1997). On the surface, it may seem that the

centralized and essentially regulatory nature of mainland European planning systems may well be ill-suited to the attraction of FDI (cf. Healey
and Williams 1993). It seems clear that even the comparatively flexible
British planning system has, in some instances, hindered development
(Healey and Williams 1993; Evans 2003). This gives rise to the notion
that the varying form of planning systems across Europe and their
ability to become more flexible to meet inward investment objectives
either support or inhibit different European regions to attract greater or
lesser FDI. And yet planning's relationship to broader regional economic
development issues remains under-assessed.

A UK government report (ODPM 2003b), for instance, highlighted
just how contentious and yet unresolved this issue has been. For example,
problems associated with passive landownership and land valuation
overshadowed planning as a constraint on land supply and, by implication, economic development – including that through FDI (Adams,
Russell and Taylor-Russell 1994; Adams et al. 2002). Moreover,
although planning systems may, in principle, embody important 'non-
tariff barriers' (Healey and Williams 1993) to FDI, there is evidence to
suggest that, in practice, planning has been an important part of rules-
based competition for, or the incentivizing of, FDI (Tewdwr-Jones and
Phelps 2000).

It should not be surprising that different views of planning and
spatial strategy-making as a constraint coexist within particular
national contexts. In fact, a key feature in respect of the above is the
geographically unbalanced nature of economic growth, land and property markets and hence the policy latitude open to planning system
responses within national territories and across Europe (MacLennan
1995). With the heightened competition for FDI across Europe recently
and probably in the future, there are signs of renewed inter-authority
cooperation and strategic planning at the city–region scale (Tewdwr-
Jones and McNeill 2000; Harrison 2007), and as Brenner (2003) notes:
'metropolitan governance is today being mobilized as a mechanism of
economic development policy ... to enhance place-specific socioeconomic assets' and unblocking growth constraints, as in the case of
the Cambridge high-technology cluster (While, Jonas and Gibbs 2004).
Critically, centrally conceived 'one-size-fits-all' national planning policies are unlikely to match the needs of a Europe of the regions in which
divergence in economic performance remains the order of the day. With
the accession of Central and Eastern European countries, the tensions
between the planning and FDI needs of overheated 'core' capital city
regions and lagging 'peripheral' regions are likely to be greater still.
Ironically, the push by national governments to encourage FDI within
these regions has occurred simultaneously to the rolling out of regional

devolution, thereby reinforcing aspects of the central state (Phelps and Tewdwr-Jones 2001).

The spatial planning implications for FDI

Clearly, as part of the continued trend across Europe towards a Europe of the regions (Keating 1997), with greater decentralisation and regional autonomy (Batchler and Turok 1997), development agencies and government bodies adopt proactive development strategies to ensure the economic growth of particular regions. This economic growth strategy, founded on competition between cities and regions, is not necessarily led by or constrained within spatial planning frameworks, but is rather led by economic development personnel and political actors; their active bidding for FDI places regions on the global map as possible locations for multinational companies' mobile investment. Given the scale and employment size of these developments, politicians and economic developers are more than aware of the possible positive impacts for existing firms in their locality, and of the economic benefit to their regions.

During the 1980s and 1990s, certain countries within Western Europe were particularly successful at winning these developments (Cooke and Morgan 1998), but since then strategic development projects have been more spatially concentrated in Central and Eastern Europe (Carstensen and Toubal 2004). This spatial unevenness is resulting in the promotion of competitive strategies by western regions of Europe as they attempt to out-compete the new accession countries of the EU where economic and labour conditions are more favourable (Bevan and Estrin 2004).

Examination of examples of FDI (such as BMW's development in Leipzig, Germany; LG in Newport, UK and Volkswagen/Ford in Setúbal, Portugal) indicates that each of the multinationals have been reliant on large-scale financial incentives offered by national and regional governments to support the investments in particular locations (Moniz 1994; Phelps and Tewdwr-Jones 1998; Lung 2004). The European Commission's competition laws have been checked, but the EU has given approval for the incentives packages offered in each case. The finance used has not been EU money, but rather that of individual member states. In all cases, the planning process has played a less than significant role in the investment process. The attraction of companies to particular regions is not related to traditional economic matters alone. As Moniz (1994: 1) highlights: 'The question where to locate production sites do not lie on labour costs or technical competencies. The so-called comparative advantages can show up from the type of

Box 4.2 Manipulating a planning system for short-term economic gain

During the 1990s, the UK witnessed a significant amount of competition between the regions of England, Scotland and Wales for scarce and prestigious FDI. Large-scale 'flagship' inward-investment projects, bringing perhaps thousands of jobs to the 'winning' regions, were attracted to particular regions of the UK just as the ESDP and questions over balanced competitiveness were being discussed; Toyota in the East Midlands, Samsung and Siemens in the north-east of England, Hyundai in Scotland and LG in Wales were some of the most notable examples. All were characterized by an intense degree of interregional competition, with regional-level institutions of governance providing innovative and competitive packages of aid to the prospective inward investors.

LG in Wales

The Welsh Development Agency (WDA), a governance institution since merged into the Welsh government, had recognized in the 1980s that in order to attract the most prestigious foreign companies to South Wales, there was a need to identify appropriate greenfield sites that were physically large and unconstrained by the surrounding area; free of contamination (thus focusing on greenfield as opposed to brownfield locations); and readily accessible from the strategic transport network. Most importantly, the location of any such site had to be within a positive planning framework that allowed development on the scale required. With financial assistance readily available in the form of government subsidies, the site would have to be supported by a consensus of government agencies which, together, possessed a track record of success in attracting similar projects. Taking into account all these requirements, a greenfield site to the south-west of Newport, in south-east Wales, was identified as a potential location. The site identified – 'Celtic Lakes' – was widely regarded as the most prestigious industrial development site in South Wales by virtue of its location adjacent to major strategic transport arteries and its scale as a greenfield site. For this reason, and given the support the site received from Newport County Borough Council and the WDA, among other groups, the LG industrial site was viewed as a 'golden strategic site' within South Wales.

The site for this major strategic development was land at, and adjacent to, Imperial Park, south of the A48 trunk road and M4 motorway at Coedkernew, in west Newport. The land was bounded to the south by the London to South Wales railway line, to the north by the A48 and to the east by the Celtic Lakes Business Park, and extended over an area of 145 hectares (345 acres). The consultants to the LG Group submitted an outline planning application to Newport County Borough Council in summer 1996 and the Highways, Transportation and Planning Committee of that authority deter-

$\rightarrow$

→

mined the application on 3 September of that year. The planning application was submitted by the WDA on behalf of the LG Group, who sought permission for the construction of an integrated plant for the manufacture of television monitors, colour-picture and picture-display tubes and other electronics equipment on 'Development Area 1' (on behalf of LG Electronics, Inc.) and for a wafer fabrication and assembly plant on 'Development Area 2' (for LG Semicon Co. Ltd).

The development area contained, in planning terms, two distinctly separate parts: Development Area 2 (host to LG Semicon) was on the eastern half of the site, which was land allocated for industrial use as part of the Celtic Lakes Business Park; Development Area 1 (host to LG Electronics) lay in a greenfield area on the western half of the site. In addition to these two development sites, a third area to the south was also earmarked by the applicants for possible future expansion and mitigation measures, although it was unclear what proportion of this site would be taken for development. Development Areas 1 and 2 would involve the construction of very large factory units, ancillary buildings including offices, wastewater-treatment plants, staff accommodation, earthworks, the creation of parking and servicing areas, the construction of roads, landscaping and the creation and rerouting of various water bodies to replace some of the land-drainage channels that would have to be removed. In addition, LG's insistence that there was to be no public access to the site necessitated the rerouting of a national 400KV electricity-grid power line which ran across the site and the stopping up of two public highways, Duffryn Lane and Celtic Way, and the diversion or possible extinguishing of two public footpaths.

At £247 million, the size of the total incentives package of assistance agreed for LG's investment was extremely controversial – prompting claims of rule-bending which were later dismissed. From a planning point of view, the developments were dealt with reactively rather than proactively. There was an adopted local development plan over part of the site but this was proving to be a barrier to the LG proposal. If Newport determined LG's application in the spirit of the plan, it would have to reject it. Following collaboration between the various agencies, Newport conveniently withdrew the entire plan thereby proving no planning framework locally and also no barrier to the scheme being approved. Also, the planning application itself was determined in just two days, a far cry from the usual standard eight weeks it takes a routine planning application. The clear question here is to what extent could spatial planning lead the process of negotiating a sudden major investment opportunity, or would it be a follower in a decision already made elsewhere in government about delivering the scheme on the ground.

For more information and debate, see Phelps and Tewdwr-Jones 1998, 2001; Tewdwr-Jones and Phelps, 2000.

available infrastructures, on the location, social environment or even on the political and fiscal.'

All regional authorities have used strategies to promote the region, galvanize institutional support among a range of relevant actors, and develop a team approach. But these strategies have not been spatial by nature. If planning has played a part, it has been to remove the impediments to development, given that the investment deal had been won in each case prior to securing planning approval (see Box 4.2 for an illustration of the relationship between regional economic development and the planning process).

This is the reality of the market: the continued move towards regionalization across Europe is creating enhanced regional competitiveness between and sometimes within regions. Economics, politics and the power of multinational firms are setting the framework for major inward investment developments that have strategic significance. National and regional finance is assisting the development decisions. The key question therefore is, what role can planning really play in achieving more 'balanced competitiveness' and in providing spatial certainty and cohesion across and between territories?

Implications for and the future of European spatial policy

Drawing down the benefits to territories

A degree of convergence in European planning systems was already detected some time ago (Healey and Williams 1993). However, even if there are reasonably commonly felt pressures of inter-locality competition and regulatory arbitrage by foreign direct investors, there nevertheless remain important differences in the structure, consistency, administration and nature of national and sub-national planning systems alongside differences in the dynamics of land and property markets within Europe. These differences have periodically been documented and their implications for the likes of housing markets explored. There appears to be a dearth of systematic studies of variations in European planning systems and their impacts on economic performance, a large part of which rests on the contribution of FDI to national and local economies. Environmental appraisals and sustainable development obligations across the EU have increasingly provided a benchmark against which to evaluate individual projects, but do not capture subtle differences comparatively across the territory in land, infrastructure and regulatory permeability.

What is required is a study to uncover the mechanisms through which there is or is not a degree of convergence in planning for FDI in the EU and in the role of member states in creating conditions to enhance regional economic growth. This 'internationalization of the state' occurs in less overt, more concrete, terms through ad hoc and Commission-sponsored transnational cooperation through which there is the prospect of knowledge transfer and the transformation of institutions and their norms. The picture is complicated further still by the proliferation of quasi-governmental bodies such as investment promotion agencies (IPAs), EU initiatives, entrepreneurial cities, and competitive regions across Europe that frequently benchmark the rapid transmission of what may be termed 'best practice'. Multinational enterprises (MNEs) themselves exert pressures on local and central governments, not least in the expediting of planning processes, by virtue of their experiences of operating in many nations globally. Intermediaries such as location consultants also play a role in transmitting particular norms and practices regarding the successful attraction of MNEs – including presumably those relating to planning – among potential host countries. The reinvention and reinvigoration of spatial planning rest significantly on the acquisition of new attitudes, and of skills of persuasion on the part of professional staff (Harris 2001; Healey 2001) and, indeed, elected local politicians, as has been seen in an improved UK planning system. Finally, the planning profession itself is unevenly developed across Europe with different disciplinary orientations and credentials (Healey and Williams 1993; Maier 2010), which is likely to exert an effect upon practices in 'territorial cohesion' and planning for FDI. Historically in the UK, for example, economists' lack of influence on planning has been evident (Evans 2003; Barker 2006). The influence of economists may be greater given the sectoral planning legacy of Central and East European countries, while architects (rather than land-use planners) exert a more widespread influence on mainland Europe (Healey and Williams 1993; Nadin and Stead 2008).

These considerations indicate that:

> competition for investment is not just any kind of competition. Unlike competition in goods markets, there can be no presumption that competition for investment is efficiency enhancing ... it clearly has the potential to result in races to the bottom in terms of wages, social protections, environmental standards, and tax base degradation ... Conscious intervention is necessary to prevent these negative outcomes. (Thomas 2000: 271)

Therefore, liberalization in advanced nations has not been associated simply or directly with deregulation per se, but also with creative processes of re-regulation (Vogel 1996). The challenge remains, as Healey has noted, to remake planning and effective national and local institutional capacities – including those pertaining to planning – capable of the 'drawing down of benefits from companies into the social and economic life of a place in environmentally sensitive way' (Healey 1997: 202). This might involve a broader vision of 'balanced competitiveness' as contained in the ESDP (CEC 1999). Here, an emphasis upon polycentric development might inform a shift towards viewing FDI and planning as ingredients in the production of economic growth in regions away from concerns to redistribute to, or compensate such regions (Amin, Massey and Thrift 2003). This, in turn, is likely to rest on the regionally differentiated practice of planning as a regulatory and facilitative activity.

The paradox of balanced competitiveness

In terms of the form of European spatial planning as well as the principles of the ESDP and territorial cohesion in the future, regions and national states may already recognize the benefit of and commitment towards European spatial development. As the European Community increases in size, with enhanced markets, greater territorial competition and economic unevenness, it is right that issues such as sustainable development, balanced competitiveness and territorial cohesion are assessed in a meaningful way across the continent. The interests in these issues are checked by an economic and political expediency for the regional advantage that is becoming more apparent in different parts of Europe, in order to address growing regional economic disparities and to market territories as major players in the global arena. But this behaviour may run counter to the accepted principles of European spatial planning as governments, government agencies and non-governmental agencies become more entrepreneurial and competitive.

Wooing major multinational companies, identifying land, the availability of cheap labour, the offer of incentives and the hard sell between particular companies and individual city-regions are the factors that carve out customised spaces for businesses. Finance plays a significant part in this wooing process: older industrial regions, recipients of EU structural funds, form a dependency culture on the Commission for their economic development; 'successful' EU regions (in terms of their economic profile and growth) rely on national and regional governments' finance to create their advantage, bound up with strong institutional capacity and presence. The link between spatial planning policy and financial incentives must be addressed more prominently in the future if spatial development strategies are going to make a difference and contribute towards the goal of territorial cohesion and balanced competitiveness. But this also means the planning culture has to change, and the knowledge of the economic processes accumulated in the planning policy-making system has to be garnered and optimized to ensure the effectiveness and efficiency of future spatial policies

Conclusions

Attempting to develop European spatial planning further politically may be a goal worth pursuing. And attempts by the European Commission in the wake of the ESDP to make enhanced links between spatial development policy, land-use decisions and finance should be welcomed by making qualifications about the allocation and spending of EU structural and cohesion funds. These attempts have assisted in promoting greater spatial awareness within and across a range of territorial scales, and in reinforcing the role of planning in development decisions. But the spatial planning practice relationship between a reliance on the knowledge of existing spatial situations and regional economic development, and an economic logic of profit maximization, remains out-of-synch and unrelated at present. National and regional development actors have preferred to negotiate with multinational companies directly and impose minimum externalities on firms as part of an incentives package to attract industries to particular territories. Such incentives, resting on finance and the creation of customized spaces, rely on bargaining, negotiation and flexible institutional structures and strategies, and do not build upon accumulated spatial knowledge.

Previous instances of FDI suggest that firms are highly mobile and require fast decisions on potential locations, and regional authorities are either successful or unsuccessful in attempting to embed companies into particular territories. Faced with market concentration, lucrative financial incentives, the availability of land and cheap labour, and political and economic actors who are enthusiastic to attract companies partly on the latter's terms, planning becomes an externality in itself rather than a promotional tool. But there are differences between regions in the form of inward investment attraction and the degree to which companies are encouraged to embed to support the region's economy more broadly. In some cases, there has been a noticeable absence of planning in the attraction process, making attempts by governments to extract gain from companies problematic. This could be one step in the right direction in the future, where planning – having arranged incentives to attract a firm to locate to a region initially – then utilizes the gain extracted from the development as a basis for further development on the site and as a way of embedding the company within the territory.

There are challenges in achieving a more embedded form of economically aware spatial governance, particularly in linking up the skills of planning practitioners with other communities of practice. But overall such an approach could be thought of as a robust form of strategic spatial development and territorial cohesion.

It is possible to identify European spatial planning and national and regional spatial planning strategies as playing a proactive role in territories to identify spatial locations and create the broad conditions for territorial development. Specific attention could be devoted to the relationship between finance, financial incentives and land. It may also perform a role in developing institutional capacity, team-building and collaboration between a range of relevant actors to ensure the delivery of development and the removal of potential barriers at the appropriate stage once a multinational company has expressed interest. Spatial planning may also assume a reactive role after a company has been approached by regional actors or when regional actors have already secured a firm's interest. Thus the role of spatial planning would not be in the regulation of development but rather in the attempt to territorially embed companies by integrating disparate development opportunities into a more cohesive whole, directly related and linked to the inward investment industry and site. Though, the ability of the market and the dominance of multinational companies to select strategic sites for investment will continue in the years ahead as the EU pulls out of recession; as the EU territory expands, so too will the competition between city-regions in the attraction and wooing of companies to customised sites. Nevertheless, if European territorial cohesion is going to play any sort of role in planning for territorial development, it must be recognized for its limits and opportunities in the regional economic development process – a process that will always remain highly political.

It can be agreed that the existing dissemination and influence of the European spatial planning discourse clearly feeds the emerging paradigm of Europeanization in the field of planning studies. Let us remember, finally, that the word Europeanization may be somehow misleading; its suffix '-ization' almost induces a normative bias towards perceiving it as a 'standardization' of European origin. However, the diversity of observed clusters or 'macro-regional perspectives' is good evidence of how unsettled Europeanization as a line of inquiry within planning still is. The regional degree of change varies depending from institutional adaptation dynamics to personality-based processes and political preference, as illustrated by the UK example where Dühr et al. (2010: 363) describe Europeanization in planning as a process that 'dares not speak its name'. Nonetheless a common European spatial planning language has emerged and different member states are now being comparatively analysed not only based on their planning traditions but on their different adaptation patterns to a common influence or, metaphorically, on how they are speaking this language. The policy context, namely the territorial impact agenda over the next ten years, may provide further developing ground for this adaptation. Future challenges for Europeanization as a conceptual research framework lie at two areas. These are, first, the creation of indicators that would facilitate further operationalization of a greater number of richer comparisons and, second, the mechanisms of Europeanization, so that one can better understand whether they may work, as well as where and how.

Chapter 5

National Spatial Planning and Political Discretion

Chapter 1 set out the ways in which spatial planning and land-use management has been stretched in all directions over its history to accommodate disparate agendas, changing needs and political preferences. Chapter 2 then went on to consider the different drivers of change as they presently affect land and land demand, and the trends likely to occur over the next three decades in certain substantive fields such as economic growth, transport, infrastructure, energy and water supply and the land-use consequences of those trends. Governments have consistently employed land use and spatial planning to intervene in the management of the land and to give shape and direction to change. Indeed, the planning system was first created statutorily by central government over a hundred years ago in order to address key problems relating to housing problems in inner-city locations, the welfare and health of citizens and to avoid overcrowding and high densities. But, interestingly, in the early 1900s Parliament itself did not award itself direct powers to plan. The power of intervention, new state housing development and the regulation of private housing development was handed over to local government, even if Parliament itself had recognized the need for the state to become involved. In the following decades, central government did acquire planning powers of its own but only as a consequence of World War II and the need to rebuild cities, infrastructure and the economy in the national interest. Since 1945, central government has retained these powers, allowing a minister of the crown to set out legislation, make policy and to take decisions on key development projects, while also permitting the monitoring of local authorities in their operation of the planning system. These powers have changed dramatically since the mid-1940s and have ebbed and flowed according to political ideology, the fate of planning more generally, and the changing role of government and the relationships between different arms and layers of the state (Tewdwr-Jones 2002).

In the 1980s, as part of a political ideological conviction to roll back the state, the then government withdrew some of the provisions of the planning system to allow the market, rather than the state, to lead on development and land-use matters, usually through property development and urban regeneration. Local authority powers were curtailed while at the same time central government actually centralized the parameters of planning (Thornley 1991) by setting out the issues that planning locally had to address. Although this has been labelled as a withdrawal of central government – in being seen to lead the planning system in a way that previous governments had done in the spirit of the late 1940s welfare state legislation – the 1980s actually represent a period when government awarded itself additional powers, albeit in a different style to that existing before 1979. The irony here is that, in order to implement a 1980s programme of permitting economic growth, giving a more prominent role to the market in land use and development interests, and bypassing local authority planning powers, central government had to adopt greater centralist tendencies in order to impose its agenda against local opposition. And somewhat tellingly, since 2011 the Coalition government's programme, which has involved stripping away aspects of state-led strategic spatial planning coordination and decentralizing planning powers to neighbourhood groups under the guise of localism and the Big Society, is also an example of an imposed centralized agenda. All parts of England are expected to implement the new legislative programme. So it would be foolish to think that in the spirit of regionalism or localism, or a political commitment to enhance citizen involvement in land-use decisions, that central government conveniently withdraws from the picture. It is true that some powers and functions are relinquished, but in other respects Whitehall merely adapts and takes on a different role. During these moments of political posturing, the key question to ask is whether central government relinquishes the right sort of duties and retains those issues of a national interest it should act upon. And more pertinently, in any shift by central government in favour of decentralization or localism, what serves as the national interest and what conforms to the notion of planning as a matter of national significance?

After 1999, devolution in Wales, Scotland and Northern Ireland further fragmented the meaning of national in policy and planning terms (Tewdwr-Jones and Allmendinger 2006). During the 2000s, the push towards regional spatial planning in England also rebalanced national planning matters towards sub-national interests (Haughton et al. 2010). With so much of a push towards making planning a non-UK-wide phenomenon, through devolution, decentralization, regionalism and localism over the last 20 years, it is increasingly questionable whether the UK now possesses anything that could be regarded singularly as 'a planning system', since so much has changed spatially and within policy-making institutions and processes across different parts of the country. The planning polity now comprises at least four different systems within the constituent parts of the UK. Planning in the UK is now plural and increasingly divergent as devolution to the Celtic countries enters a period of maturity and even more differentiated planning arrangements.

The UK still possesses a national government, of course, and policies are formulated within UK government on certain topics for application across the whole of Great Britain and Northern Ireland, and planning's importance within government and politics should not been underestimated. But to what extent can the UK government now claim a remit over securing national consistency and coordination within spatial planning policy and on land-use matters, a remit it had possessed for over 60 years? Does central government really take its sticky fingers off matters relating to spatial development in the spirit of regionalism or localism? This is the theme of this chapter.

The Enigmatic Role of National Planning Policy

The role of central government in addressing spatial planning and land-use change has undergone amendments over the last 30 years. This has been the consequence of the changing role of the state, an ideological preference on successive governments to roll back the central state in favour of sub-national and local levels of governance, and also because central government has rarely provided national direction on spatial matters but has relied upon other means to influence the policies and decisions on land-use change led by other tiers of government or even by the market. Enacted during an era when the thoughts of top-down control and authoritarianism were inappropriate and unnecessary, the postwar planning system in Britain was created in a way which bolstered local democracy and accountability by awarding most planning powers to the level of government closest to the people. At a time when direct citizen involvement in planning remained decades away (public consultation on planning matters was only introduced after 1969), the democratic and transparency issue would be revealed in planning through a reliance on planning committees of local government and the work of elected representatives. Issues of more than local interest, such as major infrastructure issues, would be resolved through exceptional means where central government ministers could retrieve development proposals for their determination following public inquiry.

Although this system may seem like the ideal means by which issues could be dealt with locally, it did raise the issue about whether some matters were of national interest and required national policy, and how these matters would then be prescribed or actioned by a separate and independently elected tier of government. Step forward, then, national planning policy – not only statements of national interest but rather national planning policies covering a wealth of planning and land-use issues and projects that were in the preserve of local government decision-making.

The provision of national planning policy from central government to local authorities and property developers to shape urban land-use policy and practice has been a feature of the planning system in Britain since the 1940s (Tewdwr-Jones 2002). This policy, however, was never released in any consistent form and has occasionally been subject to criticism by commentators (Bruton and Nicholson 1985). While the original postwar role of national planning policy was to provide strategic direction (Switzer 1984), central government has modified its planning remit and for the most of the last 70 years has utilized its land-use obligation to set parameters on detailed planning control and policy matters at the local level. The nature of central government intervention in local land-use matters has therefore changed over time. The current form of national advice in England, Scotland and Wales is contained within the series of national planning policy guidance notes: Planning Policy Statements (PPS; formerly Planning Policy Guidance) in England, National Planning Policy Guidelines (NPPGs) in Scotland and Planning Policy Wales (PPW).

The land-use planning process changed very little between the 1940s and the early 2000s. Planning was primarily restricted to considering land-use issues through the management and coordination of policy at various levels of administration by a variety of agencies and actors. Implicit to the operation of the land-use planning system was a national coordinating level, where the social, economic and environmental needs of spatial areas can be addressed in an integrated way. Although this suggested that planning could only be operated effectively when land-use issues are considered strategically (Bruton and Nicholson 1985; Rowan-Robinson, Lloyd and Elliot 1987; Breheny 1991), the provision of a national element of strategic coordination by the central state was seen as an essential ingredient in physical development. As Diamond (1979) remarked, strategic planning set out a frame of reference for the organization of planning at the lower tiers of administration. The planning process was managed and implemented by national and local tiers of government and was hierarchical as a policy framework (Tewdwr-Jones 1996). Although there was never a meaningful national physical plan in England, Scotland and Wales, central government always provided a clear approach in determining and promoting planning policy to be operated across the various government scales. Rather than developing a statutory national physical plan, the government preferred to rely on a system of discretion rather than prescription, a process where central government sets down the legal framework and broad policy for local government to interpret.

When Britain was in the throes of World War II and the country was concerned about how it should commence rebuilding itself, physically, economically and socially, central government was charged with taking a lead in providing strong national direction and coordination. Indeed, it was during this period that planning was formally given a role in bringing about physical change, a response to the recognition of starting anew, and that those changes could only be coordinated by the state. One of the first pieces of planning-related legislation that emerged in Britain to secure this national planning lead was the Minister of Town and Country Planning Act 1943. Under the provisions of this Act, a central government minister was charged with overall responsibility for development, environmental protection and physical rebuilding, and these essentially became the core building blocks upon which statutory land-use planning was based. The minister was charged with the duty of 'securing consistency and continuity in the framing and execution of a national policy with respect to the use and development of land throughout England and Wales' (Section 1). The role of central government in overseeing a national policy approach to physical planning and in ensuring that national policy was implemented by government planning agencies was therefore placed at the heart of the emerging statutory planning legislation. Whether the framers of this statute intended to extend this duty to detailed local planning matters at this time, in addition to strategic direction, however, is difficult to determine.

The duty on the part of central government for land-use planning has been fulfilled by successive planning ministers since the 1940s. Different ministers, and governments of different political persuasions, have used this obligation to define the role of the planning system by a variety of methods, including direct intervention in local planning issues, providing national policy advice and passing planning-related legislation. Although section 1 of the 1943 Act was repealed in 1970 (when the office of Secretary of State for the Environment was created), the duty of central government in planning did not change drastically. However, the interpretation of the duty has modified according to how interventionist planning ministers have been when in office. In 1958 Enoch Powell, as planning minister, was questioned on the role of the minister's duty as set out in the 1943 Act, and provided a characteristically terse answer by stating: 'You must regard those words as a piece of flotsam left on the beach by the receding tide of post-war optimism' (quoted in Switzer 1984: 74).

The exact role of central government in planning has therefore been modified; following the rebuilding of the British economy in the 1950s, there was no need for a minister of the crown to frame national policy on planning since local government agencies (charged with implementing land-use planning at the local scale) could coordinate and develop future physical land-use change by negotiating with developers and later the public without the necessity of involving heavy central-state intervention. However, as the British economy has ebbed and flowed in the period since, central government has retained its overriding duty to intervene in the land-use planning system to achieve both economic recovery and to reflect party-political mandates, but not consistently. This explains why there has never been a consistent form of policy documentation to reflect central government's planning agenda. The various devices used by central government ministers to amend or change planning practice have included the introduction of planning-related legislation; the issuing of policy advice (particularly in government White Papers, departmental circulars and policy notes); providing planning decisions (through central government call-in applications and the appeals process), and ministerial speeches.

Centralist agendas, local responsibility

In January 1988, in response to the calls for national planning statements and as an acknowledgement of the need for national strategic direction in land-use planning, the government issued the first in a series of Planning Policy Guidance Notes (PPGs), jointly for England and Wales at the time. The aim of the PPGs (later to become Planning Policy Statements (PPS)) would be to 'provide guidance on general and specific aspects of planning policy' and were 'intended to provide concise and practical guidance on planning policies, in clearer and more accessible form than ...' (DoE/WO 1988). Nine documents were originally released covering the following issues: General Policy and Principles, Green Belts, Land for Housing, Industrial and Commercial Development and Small Firms, Simplified Planning Zones, Major Retail Development, Rural Enterprise and Development, Telecommunications, and Strategic Guidance for the South East. No justification was made as to why these topics were selected rather than any other planning matters, and no indication was given over what time scale they would apply or be reviewed. The first three documents in a separate 'Minerals Planning Guidance' series were also published at this time.

The strategic function of national planning policy was therefore recognized as part of the overriding duty on the part of central-government planning ministers stemming from the 1943 legislation. But in addition to providing the UK government's perspectives of issues of national and strategic planning importance, national planning policies could also be useful in achieving a convenient way of monitoring the planning system across various geographical and spatial scales, and thereby ensuring a high degree of uniformity in local authority decision-making. More tellingly, the policy statements could also be utilized by central government to ensure its own agenda with regard to spatial planning and land use could be taken into account and acted upon by different agencies of the state. In this respect, they have been far too convenient a mechanism for ministers and central agendas to hide behind, while simultaneously espousing certain principles and publicly declaring their anathema towards top-down prescriptions. Policies such as out-of-town shopping centres, urban regeneration, housing development, windfarms, telecommunications masts, even all-seater football stadiums, were all favoured and 'talked up' at various times in national planning policies, but were politically and publicly contentious projects that local-authority planning committees had to deal with themselves on the ground. This is somewhat ironic, since the great explosion in the provision of national planning policies to local government occurred under successive Conservative administrations just at the time that Conservative ministers themselves were claiming a rolling back of the central state and giving a greater priority to market interests. But faced with a great deal of local opposition to some of these policy themes – such as housing development in the countryside, or favouring out-of-town shopping centres over high-street retailing – it was actually a rather effective way for publicly unpopular policies to be realized one step apart from claiming direct ownership. Under the Labour administration after 1997, this provision of national policy continued, although not at the same frenetic pace.

National planning policies can therefore be effective in achieving both strategic overview and local consistency, since they can be used to react to land-use problems, to reflect changing political priorities between different governments and ministers, without the necessity to instigate long and complex legislative changes, but also to oblige local authorities to consider issues of relevance to central government. The documents have offered policy advice in relation to land-use planning on different aspects of planning in general terms to a variety of audiences. They have been neither statutory nor legally binding on the people or agencies who have used them. However, national planning policies can take on the form of influential policy drivers since their contents affect all planning functions (policy formulation and implementation) operating at every level of planning administration. They have been 'the muscle, or sinew, that holds together the skeleton of the planning system' (Chapman 1995). In the 24 years since 1988, the government extended the series to 25, and reissued many during this time.

Central government has ensured that the contents of its own national policies are reflected at the local level by the statutory and policy arrangements existing between different government scales. Since the mid-1980s, local planning authorities have had to take account of national policies in carrying out their planning duties (DoE/WO 1992). If they wish to depart from established government policies, they will have to demonstrate comprehensively the locally justified grounds for departure. As a result of this requirement, planning practitioners have often seemed uncertain of the exact status of national policies in the planning system. For example, on what occasions can local circumstances outweigh national policy? It has been illustrated in research that local planners have accepted national policies as statements of government policy, but have seen and welcomed them more as informed guidance on a variety of substantive areas associated with land use and spatial change, without a recognition about the possible political steer which they are imposing on local issues or the formulation of local agendas (Insight Social Research 1989; Land Use Consultants 1995; Tewdwr-Jones 2002).

The nature of topics covered by the policy statements since 1988 has varied between detailed land-use matters and more general strategic issues such as transport and retailing. It is interesting to note that the decision to release national policies on some subjects but not others has been the consequence of ministerial preference and not the result of particular land-use changes or spatial needs territorially. In the light of the key issues and drivers of land-use change outlined in Chapter 2, it is revealing to note that in 2010 there were no national planning policies in relation to population and demographics, health differentials, infrastructure, railways, economic development, urban regeneration or biodiversity. The policy direction has therefore been in one direction – top-down, from central government to local authorities – and there has been very little way that issues of concern at the local or regional levels, relating to land use and spatial development unevenness, have been considered and addressed in terms of their national implications. This is of concern if some future drivers of land-use change will cause changing patterns of land take, as well as human behaviour, but are still dealt with on an incremental basis. The context for managing these trends within government and by national policy will partly be dependent, however, on the structures within which planning resides and the opportunities to gather intelligence on land-use change to enact policies.

A national spatial remit in an age of decentralization

The importance of the UK national policy context is recognized in facilitating government policy objectives relating to the economy, society and the environment, and in delivering EU directives and global treaty commitments. The sorts of drivers of land-use change highlighted in Chapter 2 on changing demographics, climate change, economic recovery, infrastructure provision and energy needs are all of national importance and significance and warrant some form of central government involvement in addressing the issues both now and in the future.

As the UK becomes more concerned about global economic triggers, climate change impacts and population increases (both from within and possibly from migration overseas), the UK governmental and planning structures have fragmented practically and ideologically. Whereas this is only to be expected from devolution processes, it has been exacerbated by the hollowing-out of sub-national political and governance arrangements, making it more difficult to address the spatial and land-use impacts of these changes over time. The reliance on the locality and the neighbourhood in the revised English planning process may resolve site-specific issues and give local people a greater voice in determining the extent and pace of change in their own backyards, but it is hardly the arrangement to be relied upon to address regional differences in energy provision, water shortages, failing infrastructure provision, or even the uneven spatial differences in unemployment. Both Scotland and Wales are in the process of creating country-specific planning and governance arrangements, comprising new national spatial frameworks, land-use change maps and sub-national plans to provide the evidence base and trends and potentially address these threats in an integrative and robust way. The same is not true of England, nor has it ever been the case with regard to the UK as a whole. The future enhanced European context of spatial planning and territorial cohesion, as discussed in Chapter 4, will in all probability strengthen the spatial policy processes within the new structures of governance currently being put into place as part of the implementation of devolved assemblies in Scotland, Wales and Northern Ireland, and potentially place these parts of the UK at an institutional advantage over England. While this dual push is occurring towards European spatial planning and devolution, we need to pause and assess whether a UK-wide approach to spatial planning and land-use change will be required in future and how UK national policies and decisions could potentially impact upon devolved forms of spatial planning processes. This is not a question of devising some sort of grand national plan; rather it is more to do with ensuring the UK-wide effects of land-use change and the territorial and spatial differences within the UK are recognized sufficiently and serve as a basis for possible future action. At the present time, these UK-wide assessments are largely off-radar.

The Labour government's review of the planning system, published by the Department of Environment, Transport and the Regions in 1998 (DETR 1998b), emphasized that the basic principles of the planning system at that time did not need to be fundamentally altered, but certain dimensions were missing. These missing dimensions included the European context for planning at national and regional levels, a clearer statement of intent on nationally significant development projects, the strengthening of regional policy-making, and the use of fiscal instruments such as incentives and taxation and their integration into the planning framework. In the years since this statement, a great deal has happened. The future of the planning system Green Paper released in December 2001 advocated the replacement of the then development plans and the formulation of enhanced RSSs in England. National planning policy would then increasingly focus on nationally and regionally significant projects and problems (DTLR 2001a). In the ensuing legislation, the Planning and Compulsory Purchase Act 2004, these new regional and local spatial frameworks were devised at the sub-national level and were intended to be as much integrative strategies across various policy sectors as they were planning documents. The national issue, for the moment, remained unresolved.

In the early to mid-2000s, the process of national planning policy became a matter unique to each of the three British countries, and this is the system currently retained. Since then the Scottish and Welsh governments have commenced developing further their own national policy perspectives divergent to that laid down in England. Wales had already strengthened its national spatial policy by preparing a revised version of the Wales Spatial Plan (Welsh Assembly Government 2005). In Scotland, a similar exercise created a National Spatial Planning Framework (Scottish Government 2008) and, separately, a National Land Use Strategy (Scottish Government 2011). England, on the other hand, did not embark on an English spatial planning exercise but rather retained its narrow land-use-focused national planning policies (the PPSs), but had no plans to develop anything stronger at the all-England level, preferring to rely on the new broader post-2001 RSSs (see Figure 5.1).

The short-lived Infrastructure Planning Commission and national agendas

The national agenda in England was finally considered through the Planning for a Sustainable Future White Paper of 2007 and enacted through legislation the following year in the Planning Act 2008. This created a new way of determining development and infrastructure projects of national significance, including new railways, motorways, airport, power stations, reservoirs and power lines (see Figure 5.2). The government proposed to establish an independent Infrastructure Planning Commission (IPC) to take charge of major planning projects that previously had been the subject of long, expensive and adversarial planning inquiries, such as Heathrow Terminal 5 (see Box 5.1). The second relevant provision was for enhanced national strategic planning policy, setting out medium- to long-term planning requirements over a 25-year period, cutting back on detailed policy guidance and focusing more on nationally relevant issues. The intention at the time was to streamline

Figure 5.1 *Regions and nations in Britain*

The so-called 'standard regions' of England, based partly on historical boundaries and regional identity, have formed the administrative areas for regional planning and policy attempts throughout the last 100 years but have not always reflected flows. London and the Greater South-East, for example, comprises three standardized regions.

the planning system, and the proposals illustrated the degree to which central government still called the shots on the form of planning existing in the regions and locales of England, but also set out a national case for government on spatial planning matters. Ruth Kelly, then Communities Secretary, referred to the proposals as delivering 'a planning system fit for the 21st century' (HM Government 2007a). In the year of the sixtieth anniversary of the Attlee government's creation of modern planning, the reforms were intended to introduce radical changes to the spirit, purpose and process of planning. But the reforms generated criticism from environmentalists and community representatives, concerned at the prospect

Box 5.1　The planning saga of Heathrow Terminal 5

Plans for a fifth terminal at London Heathrow Airport originated in 1982 as part of a larger debate about capacity and developments at all of London's airports. The Richard Rogers Partnership was commissioned to design the new building and a planning application was submitted in 1993. Given the strategic nature of the project, the application was 'called in' by the Secretary of State for determination and a Public Inquiry announced. This commenced in May 1995 and lasted until March 1999; sat for 524 days, heard 700 witnesses, generated over 100,000 pages of transcripts and cost £80 million. The Secretary of State finally made a grant of planning permission in November 2001 and the official opening occurred in March 2008, some 26 years after the original proposal and 15 years after the submission of the planning application.

This case has been cited regularly as the reason why the planning system needs urgent reform, and to emphasize how cumbersome the bureaucratic arrangements have been for the delivery of major infrastructure projects. But without a national planning policy on airport development, a great deal of time was given over at the Inquiry to discussion of principles of aviation expansion and the environmental damage of air travel per se, not only in relation to possible impacts of the Terminal 5 project. There was also a perception that the Inquiry was being used strategically by the government to implement a project it wanted to see implemented in the face of strident local opposition. The rules of the game meant that the Inquiry indirectly enabled the most powerful groups, in this instance the British Airports Authority (BAA), the developer of Terminal 5, to champion its interest against other groups that lacked resources and the means to counter claims.

The Labour government implemented an alternative planning decision-making system under the Planning Act 2008 with the establishment of the independent IPC and the release of national infrastructure policy statements. This was opposed by many campaign groups on the grounds that it went against local democratic involvement opportunities. Supporting the opposition, the Conservatives favoured a return to more localized decision-making. In 2011, the IPC was amalgamated into the Planning Inspectorate Agency (PIA).

of a 'free-for-all' on development issues and the state imposing its will over local areas while removing local discretion to determine planning projects. Business leaders, on the other hand, welcomed the proposals that were intended to assist in economic growth and build on Kate Barker's recommendations on planning and the economy of 2006 (Barker 2006). But Barker was only one influence; other commissioned reports on specific sectoral changes also impacted on the White Paper, including the Eddington transport review (Eddington 2006), the Stern climate change report (Stern 2006) and the Lyons report on local government (Lyons 2006).

The White Paper attempted to strike a balance for future environmental protection, economic growth and sustainable development. Critics remarked that the proposed IPC would ride roughshod over local democratic processes. But individual local authorities have rarely determined such major proposals since they have been 'called in' frequently by the Secretary of State, as the potential impacts of such development may be felt beyond the boundaries of one local authority area. In the context of stronger national policy steer, the IPC would still be required to make recommendations to the minister who would ultimately be responsible to Parliament for the decisions taken. One could argue that developments in the national interest require national politicians to act; it is not necessarily a dent in the democratic process, it merely uses a different type of democratic process from that used to determine small household planning applications.

The IPC, approved under the Planning Act 2008, was formally established in 2009, but the Conservative Party in opposition had already announced its intention to abolish it if it was elected to government

Figure 5.2 *New rail links and the desire for fast connections: Canary Wharf station, London*

Recent new infrastructure funded in part by central government has tended to privilege the financial area and eastward growth of London with the provision of the Jubilee Line, the Crossrail scheme and the Channel Tunnel Rail Link (CTRL). Successive governments have viewed these projects as vital to the national economy.

(Conservative Party 2010). And so, one month after the Coalition took office in June 2010, the abolition of the IPC was announced, and its functions transferred to the 'Major Infrastructure Planning Unit' (MIPU) within a revamped Planning Inspectorate Agency. Decisions on large development projects would be taken in future by the Secretary of State directly. The promised strategic national policy statements have been released but are formulated by different government departments; the Department for Energy and Climate Change releasing policy statements on Energy, Fossil Fuels, Oil and Gas Supply and Electricity and Nuclear Power; the Department for Transport releasing statements on Ports, Transport Networks and Aviation; and DEFRA releasing national policies on Water Supply, Hazardous Waste and Wastewater Treatment. To date, all the statements, with exception to that for Nuclear Power, lack a spatial dimension. Geography is completely absent. One can understand why central government may be reluctant to stipulate the selection of particular local sites, but this lack of spatial detail undermines the idea of a new central government steer on matters of national importance. Furthermore, under the provisions of the Localism Act the national policy statements will also be subject to Parliamentary approval, and so the determination to open up the process in the interests of democracy could well delay the implementation of major infrastructure projects, which is exactly what the 2008 Act and the Localism Act proposals were attempting to avoid.

And so the likelihood is that ministers will come under the same pressure to take quick decisions on major development projects following public inquiries as their predecessors had in the 1980s and 1990s. A desire for faster decision making while enhancing democratic opportunities may yet conspire to slow down the process even further, and without a geographical dimension in the national policy statements either, decision making for major projects will remain adversarial and combine issues of principle with issues of detail. This is the revised planning regime after 2012 and relates to projects of national significance. But an equally problematic area is one where the government or an individual minister wants to be seen to be doing something about a problem but is constrained from doing so by the governmental framework or by the principle of subsidiarity that successive governments have advocated. Under the 2011 reforms, the government also prepared a new NPPF, a slim policy statement setting out key planning objectives but essentially replacing all 25 national PPSs in England with a much briefer document, the most controversial aspect of which was creating a default 'yes' position on all land that was not designed as Green Belt or an Area of Outstanding Natural Beauty (AONB), and where no up-to-date and relevant local planning framework was in place. This approach, dubbed a 'presumption in favour of sustainable development', has proved to be the most contentious part of the 2011 reform programme, with opposition emanating from countryside groups and, indeed, members of the Tory party in the shires against the pro-development agenda of both the Treasury and the Department for Communities and Local Government (DCLG) (see Box 5.2).

On the vexed subject of affordable housing, in 2007 the then Prime Minister Gordon Brown publicly committed the government to providing over 300,000 new houses per year, to meet demand but also in an attempt to deal with the unaffordability issue. On the surface, this is of course a fine objective. The problem is that it is not the government that builds or gives planning permission out locally for new development schemes. The state's role in house building ended in the 1980s, and so a planned provision of housing locally is always a matter for negotiation between housebuilders and local planning authorities. And although there were planning mechanisms in place up until 2010 to ensure that 300,000 figure would be cascaded down to regions, counties and districts, once the local scale is reached it becomes one of argumentation on a specific site, involving local people with diverse views about the merits or otherwise of building on greenfield and brownfield sites. New government incentives were on offer to local authorities to allocate more land than has been earmarked for new housing both under Labour and under the Coalition, but this may cut against locally agreed plans that may, by democratic virtue, attempt to restrict growth. South-east England, already a development hot spot, has long been the focus for argumentation in this respect as local battles emerge over the fate of individual plots of land.

Finally, these contentions relate to England-wide matters. It also remains uncertain as to the position of any UK perspective in the light of the greater devolution of powers to the three other countries. The RTPI progressed a feasibility study into the provision of a UK National Spatial Planning Framework (Wong et al. 2000), and although giving commitments towards devolution, this has always been thought of as potentially running counter to political thought and developments. For the moment, however, the UK possesses a kaleidoscopic framework of planning policy processes, with the word 'national' meaning different things in different contexts, both geographically and politically. This is also compounded by a simultaneous emphasis on transnational and supra-national spatial planning developments between the nations and regions of the UK and other parts of Europe (Alden 2001; Tewdwr-Jones and Williams 2001).

The future of land use and planning reform

The role of central government in spatial planning and land use in England has been undergoing change for at least a decade, and this

Box 5.2 The National Planning Policy Framework (NPPF)

The Coalition government released its draft NPPF in July 2011, a radical streamlining of over 1,000 pages of existing national planning policy in England into a simplified and consolidated 58-page document. Since its release, the NPPF has had the same status in law and policy as other types of central-government planning policies, namely that local authorities are obliged to have regard to its contents in formulating their own plans, and it can be a material consideration when planning applications are determined.

The most controversial part of the NPPF is the creation of what is called a 'presumption in favour of sustainable development'. In planning there has always been a presumption in favour of development. This means that local planning authorities will always give permission for new development where it can, unless there are good reasons to stop it. In fact the presumption originates from 1922. In 1991, the presumption was modified to become a 'presumption in favour of development that accords with the plan', meaning that the default 'yes' position to new proposals would occur where those plans were in conformity with an up-to-date and relevant local plan. Under the NPPF in 2011, the phrase 'sustainable development' was included in the presumption, and the Chancellor of the Exchequer, George Osborne, went on to define 'sustainable development' as economic development and growth, a somewhat different interpretation to most academic and previous government views, which had considered it to comprise, basically, economic growth, environmental protection and social inclusion. The presumption has been accompanied by the abandonment of brownfield land targets that prioritized existing urban locations for development rather than the urban fringe or countryside. This implied that all land that was not designated as Green Belt or AONBs would be subject to a default 'yes' position, and that the NPPF in effect ensures this application by requiring local plans to conform to its content.

The NPPF and the presumption caused an outcry from countryside and amenity groups in summer and autumn 2011 with a campaign organized by the *Daily Telegraph* against the government's pro-growth presumption, supported by several other national newspapers. The government's supporters maintained that the presumption was the only effective way to ensure essential growth at a time when the UK remained vulnerable economically. Critics pointed to previous attempts by a Conservative government in the 1980s to impose a pro-growth agenda and allow development in the urban fringe against the wishes of local people and Conservative-voting shires. At that time, the government backed down and revised its planning reforms to allow more local choice in development decisions, and this led eventually to the revised 1991 presumption.

revised role has had significant implications for not only national policy but also for the role of the central state in relation to local government, the issuing of central government preferences for land use, and indeed the opportunities for public involvement. The Localism Bill was introduced into Parliament by the Secretary of State for Communities on 13 December 2010, heralding what the minister promised to be a radical reform of the planning system. If those words seem familiar, it is because previous incumbents have described recent planning bills in much the same way (Stephen Byers in 2001, and as we saw earlier, Ruth Kelly in 2007). The bill was not without controversy and went through a tortuous process where both Houses and the government agreed to over 240 amendments – more than was in the bill to start with. The bill was supplemented with the Chancellor's Budget Financial Statement of March 2011 with its focus on deregulation of the planning system and its economic interpretation of sustainable development. Finally, the release of DEFRA's new environmental White Paper addresses ecosystem services and the valuing of land (HM Government 2011).

Despite the experiences of the 1980s when government successfully deregulated large parts of the planning process, allowing the market a more prominent role in land-use decisions and an increasing reliance on alternative policy and decision mechanisms to local authorities and local development plans, central government has been reluctant to let go of some responsibility on land-use matters. Previous attempts by government to reform the planning process occurred under the Planning and Compulsory Purchase Act 2004, the Planning Act 2008 and the Local Democracy, Economic Development and Construction Act of 2009. The Localism Bill promised to revise planning decision-making processes once again, introducing some bold ideas that have as much impact on forms of local democracy as they do on land-use planning per se. Some of these new revisions dismantle aspects of the processes put in place under the Labour administration in the period 2004–10. These include the abolition of RSSs, national and regional housing targets of central government, and – as we saw earlier – the IPC, the latter only recently charged with assessing major development projects of national significance.

The bill, perhaps controversially, was not preceded by a White Paper on planning issues per se, but rather mirrored the Open Source Green Paper launched by the Conservatives just prior to the General Election (Conservative Party 2010). The Green Paper reflected the ideological belief in localism and the much-lauded Big Society and its application to planning:

> we need a planning system that enables local people to shape their surroundings in a way that ... is also sensitive to the history and character of a given location ... Our conception of local planning is rooted in civic engagement and collaborative democracy as the means of reconciling economic development with quality of life ... the planning

system can play a major role in decentralising power and strengthening society.

At face value, then, these principles suggest potential reforms that support place-based distinctiveness, a deeper understanding of land locally, and an opening-up of policy and decision making to wider sections of society, all of which potentially conform to issues discussed in Chapter 2 of this book; these issues relate to strategic and spatial matters. The government began a process of dismantling high tiers of strategic spatial policy, at national level in England and in the English regions, in favour of a rescaling of policy and decision making to the local authority or neighbourhood levels. This fitted ideologically with the notion that there had been too much top-down policy in the past, especially in addressing housing need in the Home Counties, with many people residing there remaining opposed to new development. But of course it also means that high policy-tier commitments, such as renewable energy targets, for example, will be much more difficult to achieve if decisions on windfarms are to be left to incremental neighbourhood decision-making.

The other striking issue is two slightly different approaches towards the land that exist within government. The Localism Bill was supported by community, voluntary and environmental groups around the country, eager to take up the new decision-making powers that the ministers trumpeted. This is a fundamental shift away from not only the planners but also local authority councillors. That is one agenda. The Treasury perspective is, however, a little different and underlies the Budget Statement. This agenda, naturally enough, reflects a market perspective and talks about the need for economic growth post-recession, deregulating more of the planning system, abolishing brownfield development targets, allowing more of a 'free-for-all' on greenfield, edge-of-town non-green-belt land, and reintroducing a 30-year-old policy, Enterprise Zones, where planning permission and regulation are not required. And it is this latter agenda that has been translated into the default 'yes' position to development proposals, reflected in the phrase 'presumption in favour of sustainable development' included within the National Planning Policy Framework.

Clearly, there is potential for contestation here in the same location, with neighbourhoods and developers having two very different viewpoints about what should be done and by whom. As soon as the Budget Statement was released in 2011 one could see the potential for battles raging on urban periphery land in green fields in the Home Counties, with local people opposing development, and the housebuilders saying their projects support economic growth. And in the late summer and autumn of 2011, an effective campaign was launched by pro-countryside groups like the National Trust, the Campaign for the Protection of Rural England (CPRE) and the Royal Society for the Protection of Birds (RSPB) against the National Planning Policy Framework (NPPF) and the pro-development agenda of the Coalition, with national newspapers mounting a defence of the existing planning system as a balanced and neutral decision-making framework.

Local authorities are not abolished under the Localism Act, and in fact are still to prepare simplified local development plans and deliver public services in partnership with health bodies, transport providers and other social infrastructure groups. So one could argue that some of the local and neighbourhood agenda will have already been determined by the time neighbourhoods are asked to make judgements on schemes.

The key aspect of the proposals relates to changing responsibility for who makes decisions about planning and land-use development proposals are as follows:

- Nationally significant projects – the abolition of the IPC and replacement with an MIPU within the Planning Inspectorate, a greater reliance on ministerial decision-making and project-specific parliamentary bills and parliamentary approval of national policy statements.
- A new England-wide national planning framework, a short statement on key planning issues in place of all previous national planning policies which have been deleted from the CLG website (although remain in extant in the eyes of the law); so national policies on retailing, housing, energy, flooding, telecommunications, heritage, nature conservation, waste, minerals, sport, leisure, etc., as they are addressed through and acknowledged statutorily by planning are reduced to a few paragraphs.
- Housing provision – the abolition of centrally released, regionally and locally translated new housing provision figures and their perceived 'imposition' on local communities.
- Regional and strategic differentials – the abolition of RSSs (as already announced by Labour in 2009, in fact) and Integrated Strategies (not implemented prior to the General Election), abolition of the Regional Development Agencies (RDAs) and Regional Partnerships.
- Economic development and infrastructure – new Local Enterprise Partnerships (LEPs) in selective locations (already announced), amalgams of several neighbouring cities and locales for coordinating economic growth agendas, with new Infrastructure Plans to be prepared by upper-tier agencies.
- Enterprise Zones reintroduced that remove the need for any form of planning permission within their boundaries, and can be on a scale and extent much wider than the previous 1980s examples (e.g. Manchester airport's designation, where peripheral development in

the form of logistic and support services, retailing and warehousing are now exempt from planning control).

- The introduction of a statutory duty to cooperate, a clause agreed to in the House as the bill was debated, where local authorities are obliged to cooperate with neighbouring authorities on matters of strategic land-use interest.
- Local planning – the retention of a simplified form of local plans, but with greater use of council tax receipts, tariffs and incentives to shape the location of projects and determine development – valuation will play a more prominent role here.
- Participation – the encouragement of 'collaborative planning' with greater use of local referenda, possibly enhanced powers given to parish councils, the creation of local housing trusts, and direct people power rather than local authority committee decision-making.
- Neighbourhood forums of local people to be permitted, comprising 21 members of the public, who will be able to formulate neighbourhood plans and designate areas where no permission is required for new housing to meet local needs.
- Neighbourhood plans to be allowed to be drawn up and approved by businesses or developers for the first time, rather than the local authority or the public; questions remain as to what would happen with two rival neighbourhood plans in the same location prepared by the community forum and by the private sector.

The 2010 Green Paper had previously also floated the possibility of a policy 'presumption in favour of sustainable development'. This was absent from the Bill originally. But, in the event, it was the Budget Statement of March 2011 where this was addressed, with the Chancellor defining sustainable development as 'job creation and economic growth', somewhat in contrast to just about every other government policy document in existence and to every academic interpretation of the phrase.

The reaction from the professional community has been somewhat negative. At the time of the bill's progression through Parliament, the Secretary of State remained embroiled in the courts over his unilateral announcement of the abolition of RSS last summer prior to parliamentary debate and the publication of the Localism Bill. Interestingly, it was housing developers that took the legal action, not regional or local authorities, signalling the degree to which the market preferred having the certainty of regional plans in place, since they prioritized medium- to long-term phased strategies for places but also related housing directly to infrastructure, transport and commercial needs in a coordinated way.

Who determines nationally significant projects that have a localized impact will remain controversial. The abolition of the IPC will not remove the need for national planning; in fact most of the IPC functions will be transferred across to the Planning Inspectorate Agency. So we should expect to see proposals come forward for new high-speed rail lines, new power stations and other 'big bits of kit', although there could be interesting debates not only about the merits but also the principles of development bound up in the detail of each project – in much the same way that the Heathrow Terminal 5 Inquiry found in the 1990s and the exact reason why the previous administration established the IPC and new national policy statements in the first place.

There is also uncertainty about whether a reliance on localized decision-making and ad hoc ministerial decisions could ever meet national and international obligations on climate change or energy provision. How will the UK renewable energy targets for 2020 be achieved, for example, if each project will be determined via neighbourhood forum or by local referendum?

The LEPs were announced in June 2010 and by the time of the publication of the Local Growth White Paper in October of that year, the initial 24 were announced formally. The LEPs are intended to provide the strategic leadership and long-term vision for private sector-led economic renewal in their areas. They are intended to integrate with local authority decisions and will be able to access a Regional Growth Fund and other sources of funding. One suspects that these bodies will take on more strategic-level duties over time as issues of a strategic nature are not addressed locally or within neighbourhoods, but that remains politically contentious at the moment.

There could be 40–50 LEPs designated in total eventually, in place of the eight RDAs, and it will be interesting to see the degree to which they are able to hold together different local authorities and political allegiances to work together on strategic issues, and also whether they are able to overcome local rivalries and competitive bidding, especially where the Localism Act's duty-to-cooperate powers oblige local authorities to get together. It may also be the case that some strategic issues would require collaboration between neighbouring LEPs, which could result in a form of regionalism emerging incrementally in the future around specific issues or projects.

LEPs will undoubtedly become vastly more important in the near future as the key local framework to agree resource and investment priorities. But there could well be a two-tier approach across the country, as areas without an LEP may be at a disadvantage.

On the positive side, the reforms should lead to a greater role for community leadership and the opening up of local planning to enhanced democratic control, bringing 'others' into the decision-making process for the first time. This is not new – there have been innovative public participation exercises in local planning for some time – but to date they have not been widespread and there have been difficulties in translating the outcomes into policy and decision contexts.

Local uniqueness and diversity may start to underpin decisions – all places are different, so place assets may be considered in future. The market will probably adjust to the new system, as the market always does, and perhaps there will be innovative arrangements emerging that start to align incentives with regulations, linking strongly land decisions, spatial change and financial tools. Furthermore, this strengthens the need for local and strategic intelligence to underpin community decisions for two reasons. The first reason is to ensure a more robust decision process resilient to appeal and challenge from aggrieved individuals. The second reason centres on localism itself, by generating more information about places, how they change, analysing the options available, and assessment of the implications of those different options. For good local sustainability purposes this seems to be an essential prerequisite. Discussion about evidence and data generation becomes more salient here if there is to be an avoidance of incremental decision-making together with assessment of the wider strategic implications of this. The difficulty remains how to discuss and address strategic intelligence issues relating to land use in future without being seen to be top-down or authoritarian, especially where the spatial strategy and national policy mechanisms previously available have been, to all intents and purposes, removed.

In recent years, local authorities and other bodies have collected and commissioned a significant amount of place-based intelligence that could usefully support the transition to community decision-making. This has included information on social infrastructure, land-use changes and biodiversity and ecosystem services, all related to the uniqueness of locations and land capacity. There has been an entrepreneurial spirit in many local authorities, but more work is required, including the greater use of modelling that links science to decision making on environmental capacity grounds. So there could be a new and significant role here for planners and others to inform the decision process and also to ensure that all the hard work and resources collated over the last ten years are not 'lost' in the transition to the new system. Changing the process to allow different people to take the decision does not mitigate the necessity for robust and resilient strategic and local intelligence. But more worryingly, if these issues are left to local neighbourhood groups, there is great uncertainty as to whether the groups could afford to commission studies, or monitor the effects. What happens in the absence of policy evaluation and monitoring? And would the private sector step in?

The reforms also unleash opportunities for mediators and translators in the system to help communities make sense of the options available and their implications, and to liaise with developers and others responsible for investment and public services. Planners could perform this role if they are ready to embrace a very different role for themselves. But equally the mediation role could be performed by other professionals with the necessary synoptic skills. Where all this places the role of elected local representatives is anyone's guess, particularly if local referenda are used over local authority decision-making. Can you really mix partici-patory democracy with representative democracy? And, no doubt, the degree to which individuals and communities respond to the new collab-orative arrangements will be patchy, at least initially, in different parts of England. Some communities will be resistant to all types of change. Parts of the Home Counties may resist development, reflecting not just NIMBY ('not in my back yard') attitudes but rather the spirit of BANANA (build absolutely nothing near anything/anyone).

And there is real concern about the degree to which communities will be able to make informed decisions about the merits of development projects without a reliance on professional planners, expert mediators and an intelligence and land-use evidence base. Expect representatives of the housing and retail sectors to start knocking on doors in communi-ties very soon with their incentives for new development, something that communities had been protected from until now by the local planning authority, professional planners and councillors performing that demo-cratic negotiating role on their behalf.

Will all this lead to a very different type of environment from the one we are used to? This is difficult to judge at this point in time. Certainly it is easy to speculate about the degree to which some communities will oppose development at all costs and, following negotiation and compro-mise, settle for lowest-common-denominator solutions. Developments could be pushed to locations of least resistance, adjacent to existing 'weak locations' around, for example, motorway intersections, logistics and distribution depots, boundaries with neighbouring settlements, or recent housing sites. Interestingly, Thomas Sharp coined the phrase 'neither here nor there' in the 1940s to describe these sorts of locations (Sharp 1940), and Ian Nairn referred to these sorts of edge development as a form of 'subtopia' (Nairn 1955; see Figure 5.3). Or, with a lack of significant public finance available in future, development could occur where local public services are currently located, a form of agglomera-tion, leading to property and land-price inflation in places that have previously not experienced significant pressures. Or could we see devel-opers, realizing that they are being asked to pay more for infrastructure and services for each community, become more interested in branding the places to reflect their investment? The rebranding of the negotiated planning gain provided as part of recent Tesco store developments into 'Tesco Towns' may just be the start of things to come.

There are clearly major implications for democracy at all scales; there are potential fundamental shifts in the way this country takes decisions

Figure 5.3 *Out-of-town shopping centres and changing behaviours: Southampton*

Enabled by central government national planning policy in the 1980s and 1990s, out-of-town shopping centres and warehousing were based around car journeys and located outside existing urban areas. When the impact of the policy was viewed in practice, government amended the policy to favour town-centre retailing to encourage the vitality of the high street and reduce car journeys for sustainability reasons.

that could affect the pattern of land and the shape of towns, cities and neighbourhoods. The reforms, originating from both the CLG and the Treasury, are likely to generate more intense debate and contestation about individual land parcels and their future. One expects that a big conversation about land, our land values and place identity and even nationality could occur, and there may be political ramifications of this (who wins, who loses, who's genuinely local, etc.). So there remains a need to foster a debate about the land, even if decisions on land are no longer a remit of top-down government. One doubts that clear national objectives for land use will ever materialize, although the Scots and the Welsh have already gone down this path – the Scots producing their own strategic land-use strategy in 2011 and integrating this with their existing National Spatial Framework.

The reforms could lead to a greater understanding and recognition of the diversity of places and their assets, both from a biodiversity perspective but also an economic one. Many outside central government departments are undertaking a deeper assessment of land, and utilizing scenario and modelling work to inform choices and, possibly in some cases, to attempt to influence arguments. This could then lead to the promotion of place-based governance and growth, based on the realization of opportunities and assets, not now led by government but rather by a range of alternative organizations. And this is an important point because of international interest – the OECD is promoting place-based growth as a paradigm globally, while the EU's 2020 Agenda will lead to member states having to address Territorial Impact Assessment (TIA) at some point in the near future. TIA could link in well to place-based assets and ecosystem services. Above all, the possibilities suggest that a strategic overview of the implications for land-use changes will still occur even if there are no formal strategic plans in place in England; academics, policy organizations and environmental bodies will still consider the synoptic and wider matters of land-use change even if it is unfashionable in government. What goes around, comes around. If other groups are still performing that strategic and synoptic role at present, it may be useful for government at some distant point in the future.

Chapter 6

Regionalism and Regional Strategies

The history of strategic and regional policy has developed over the last 100 years. There are various terms to describe this tier of policy making that sits between central government at the national level and local government at the local level. It has been described as forms of sub-national, regional, sub-regional, strategic and supra-local scales. These terms possess one common element: they refer to the scale of policy and decision making that occurs on a wider basis than one individual local authority area, and below the level of the nation as a whole. This could refer to the country sub-divisions of the UK (England, Scotland, Wales and Northern Ireland), or to the different divisions of England (into regions – South-East, North-East, North-West, etc.), or into counties and districts.

Regional planning first emerged in the UK after World War I, in response to the declining economies of some parts of the country and, in certain places, the impact on employment caused by losses in coal, iron, steel and shipbuilding. At that time regional policy occurred incrementally and focused on those regions that had been reliant traditionally on heavy manufacturing industries. During the late 1920s and 1930s, as severe economic depression kicked in, a more prominent form of regional planning occurred in an attempt to create new employment in the north of the UK, a feature made even more stark by the establishment of new industries based on the car industry and white goods manufacture in the south of the country. World War II had the effect of boosting the northern regional economies for a time, in the name of war and armaments production, but the pronounced North–South divide remained a problem from 1945 onwards. Regional planning has been used at different times by different governments to resolve the North–South differentials, but it has always been temporary and somewhat piecemeal. In addition to the 1930s, the UK experimented with regionalism in the 1960s but it soon was neglected.

The (re)emergence of the regional level of governance and planning within Britain in the period 1997–2010 occurred partly as a result of changes outside the UK, including the continuing failure of northern regional economies against better regional performances in the south of

England (HM Government 2002), the 'hollowing-out' of the nation-state (Ohmae 1995), globalization (Brenner, 1999), changes in governance (Stoker 1990), resurgent national and regional identities (Keating 1997) and developments within the EU (see Figure 6.1). Policies aimed at creating a 'Europe of the Regions' (Jonas and Ward 1999), together with proposals on spatial planning and the EU Structural Funds (Batchler and Turok 1997) and inter-territorial cooperation at the regional level through the INTERREG III initiative and the European Spatial Development Perspective (CEC 1991, 1994, 1999), have all directly and indirectly promoted the regional level. Within Britain, changes in regional policy and governance were a priority of the New Labour government after its election in 1997. A swathe of constitutional reforms, including devolution to the Scottish Parliament, the Welsh Assembly, the Northern Ireland Assembly, the introduction of RDAs, regional chambers and the faltering introduction of elected regional assemblies within England all added an impetus to the more modest institutional changes towards enhanced regional planning introduced under the Major governments between 1990 and 1997. Some aspects of this agenda were not carried through to fruition, however, with the democratic arm of the reforms, elected regional chambers, being abandoned in 2004 following a public referendum on the establishment of a regional assembly in the North-East. Regionalism in England limped on until 2010, when the Coalition government embarked on dismantling the regional governance and planning scale.

Academically, over the past three decades there have been a number of important theoretical developments in our understanding of the continued significance of sub-national territories within an ever-more closely integrated global economy. Initial interest focused on reinvigorating the theory of agglomeration (e.g. Scott 1983, 1986) and analysing the local outcomes of and responses to global processes of restructuring under the localities rubric (e.g. Cooke 1989). Since the 1990s, theoretical interest has centred on tracing the 'new regionalism' produced from the rescaling of political processes (Jessop 1996; Keating 1997; Lovering 1997) and the autonomous institutional capacities of regions to organize for economic development (Amin and Thrift 1992, 1995; Scott 1998). A major focus of work throughout this time has been on understanding the institutional capacity or 'thickness' of regions and the possibilities for building such capacity.

A variety of theories speak to the possibilities for institutional capacity-building at the regional or sub-national scale – the affinities among them having not been lost on some of the main protagonists (Vigar et al. 2000: 43–6). Theories of 'collaborative planning' (Healey 1997, 1998), 'associative democracy' (Hirst 1994), the role of 'relational assets' in regional development (Storper (1997) and of 'institutional

Figure 6.1 *Regional economic disparities in England, 2002*

Three graphs demonstrating the North–South differences in economic statistics. GDP per head in London, the South-East and the East of England is almost twice that of the northern regions. Productivity and services also demonstrate marked differences, with the Midlands performing poorly. Migration continues to be attracted to the best-performing regions, while the numbers of deprived local authorities are concentrated in the North.

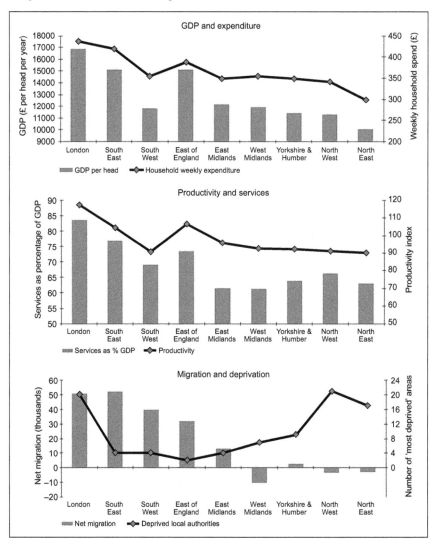

Source: HM Government (2002).

thickness' and 'interactive governance' (Amin and Hausner 1997) are among some of the most influential within the field of urban and regional development and fall within what Lovering (1999) and Jones (2001) identify as a fourth variant of new regionalist theory. The most important accounts of successful institutional capacity-building, within what can be termed the new regionalist literature, have placed a singular emphasis upon the potential for communicative and normatively regulated action. Healey's (1997, 1998) theory of collaborative planning is part of a recent tradition – including the work of Fischer and Forester (1993), Innes (1995) and Sager (1994) –within planning theory that draws explicitly on Habermas's theory of communicative action. Storper's (1997) theory of relational assets, technological innovation and regional development and Hirst's (1994) theory of associative democracy see a collective communicative rationality or normatively regulated action overcoming distortion in social action and interaction. Finally, we may group together the work of Amin (1996), Amin and Thrift (1992, 1995) and Amin and Hausner (1997) as the most open to the diversity of social action in the institutions underpinning regional economic development. While there are important differences in the origin and emphasis of each of these formulations of the building of institutional capacity, there are also some important similarities – most notably their basis in a particular type of social action and interaction.

The political determination to enhance regional competitiveness and bolster regional economic growth drove the push towards this institutional restructuring, but the degree to which particular regions could become successful was not only dependent on the existence of advantageous physical assets or resources, but 'also through the emergence of socially and institutionally mediated forms of selective co-operation between actors' (Imrie and Raco 1999: 951). These networks of institutions conform to the emerging structures of regional planning and policy that the government's various approaches sought to modify. However, as Amin and Thrift point out, 'It should be remembered that institutional thickness is not always a boon. It can produce resistance to change as well as an innovative outlook' (1995: 103). The individual characteristics of a region may therefore shape or impact upon the degree to which regions become more competitive. Di Maggio (1993) classifies networks as structural (spatially concentrated and resistant to change), strategic (less spatially concentrated and more open to change) and cognitive–aesthetic (not spatially concentrated and fluid). For planning purposes, regions are likely to fall into the first two of these categories, as there is undoubtedly an element of spatial concentration by definition. This does not, however, exclude other forms of institutional networks simultaneously existing. Consequently, it cannot be guaranteed that existing networks will automatically embrace new forms of regional initiatives, despite their general welcome; a good example of this scepticism was found in the north-east of England in November 2004, where the public voted overwhelmingly against the establishment of a regional assembly in a referendum, and thereby not only frustrated regional institutional accountability in the North-East but the then government's final phase of English regionalization. Of critical importance in the success of new regional planning and governance mechanisms in integrating with existing regional institutions and networks, therefore, will be the attitude and dispositions of those currently involved in regional policy-making and those members of the public who interact with policy-making institutional structures.

This chapter seeks to explore the form and nature of regional planning and governance in the UK after 1997, including an assessment of what has emerged with the political demise of regionalism in the period after the election of the Coalition government in 2010. The renewed emphasis upon regional planning or strategic spatial planning after 1997 produced a new impetus and direction for planning after the antipathy of the 1980s and 1990s. Yet this resurgence should not be seen as an uncritical endorsement of planning by the Labour government. The emphasis in change was as much on delivery of central policy objectives (especially economic competitiveness and growth and housing development) as feeding resurgent identities and cultural affiliations. As a consequence, regional planning in this period was really 'on trial'. As we shall see, this required an even greater need to 'get it right' on the part of new and evolving institutions and practices.

An overview of how we arrived at today's position

Putting aside debate on the relationship of the UK to the four devolved nations, the division of England into a number of administrative sub-national areas has a long history. It was first proposed by Winston Churchill in 1912 as part of a 'Home Rule All Round' campaign when he suggested 10 or 12 regional parliaments, including those for London, Lancashire, Yorkshire and the Midlands. The policy was never officially adopted, but it was recognized that some sort of division of England might be necessary. In the following three decades, this division occurred incrementally in specific policy sectors in reaction to needs and in response to social and economic changes. By the 1930s, several competing systems of regions were adopted by central government for the census of population, agriculture, electricity supply, civil defence and the regulation of road traffic. Furthermore, the economic crisis of the 1920s and 1930s, combined with the decline of manufacturing industry, had a pronounced geographical dimension in the UK that required central government intervention in certain regions.

Creation of some form of provinces or regions for England has been an intermittent theme of post-1945 British governments. The Redcliffe–Maud Report, following the Royal Commission on Local Government in 1969, proposed the creation of eight provinces in England, which would see power devolved from central government, supplemented by a structure of city-region local government. Edward Heath's administration in the 1970s did not create a regional or city-region structure in the Local Government Act 1972, but rather created a two-tier local government structure of counties (based on existing shires and new counties) and districts or boroughs. This structure lasted in place until the 1990s.

In the 1980s, Margaret Thatcher's government abolished the metropolitan county structure for London and the seven largest English cities, and replaced them with the existing borough level of local government. Short strategic planning statements were then released by central government to address strategic issues within the seven cities and were then accompanied by short Regional Planning Guidance documents, prepared by local authorities in each region but then approved and issued by the Secretary of State. In April 1994, John Major's government created a set of ten Government Offices for the Regions (GORs) in England, essentially satellite offices of central government coordinating on a regional basis the activities of the Departments of Trade and Industry, Employment, Transport and Environment. Local government reorganization was also implemented after 1993 in England, Scotland and Wales, but the form it took varied from country to country. Wales and Scotland became unitary, whereas England was treated to review area by area, with a resultant mix of new unitary structures and the retention of existing two-tier structures in different places. And, as a consequence of the implementation of the Maastricht Treaty, Scotland, Wales and Northern Ireland were designated as EU regions for the purpose of representation on the EU Committee of the Regions.

After 1997, the Labour Party was committed to regional and devolved government across the UK. Following referenda, Wales was granted a Welsh Assembly while Scotland received a Scottish Parliament. Northern Ireland was granted a Northern Ireland Assembly following the peace negotiations. London received a London-wide mayor and London Assembly. Further structural reforms were proposed for the English regions. These comprised three elements: the establishment of RDAs in the ten regions of England; the establishment of a statutory form of regional planning and the preparation of RSSs in each of the English regions; and the creation of Regional Chambers or Assemblies, interim amalgamations of local authorities prior to referenda determining the establishment of formal elected regional government in each region. Sub-Regional Strategies were also introduced with a statutory status to address cross-border issues. Following the failed referendum in the north-east of England, the government abandoned the policy towards elected regional government but had already implemented the RDA and RSS processes.

In the 2000s, further local government reorganization has extended unitary status to additional areas of England, while the government addressed major strategic or sub-regional economic, infrastructure and housing issues directly through the creation of the four Sustainable Community growth areas – Thames Gateway, Ashford, Stansted–Cambridge and Northamptonshire – which transcended but incorporated existing local government boundaries, and The Northern Way agenda that promoted 'city-region' joint partnership working between the cities of the North and their metropolitan hinterlands (see Box 6.1 and Figure 6.2).

In 2007, a Treasury Review recommended that greater powers should be given to local authorities and that the Regional Assemblies would be phased out of existence by 2010 (HM Government 2007b). Furthermore, as part of this sub-national review, the RDAs' Regional Economic Strategies and the Regional Assemblies' RSSs would be replaced with Integrated Regional Strategies.

Strategic regional planning issues are addressed across the UK today through the Wales Spatial Plan, the Scottish National Spatial Planning Framework and the Northern Ireland Regional Development Strategy; these are not planning documents per se but rather are corporate plans

---

Box 6.1   The Northern Way initiative

The Northern Way was a 20-year sub-national strategy established by the UK government in February 2004 to assist in the regeneration and economic development of the North of England. The emphasis was on tackling issues that could only be dealt with effectively across the North as a whole rather than by individual regions, in relation to transport, infrastructure, training and skills and economic growth. The strategy area comprised the regions overseen by three RDAs: Northwest Development Agency, One NorthEast and Yorkshire Forward.

The partnership produced *Moving Forward: The Northern Way Growth Strategy* in September 2004 and focused on four key themes: developing new city-regional plans in eight major conurbations across the North; targeted investment in line with the RDA strategies; working collaboratively in the allocation of public investment; and advising and influencing other agencies and decision makers to ensure conformity with the Northern Way Strategy. A Growth Fund was established worth £100 million and the eight city-region partnerships (amalgamations of local authorities in each conurbation) produced their own city-region development plans to target priorities.

The intention of the Northern Way was to resolve economic development differentials between the North and South, particularly the £ 30 billion economic output gap between the North and England's average. The Coalition government announced the termination of the Northern Way in March 2011.

Figure 6.2 The Northern Way spatial strategy

The spatial strategy for the North of England, 2004, arranged in an L-shape, comprising a west–east axis along the Pennines between Liverpool, Manchester, Leeds and Hull, and a south–north access stretching from Sheffield to Sunderland and Newcastle. Particular attention was given to infrastructure links across the regions and to the core city-region as economic hubs.

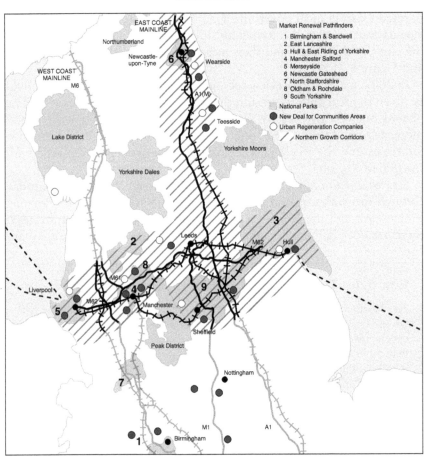

Source: Northern Way.

and have Cabinet and legislative backing. As discussed in Chapter 5, there is no UK-wide national strategic plan or national spatial framework. Rather, the UK framework has comprised all country plans for Scotland, Wales and Northern Ireland, and nine RSSs in England. London possesses a Spatial Development Strategy, or the 'London Plan'. After 2010, the Coalition government abolished the RSSs on the grounds that they precipitated top-down control of issues, particularly in relation to housing growth and numbers. While this move was in conformity with the Conservatives' ideological attachment to localism, there has been some concern that the Conservatives saw RSSs in a myopic way, looking at the housing issue but not the wider economic, environmental, infrastructure or strategic integration matters that RSSs attempted to deal with. Interestingly, the regional structure existing in London was retained, whereas all other parts of England have seen the regional governance tier abolished.

Therefore any debate about the merits of regional spatial planning has to be constructed against a recent and contemporary backcloth of:

- A political settlement through *asymmetrical devolution* to Northern Ireland, Wales and Scotland in 1997, and the subsequent extension of competence in these devolved territories.
- A *'quiet' regionalism* in England and fluid institutional architecture that has involved RDAs, GORs/Regional Co-ordination Units and Regional Assemblies.
- The failed English experiments in a new *regional civics.*
- Regional policy predicated on *endogenous growth,* reinforced through successive reforms of the EU Structural Funds and Competition Policy.
- Public-sector *'modernization'* in Public Service Agreement perform-ance targets, imposed through new RDAs (to uplift GDP/productivity in all regions and to narrow uneven regional development in the longer term) and regional funding allocations (such as the CSR Regional Emphasis Documents).
- Regional *Spatial Strategies* prepared in all regions as a broad develop-ment strategy for 15–20-year period.
- Re-emergence of provincial *metropolitan power* sought through core cities and city regions.
- Abolition of English Regional Assemblies and the failed planned introduction of Integrated Strategies and 'Leaders Boards' in 2010 caused by the outcome of the General Election.
- Abolition of regional planning and structures, the RDAs, and the dismantling of the sub-national Sustainable Community Growth Areas and the Northern Way initiative.

The rescaling of English regional governance and planning

The institutional restructuring processes that have been under way since 1997, promoting regionalism and then abolishing it, have directly affected the role of spatial planning, and its relationship with economic develop-ment within the regional agenda. There is, for the most part, a consensus that the emphasis on regional planning and policy in the early years of the Blair government had been welcomed by academics (see, for example,

Roberts 1996; Hayton 1997, Mawson 1997; Baker 1998; Goodstadt and U'ren 1999; Murdoch and Tewdwr-Jones 1999; Roberts and Lloyd 1999), regional stakeholders (British Chambers of Commerce 1997; CBI 1997; TEC National Council 1997) and others (TCPA 1997; RTPI 1992; CPRE 1994; ERA 1995), but a number of questions always remain unanswered. Such questions revolved around, for example, the ability of these proposed arrangements to integrate with existing institutional networks that evolved during the 'fallow period' of regional planning (Baker 1998), and the extent to which the new governance and policy-making processes offered something relatively different and workable.

Yet there was also a pertinent debate about how 'new' any of these sorts of arrangements were likely to be. Those with experience of previous incarnations of regional planning saw the regions once again taking their rightful place in the spatial hierarchy of planning. However, such views tended to underplay significant differences. There was a tendency to confuse regional *policy* and regional *planning*. The rebirth of the region as a level of planning was about economic competitiveness and growth but within a neo-liberal framework of supporting the market rather than supplanting it. There was also the addition of the prefix 'spatial' to planning. As was discussed in Chapter 3, spatial planning involves integration and coordination across different spatial scales and institutional and sectoral boundaries. The nature of government that dominated regional planning in the 1960s (referred to by some as the 'command and control' understanding of government) had been replaced by fragmented governance. Government required the coordination and integration of a range of public and private bodies, and planning (at the regional and local level) had been given a primary role as the spatial expression of this co-regulatory environment.

Enough is now known about RDAs, and the varying experiences of the devolved administrations, to lead some to conclude that issues such as the future scale of governance and the spatial policy dimension of the state (Jones and MacLeod 1999; MacLeod and Goodwin 1999) and accountability and coordination remained problems even after the regional governance and planning structure was being put into place (Baker, Deas and Wong 1999; Murdoch and Tewdwr-Jones 1999; Roberts and Lloyd 1999). In the context of increasing government modernization, a fragmented public sector attempting to work to private-sector efficiency alongside the continued centralization of power, the confusion caused by 'institutional congestion' of ad hoc bottom-up arrangements in place and the lack of direct accountability, some commentators had already gone as far as to call the changes in England a 'missed opportunity' (Mawson 1997). Nevertheless, the evolving forms of governance released 'a real tide of imagination and optimism ... to plan the development path of this small nation' (Hague 1990:

296). What we were witnessing was either sets of teething problems – inevitably perhaps with any new process of governance – or the apparent disappointment caused by heightened expectations of radical changes to the way Britain was starting to be governed.

The shift in institutional relations and policy processes was certainly welcome as a vast improvement on the situation during the Thatcher years, but there was a possibility that the new arrangements for economic and land-use regional planning and regional governance were embraced as a relative rather than absolute advance. There remains heated debate as to whether the creation of new regional institutions alone are able to generate successful economic strategies for regions similar to the regional 'success stories' in other parts of the EU (cf. Cooke and Morgan 1993; Hudson et al. 1997; Lovering 1999) without a deeper consideration of and sensitivity to 'path-dependent regional economic and political geographies' (Jones and MacLeod 1999). More fundamentally, questions emerged on the scale of this new regional level of governance and its relationship to the existing national and local levels of governance, including whether the regional level is the most appropriate spatial scale to 'solve' wider policy concerns in the country, if indeed that was one of the premises of the new arrangements.

The changes to regional planning and governance, meanwhile, have been examined from a number of different perspectives, with the emphasis being largely on England. However, one missing element in such analyses has been the fusion of existing and evolving regional institutions and procedures across the three nations of Britain. Of critical importance to the success of evolving forms of land use and economic planning and new governance is the attitude and cooperation of existing agencies, or 'stakeholders' in New Labour terminology, institutions and policy networks that evolved during the 1980s and 1990s. As institutional and network theory demonstrate, there are important and powerful existing interests who have the ability to facilitate or thwart the new regional policy initiatives. In order to understand what was occurring, it is necessary to delve into a little prehistory.

Regional planning, policy-making and governance before 1997

The push towards regional governance

Regional planning in England, Scotland and Wales was, to all intents and purposes, suppressed under the market-orientated ethos of the Thatcher years. Strategic and regional planning were viewed by the government at the time as unnecessary bureaucratic tiers and this attitude reached its peak when the Conservatives proposed the abolition of structure plans in 1989 (DoE 1989). The market orientation had an impact upon attitudes towards planning and the ability of planners and other to coordinate change, with the result that planning, urban regeneration and economic development issues were tackled at the local level through a combination of central government-imposed project-led development and financial incentives. This led to a more site-specific approach to planning (if it could be termed planning at all), but it was the less direct changes associated with the changing nature of government and the decline of the welfare state that made regional planning increasingly difficult. Privatization of public utilities such as telecommunications, electricity and water; transport agencies; the establishment of numerous agencies on a semi-commercial footing, such as health boards and trusts; the creation of new quangos charged with the provision of public services; and the increased centralization of power to Westminster all led to fragmentation of strategic coordination amongst a disparate group of 'providers' with the responsibility for services divided between different public and private bodies at the strategic level (Hayton 1996; Mawson 1997; TCPA 1997). A further round of local government reorganization in all three nations in 1986 (of the metropolitan counties), again in 1996 and in 2008 (with a slide towards unitary authorities) led to the abolition of the two-tier system throughout Scotland and Wales and in some parts of England (Clotworthy and Harris 1996).

The reaction to this perceived strategic policy vacuum was the emergence of 'bottom-up' forms of regional coordination and planning, especially for the purposes of economic development (Dicken and Tickell 1992; Lynch 1999). The emergence of these new forms of partnerships – ad hoc groupings meeting as and when required – led in some cases to 'institutional congestion' (Roberts and Lloyd 1999) which only highlighted the complex and inefficient division of responsibilities and functions in this new realm of governance. The strategic vacuum was partly the motivation behind the growing demands for greater coordination of regional policy and planning (British Chambers of Commerce 1997; CBI, 1997; TEC National Council 1997), but other issues were also significant. Baker (1998), for example, identifies a number of other factors that led to the renewed interest in regional planning, including:

- the recognition that many policy concerns can only be adequately addressed at a regional scale;
- the realization that local government reorganization had effectively removed a level of strategic overview in certain areas;
- the increasing role of the EU in spatial planning and development that is more focused at a regional level; and

- the path paved by the creation of regional government offices in creating a similar institutional regional framework for other stakeholders.

Tewdwr-Jones and McNeill (2000) also highlighted four factors influencing the emergence of a stronger form of regional policy-making: central government funding opportunities through 'innovative' partnerships, the emergence of regional planning, the creation of regional development organizations and/or agencies with both an urban regeneration and economic development remit, and opportunities provided by EU funding mechanisms.

In opposition, the Labour Party had begun to explore possible forms for such regional planning and governance, and this had culminated in referenda on devolution in Scotland and Wales and a consultation document on the form of regional governance in England entitled *A Choice for England* (Labour Party 1995). The emphasis in the proposals was on economic and land-use planning, but with a more accountable framework along the lines of regional assemblies, that would be adopted only if a referendum in the region returned a yes vote. Once in power, New Labour proceeded with the broad approach and effectively combined the three dimensions of its regional proposals – planning, governance and economic development – into tailored packages for the three separate countries. The distinctive social, economic and political backgrounds in each country, combined with elements such as electoral pragmatism in regional politics (Lynch 1999) and cultural and linguistic differentiation, necessitated distinctive approaches that placed more or less emphasis on the three elements.

The regional voice in England, Scotland and Wales

In respect of England, Harvie (1991) has compared the lack of a coherent regional voice with the situation in both Scotland (Paterson 1998) and Wales (Tewdwr-Jones 2002). Scotland, meanwhile, has historically had a far greater demand for greater responsibility for its affairs, including its own parliament. But with its own form of regional administration through the Scottish Office and economic development policy through Scottish Enterprise and Highlands and Islands Enterprise, the emphasis for Scotland has been on accountability, coordination and distinctiveness (Allmendinger and Tewdwr-Jones 2000b). This was certainly the agenda of planners in Scotland who had been critical of the fragmented, centralized and unaccountable approach to planning (Hayton 1997; Tewdwr-Jones and Lloyd 1997; Goodstadt and U'ren 1999) – an agenda of expectations that was fuelled by the Scottish Office themselves (Scottish Office 1999). Although greater coordination and distinctiveness could be achieved through alterations in policy guidance, Scotland also had the ability to pass primary legislation. Within Wales, the situation was slightly different, since the country has historically been far more integrated into the Union than Scotland and there was less demand for accountability as the failed referendum vote of 1979 indicates (Kendle 1997). Similar to the position in Scotland, the Welsh Office (WO) had provided regional administration with limited accountability, while the WDA had provided effective economic development policy (see, for example, Morgan 1997, but cf. Lovering 1999). The package of regional measures was tailored towards providing accountability through an Assembly with greater coordination of policy and the ability to alter policy guidance.

The English regions started from a far less advanced position. The Government Offices for the Regions (GORs), introduced in 1994, provided a much needed form of regional administration and coordination but were far more limited in their ability to enter into debate and partnership with the fragmented and congested landscape of institutions that were seeking to provide some form of land use and economic regional planning (Mawson 1997; Mawson and Spencer 1997b). They also lacked accountability at Cabinet level, since different ministers represented the different departmental interests that were all included within each government office. The decentralization package for England was skewed in New Labour's first government towards an economic emphasis through the creation of RDAs to 'level the uneven playing field' for institutional presence to match the situation in both Scotland and Wales (Tewdwr-Jones and Phelps 2000); the accountability issue, through the creation of regional chambers and, possibly at a later stage, regional assemblies, would only be addressed in Labour's second election term.

The White Paper on regional government published in 2002 (ODPM 2002b) advocated regional assemblies for the English regions. But rather than imposing tiers of government onto territories, Labour decided to arrange referenda in each of the regions to gauge whether assemblies were desired. The north-east of England was the first region selected and a postal-vote referendum organised in November 2004. The region was chosen mainly because it was considered to be the one territory where there was a strong desire for a newly elected tier of governance. The result proved embarrassing for the government, with a clear 'no' vote expressed in the poll. This had the effect of not only rejecting the prospect of a North East Regional Assembly, it also had the effect of throwing out the government's regional democracy plan as ministers did not want to risk further no votes in other parts of the country. The final phase of the regional governance policy of New Labour therefore had to be abandoned and was replaced with an ad hoc interim arrangement where 'regional chambers' or less formal 'regional assemblies' met comprising various local authorities and other bodies within each region.

One element that has been common to all three countries, even in those agencies sceptical about new institutions of democracy, is the need for emerging governance institutions and policies to work and cooperate with the plethora of existing formal and informal institutional arrangements and networks. Ironically, it is this need that has generated a desire for enhanced strategic and regional coordination, to ameliorate 'silo mentalities' on the part of the different service providers and to ensure joined-up government. Many of the agencies and networks that emerged in the strategic vacuum of regional planning and policy in the 1980s and 1990s were a pragmatic response to the need for coordination and promotion, however: 'These agencies performed an important role in facilitating national policy priorities into a sub-national agenda whilst seeking to organise local authority activities and resource commitments' (Roberts and Lloyd 1999: 517). Similarly, the Scottish Parliament and Scottish Government, and Welsh Assembly and Welsh Government in Wales, have emphasized the cooperative nature of government approaches to existing institutional arrangements. This cooperative approach is in stark contrast to the more 'top-down' and confrontational perspective of the Thatcher years (Allmendinger and Tewdwr-Jones 2000a). It is therefore likely that, despite the North East Regional Assembly referendum 'no' result and the government abandoning the plan across the rest of England partly in 2004 and the remainder in 2011, the English regional governance and democracy issue will return to the political agenda in the next ten years, since there remains a clear need for regional policy and regional planning coordination. The task of 'joined-up government' at the strategic level remains as important as ever.

RSS making

Turning attention to the nature of regional planning rather than democracy, Labour's reforms to planning were ambitious. The Planning and Compulsory Purchase Act 2004 completely reformed the planning policy- and strategy-making function at not only regional level, but also at national, sub-regional, local and community levels: RPGs were replaced with Regional Spatial Strategies; 'Sub-Regional Strategies' were introduced for the first time; Structure Plans, Local Plans and Unitary Development Plans were replaced with 'Local Development Frameworks', 'Action Area Plans' and 'Masterplans'; 'Community Strategies' were to find implementation at neighbourhood level within Local Development Frameworks; and 'public consultation' was to be replaced by enhanced public participation.

The second aspect of the reforms concerned scale and uniqueness. Prior to devolution, the UK government expected planning to be devised and implemented uniformly across all parts of Britain: one country, one system. But such an ethos lies counter to processes of devolution and regionalization. It also contributed to the notion that planning was failing to deliver development in the right locations, to cater for the desires and expectations of local and regional actors, and produced standardized plans and policies that did not deliver – criticisms of planning that pre-date New Labour and, even after the 1997–2010 reforms, are still rolled out by government to justify the next wave of changes. Planning after 2004 did start to become increasingly differentiated in different parts of the UK as a consequence of devolution, decentralization and regionalization (Tewdwr-Jones 2002; Haughton and Counsell 2004), although whether these changes can be attributed to spatial planning alone is a debateable point (Haughton at al. 2010). With the impetus provided by devolution and a planning reform agenda, Scotland, Wales and Northern Ireland developed their own spatial strategies separate to England with a desire for differentiation (Berry, Brown and McGreal 2001; Allmendinger 2002; Harris, Hooper and Bishop 2002).

A further issue to bolster the case for regional planning concerned the expectation of change, and particularly that of economic development and policy integration. There was now a new role for RSS-making in achieving coordination between disparate actors and strategies, more for integrated governance purposes than planning. New forms of planning were explored as tools to help resolve community, sub-regional and regional problems (Counsell and Haughton 2003), alongside a renaissance for planning as the means of achieving policy integration and coordination and the promotion of sustainable development (Tewdwr-Jones, Gallent and Morphet 2010). The emphasis here was to look at planning not as a delivery process per se, in the style of planning under the welfare state, but rather as a strategic capacity and political integration mechanism intended to cement the increasingly fragmented agents of the state, all of whom possess their own agendas, political objectives, strategies and resources, but who needed to cooperate in order to deliver projects and developments. Spatial planning was being looked at and to some extent appropriated to ensure compatible working and strategic coordination when desired. This process, which professional groups and some ministers claimed as their own, nestled under the spatial planning label at a convenient time for them, and extended the remit of planning beyond mere land-use development and the 1980s/1990s regulatory rump into a coordinative process where professional planners' duties concerned management of agency integration (Healey 1997; Lloyd and Illsley 1999).

These three characteristics of change – complexity, scale and expectation of change – within regional spatial plan-making would transform, so it was hoped, the activity and scope of planning, across scales and across territories in varied ways and at varied times. The focus on devolution and decentralization across UK planning was not limited to, for example, a potential shift from one form of spatial planning to another. Planning in the mid- to late 2000s was viewed, ambitiously, as a contributor to and a reflection of a more fundamental reform of territorial management that aimed to, *inter alia*, improve integration of different forms of spatial development activity, not least economic development. So, at one level, devolution and its implications for spatial planning must be analysed in respect of other aspects of New Labour's regional project, particularly the government's concern with business competitiveness. At another level, the reforms that privileged regional scale-policy interventions inevitably required changes in the divisions of powers and responsibilities at local and national levels. In other words, devolution and decentralization involved a major rescaling of both planning and spatial development, downwards from the central state but also upwards from the local level, and this started to have profound implications as it unfolded rapidly and unevenly across Britain within different policy sectors.

Consequently, spatial planning was deeply implicated in the re-territorialization of the British state and a number of related significant issues and areas of interest arise from such changes, including:

- The need and opportunity to integrate spatial development through new regional strategies, including activities such as economic development, housing, transport, sustainable development, energy, water and biodiversity.
- The scope for and implications of policy divergence and inter-regional rivalry.
- The tension between regional autonomy and national interest, including wider questions concerning the balance between the two and the role of the centre.
- The relationship between the evolving regionalist agenda and existing institutions, processes and stakeholders.
- The role and extent of 'region building' and the ways in which the region is discursively constructed, being politically, socially and symbolically shaped and contested in various ways.

We will return to these issues conceptually at the end of the book. But it seemed clear that the objective of this spatial transformation during the 2000s was to widen the trajectory of planning, or spatial strategy-making, in the modernization and governance agendas at both the regional and local levels within the UK. Although this started to result in new participatory processes and greater contestation on the form and trajectory of regional and local spatial plan-making, it nevertheless occurred within a planning legislative framework that remained firmly rooted within the agenda of and context provided by the central and local government state and within professional planning duties. Here, the tension surrounding the form of spatial plan-making occurred at the level of the state between the broader form of and relationship between governance and government. Issues such as housing provision, for example, became a highly contested area caught between these governance and government processes (see Box 6.2). Central govern-

Box 6.2   Housing as a function of RSS-making

Housing was a core, and controversial, feature of RSS in England. RSS was required to take account of national and regional population and household projections – such as those illustrated in Table 2.1 – and covert these figures to houses over the time period. These figures would then be used as trends for the calculation of housing figures and land supply required within each local authority area and through its own development plan, taking into account historic trend data, age cohorts and different types of households (see Gallent 2007; Gallent and Tewdwr-Jones 2007, for more detail). These figures were often not hard and fast, since they were only trends. Some plans included higher levels than the projections indicated to take into account possible economic growth rates, changing household formations and migration rates, but essentially were there to provide a framework for planning (Adams and Watkins 2002).

The problem arose between the use of trend projections and the physical manifestation of the calculations for housing land requirements. Total average annual numbers tended to be seized upon by opponents to growth and countryside and environmental pressure groups, concerned upon possible development on green fields. Housebuilders, on the other hand, complained that the figures constrained supply in areas of unmet demand. A political dynamic added to this and the debate often became heated, where politicians at different governmental levels attempted to amend the trend figures depending on whether they possessed a pro-development or anti-development stance, thereby undermining planning and reducing it to nothing more than a 'numbers game' (Murdoch and Abram 2002).

In the 2005 draft RSS for the South-East, the housing figures for 2006 to 2026 provoked an emotional and fraught political debate. The strategy offered three different levels of average annual housing growth – 25,500, 28,000 or 32,000 – with the differences accountable to recent building rates, historic trends rolled forward and higher economic growth rates. These figures were then broken down into individual counties or growth areas. A consultancy study commissioned at the time (ERM 2005) indicated that the higher growth rate of 32,000 houses per year would meet housing demands and thereby contribute to problems of affordability, but would place additional pressures on environmental capacity, transport infrastruc-

→

ment proclaimed publicly that it wanted to deliver more housing on the ground, but had little direct means of doing so. The private sector called for greater land release and more planning deregulation to allow the housing development to happen. Local authorities were the agents dealing with site-specific contentions and liaising both with developers and the public on the appropriateness of individual sites. While the regional assembly, through the RSS, was obliged to negotiate housing numbers between the clamour for certainty from the central state and

$\rightarrow$

ture, water resources, waste and climate change. Conversely, the lower, 25,500 figure would have lower environmental impacts but fail to meet existing housing-demand problems or cater for any increase in economic growth. Political allegiances were drawn to the two poles: the countryside protection group, the CPRE, supported the lower figure; the housing charity Shelter supported the higher figure. An economic lobby also supported an even higher figure, with Deloitte (2005) suggesting that in order to ensure continued economic productivity the South-East actually needed a building figure of at least 35,000 houses per year in order to deal with existing unmet demand. But all the figures were also dependent on migration patterns and changing levels of people moving in and out of the region, so any fluctuation in these would also impact on the bigger figure.

And so a debate initially about housing numbers and land supply invariably became a debate concerned also with migration, access to housing and the contribution of migrants to the labour market, and impacts on the regional and London economy. This was one of the reasons why the then government established the Barker Reviews (2004, 2006) into planning and housing and planning and economic growth. It also led to questions being asked about the housebuilders' tactics and whether 'land banking' was occurring – housing developers gaining planning permission for new housing but deliberately sitting on the land without building in order to constrain supply and keep house prices high. In turn the housebuilders accused planners of failing to set housing targets at an appropriate level to meet demand, including allowing more greenfield land to be released for new development. Conservative Party politicians, meanwhile, at both national and local levels, complained about a centralist or 'Stalinist' form of postwar planning still operating and a system which imposed housing growth figures, top down, from national and regional projections to the local level where growth was often opposed by residents It was, perhaps, inevitable that once the Conservatives gained office in government after 2010, one of their first acts was to abolish RSS in an attempt to remove the imposed housing requirements on local areas, although whether they actually recognized the wider purpose and value of RSS making is debatable. See Gallent and Tewdwr-Jones 2007 for more information in this area.

the desire for flexibility on the part of local government and the public. Faced with such tensions, spatial planning at the regional level was always going to be caught in a heavily contested arena, with justifiable claims that it was failing to deliver much at all. And perhaps, tellingly, it was the housing issue that figured prominently in the Coalition government's proposals to scrap Regional Assemblies and RSSs after 2010, thereby reducing the spatial planning role at the regional level, somewhat frustratingly, to an argument about housing numbers and little more.

Collaborative regional governance: Communicative action as the basis of institutional capacity-building

In order to assess and explain conceptually the form of planning at the regional scale existing after 1997, its rise and failure, it is necessary to extend the analysis of institutional capacity-building found in the regionalism idea by giving greater consideration to the diversity of social action and interaction and hence the possibilities for distortion in the practices through which institutional capacity is built and exercised. This is necessary in order to situate the discussion of the form of regionalism that was on trial practically and politically at this time, but also to assist in explaining why the type of regional governance established was not embedded into formal governmental structures. The normative aspects of major theories of institutional capacity-building within the new regionalism have promoted limited conceptions of the rationality of political institutional actions and interactions – essentially in terms of communicative action or normatively regulated action. In addressing the diversity of social actions and interactions implicit in institutional capacity-building, it is necessary to look to Habermas in order to distinguish communicative action from three other types of social action. This warrants consideration of the relationship between different types of social action, the manner in which they are structured and the importance of context in understanding the possibilities for regional institutional capacity-building. This becomes a possible way of extending theories of institutional capacity-building within regionalism to acknowledge the diversity of actions and hence potential distortion in institutional practices and relations. The implications of this work for ideas of institutional capacity-building within regionalism highlight the need to analyse the motivations of individual stakeholders and the way in which social action is structured through some form of state strategy (MacLeod and Goodwin 1998) or strategic direction (Amin and Hausner 1997) within actual local systems of governance. Only then can we truly analyse and understand the degree to which any new scale of governance and

spatial planning can be situated and moulded into the existing governmental, governance and planning framework and the chance by which it
becomes a fixed form within the institutional and policy hierarchy.

In keeping with notable contributions in the economic geography
literature, Healey (1997) notes how global processes of economic
restructuring are undermining the integrity of many local economies
and the position and powers of many local agents of governance. Nevertheless, what Healey identifies is a desire to build institutional capacity
anew. A 'capacity for locally informed, place-based governance' is essential to the 'drawing down of benefits from companies into the social and
economic life of a place in environmentally sensitive ways' (Healey
1997: 202). Collaborative forms of action are central to the building of
this capacity at a local level since 'the development of governance
cultures in which collaborative collective action is possible will be more
likely to resist forces leading to economic exploitation of people in
places, to limit environmental degradation ... than cultures which are
dominated by individualistic competitive strategies' (Healey 1998:
1535). 'Inclusive argumentation' is central to the development of collaborative governance (Healey 1997: 237).

There is considerable emphasis within Healey's work on collaborative
planning on the power of process and procedures to effect rational
thought, reflection and expression engendering change for the good of
the majority of stakeholders. For example:

> this new form of governance and planning involves building up
> collaborative relationships with 'stakeholders' (which became a
> popular and somewhat tarnished Blairite word) in territories, to
> generate not merely specific programmes but governance cultures
> through which territorial political communities can collectively
> address their conflicts and maximise their chances to shape their
> places and their futures in the open and diffused relationships of
> contemporary societies. (1998: 1535)

Indeed, Healey has noted explicitly the relevance of Habermas's
communicative ethics as a conceptual resource to develop collaboration,
understanding and trust (Healey 1997: 311):

> This recasts the role of urban planning in a new form, as an active
> social process through which the governance of power to regulate and
> to distribute resources which affect the qualities of places is reshaped
> by a collaborative reflection on the ideas, systems of meaning, and
> ways of acting which have been driving place making in particular
> places in the past, and a mobilisation of transformative potential to
> make a difference to place making in the future. (Healey 1998: 1543)

Despite the acknowledged idealism of these prescriptions (Healey (1999), Healey also recognizes the role of power in distorting the rationality of communicative action among stakeholders within collaborative planning so that the design of governance processes should recognize complex power relations within and between stakeholders (Healey 1997: 288). Notwithstanding these observations on the inevitability of the distorting influence of power, the picture which emerges from these formulations of collaborative and associative forms of governance is one in which distorting influences come to be revealed, recognized and, in large measure, ameliorated through communicative action. In this way, as has been argued elsewhere:

> the power dimension is viewed as a matter that can be transformed through a restructuring of power relations and social contexts, with individuals recognising and identifying the distribution of power between those actors participating within a collaborative planning exercise. Power is therefore compartmentalised... into a process to be *recognised* by stakeholders. (Tewdwr-Jones and Allmendinger 1998: 1980; original emphasis)

So the application of these ideas to the mode of regionalism in governance and spatial planning occurring after 1997 really rests on an assessment of the degree to which the actors and institutions involved were able to embrace new tiers of policy making while simultaneously acknowledging the existing structures of government. Here, the tensions surround the degree to which government and governance, coexisting, jostle for power (Agnew 1999) and create their own path dependencies and legacies which have an implication for new or emerging forms of working. Sometimes these jostling moves result in desired outcomes of the new structures and strategies, but sometimes unintended consequences occur in power relationships and in the planning and land-use implications of those arrangements. The remainder of this chapter examines the conceptual forms of working that appeared to occur in RSS-making and in the fluid governance arrangements between the central state and local government. Three issues are relevant to frame this discussion of the *determinants of territorial institutional building* are:

- the perception and reaction of agents within the governance arena;
- the rationale and motivation of agents within the governance arena; and
- the expectation and audience of outcomes of interaction within the governance arena.

Agency perception and reaction at the intersection of capacity building

By considering the process of institutional capacity-building as a form of political interaction between various actors and agencies wielding different degrees of power, motivation, interest and purpose, the acts of collaboration are played out. Here at the intersection of capacity building between agencies in governance process, the convergence of actors' rationales for involvement and participation with the policy or practical requirements of the partnership activity ensures interaction can be identified as a political and transpersonal experience.

Each agency will readily agree to sign up to the process of partnership if a strategic or local purpose needs to be met. This might be the production of a plan, a strategic framework, a vision, a work task or an action; whichever form the purpose will take, agencies will recognize the requirement to meet an end, or possible several ends. But the involvement of several agencies in a partnership to produce a strategic or local purpose does not necessarily imply that each possesses the same outlook, agenda or perception on how to achieve that end. In reality, in view of the fact that partnership between agencies of governance involves interaction between separately composed organizations, the capacity-building arena will, by its very nature, possess differing actors who can be identified by their different remits and/or expectations of what the partnership can be expected to deliver for their agency. On occasions, the motivation for participation with the arena of capacity building will be obvious. But at other times, motivation will be hidden from view, with agencies either selectively divulging information to other participants or else employing strategic behaviour to present a partial or even false perspective of their desired end as a political tactic.

For example, a partnership of governance established within a region to identify how many strategic development sites should be identified for economic development purposes will involve various agencies representing business regional and local government, planning, training and enterprise, and environmental interests. All agencies would accept that strategic employment sites need to be identified in the region in order to ensure continued economic prosperity. But not all agencies would be expected to agree on the number of sites to be planned for, the size of sites, the type of economic development suitable for the sites, the transport links to and from the development sites, the skills and employment base of the sub-region within which each site would be planned or implemented or the associated land-use requirements caused by strategic development related to housing demand, supply chains or public transport access. These are merely examples of the sort of issues and dilemmas that would need addressing by the partnership: no doubt there would be many others. But the very existence of the partnership would indicate that an attempt is being made to address the differing perceptions and expectations that would exist caused by agency interaction.

Site selection for strategic development purposes would inevitably be a politically contentious issue, and the simple identification of area for possible future development would produce concern and agitation from certain actors in the partnership. That is why some actors may not want to 'show all their cards at once', and may prefer a more selective and cautious approach to discussing matters and evaluating options. If anything, actors adopting obfuscation to discursive interaction are usually driven by political motives. A determination to appear to want to participate enthusiastically in the arena of capacity building could well be a shrewd move on the part of politically motivated actors to calculate (a) the degree of conformity or resistance to their own agendas and perceptions of the issues under consideration and (b) the motives and expectations of other participants.

Agency rationale and motivation within arenas of capacity building

In the Habermasian world, discursive interaction between actors in these arenas is epitomised by openness, interdependence and trust; all opinions are valued equally and positive attitudes generated towards finding solutions, learning practical and political settings of governance and development, not all actors will be prepared to engage in completely open and discursive interaction. Each actor present within the capacity-building arena will be there for a purpose. That purpose could be to attain a particular desired end, identified possibly as a personal goal or an objective of an individual's employer whom he or she is representing in the arena. Each actor will be aware of how he or she is representing in the arena, will be aware of how far they are able to bargain in representing their agency's position or the subject matter and will tactically listen to and react to other actors' perceptions and utterances as they proceed in the course of the meeting.

There can be a range of factors that underpin not only an agency's participation in the capacity-building arena, but also the behaviour of the individuals representing the different agencies. The rationale and motivation of the participating agency's presence and interaction in the governance arena can result from both mandatory requirements and voluntary involvement. Mandatory requirements comprise political or legal necessity; some agencies are forced to be involved in discursive interaction with other agencies of governance as part of a new political process.

A state's attempt to establish open government underpinned by greater consultation between government departments and policy-user groups and community representatives could ensure a political commitment to active participation within a capacity-building arena. These new forms of political and administrative policy-making formalize arenas of governance comprising disparate participating agencies, and could also ensure that enduring forms of dialogue, interaction and evaluation occur between the organizations that may not have occurred previously to any great degree. This political will dictates an element of hegemonic action on the part of the state to enforce, encourage or stimulate other agencies' participation in the new political forums even if the state itself wishes to portray an alternative bottom-up, open or consultative basis to policy making compared to the previous top-down approach to government and administration. This contradiction, between fostering local or regionally scaled policy-making arenas within which the nation-state listens to participants' perceptions and viewpoints while nevertheless controlling the process that occurs, is not necessarily problematic. The important aspect for participating agencies to consider in this context is the degree to which they should expect radical change, or the controlling agency permitting and stimulating debate that could eventually see an agency's objectives fully met. In other words, it is necessary to keep expectations in check in order to avoid building up false hopes simply as a consequence of the agency's presence and interaction within the capacity-building arena.

Other factors that could determine agencies' involvement in the participatory arena include financial or democratic issues. A local authority, for example, may well discover that it has to be seen to be participating in an arena of capacity building in order to be eligible to bid for government funding for particular projects. By entering the arena and forming partnerships with other institutions an agency could not only be representing a broader section of society, but also creating the conditions that could lead to partnership.

Participating agencies could also be driven by 'softer' factors, however. Voluntary organizations, for example, may wish to enter into institutional capacity-building as an attempt to influence proceedings that were previously exclusionary and hierarchical; this arena could provide them with an opportunity to advance more formally and systematically their own agenda and objectives. They may also be present to learn more about the issues under discussion or about other participants' perspectives and viewpoints. They could also participate within the arena simply to be heard more prominently as a voice representing a common membership. Finally, individuals within the arena may wish to explore their personal desires and objectives, either in their own right or in the ways in which they present and debate contentious matters. This

is the most difficult factor to consider academically since personal opinions and individuals' styles cannot be hypothesized easily. Personal
opinions and utterances and individual motivation and behaviour are
individualistic, and attempting to uncover these can be beyond the scope
of not only other individuals' perceptions but also social-scientific study
on networks and partnerships within arenas of governance.

Agency expectation and audience when participating in capacity building

The third aspect that determines how the intersection of capacity
building proceeds is the expectations of the participating agencies in
relation to the different audiences they are required to present to. Since
participating organizations will be present within the partnership for a
clearly identifiable purpose (to represent communities, political masters
or policy groups; in problem solving; new forums of dialogue; the attraction of finance or the allocation of existing resources, for example), it is
correct to surmise that each organization will be expected to report back
to a larger institution or group of individuals on the outcome of the
partnership interaction and dialogue. It is that broader constituency of
the partnership – as the ambassadors of the constituencies grapple with
their interests in addition to debating the policy issue, problem or task –
that precipitated the formulation of the arena in the first place. This is
particularly true of forums that comprise representatives from various
tiers of government; how to meet national policy priorities, for example,
in relation to regional governance when interacting with local authorities and community associations.

Each actor present will be extremely aware of the political and policy
parameters within which dialogue can occur as determined by his or her
own constituency. Although signing up to partnership, each actor will be
eager to send signals out to the audience that matters are in progress,
under consideration, achieving desired ends or going badly. These signals
can be accomplished through interactive dialogue between the ambas-
sador and the constituency in formal and informal settings outside the
capacity-building arena, but can also be achieved through media reporting,
media briefings, covert meetings and other forms of communication.

The requirement to present an issue, argument or choice to particular
audiences possibly in different ways and in different styles represents
dramaturgical action on the part of the organization. Each participant
in the partnership process will recognize this 'reporting-back' requirement of each other, whether formally as a requirement of the institution's presence in the arena or confidentially, behind closed doors. The
problem in conceptualizing this activity is that a great deal of dramatur-

gical behaviour occurs out of sight or undetected, since mere analysis is sometimes unable to compare the utterances and communications of the same organization to different audiences simultaneously. There are separate scalar priorities or participants to different agencies and the remit of the range of institutions participating. On one level of governmental interaction, this could involve meeting audience expectations at the cross-national, national, regional, sub-regional or local levels. Alternatively, the range of agencies could dictate that the audiences are the public, private, governmental, quasi-governmental, public–private partnership or voluntary sectors. In the case of regional economic development, the audience could dictate that the audience could be composed of the national government and various departments, local government, business groups, an inward investor, the media and the wider public.

A related issue to the question of audiences and expectations is whether the partnership or collaborative process has been established as an ad hoc initiative for a particular project or problem (and therefore temporary) or as an enduring form of new political formulation. The dichotomy here of the consensus, dialogue and the search for common understanding (between the institutions) within the arena, compared to the retrenched, independent and possibly conflicting positions of the separate agencies outside it, reveals perhaps the fragility upon which some partnerships are resting: all smiles around the table; disagreement and conflict outside the meeting room. It is this uncertainty – the extent, duration and form of agreement and mutual learning in collaborative processes of governance between the various actors – that indicates the problems for regional, national and local governments in establishing and relying on the partnership approach to an unnecessary degree.

Conclusions

Let us conclude by returning to spatial planning specifics. In marked contrast to the situation in planning before New Labour were elected to office, the creation and promotion of governance styles at the regional level after 1997 led to the welcomed reduction in the role of the nation-state in determining the fortunes of sub-national territories, or so it was hoped. But such decentralization and devolution processes, structurally and institutionally, were overlain by simultaneous policy-making transfers from the centre to both the region and the locality. This twin process of institutional decentralization and policy transfer created a fusion of different styles of government and governance across the UK territory and became fluid and difficult to comprehend. Different government styles and structures became apparent in England, Scotland, Wales and Northern Ireland; very soon, a similar mix of styles began to be apparent within planning processes within the four territories. The partial abandonment of the regional democracy push in England after 2004 left the English territories in a sort of democratic limbo, but that did not mean that the task of regional strategy-making and regional spatial coordination stopped then, or was terminated after the Coalition government's abolition of the remainder of the regional institutional mechanisms after 2010. In the latter 2000s onwards, that process continued and new forms of planning and new partnerships continued to evolve in very different ways in very different places, but centred on specific policy sectoral issues, such as housing, transport or waste.

One of the problems for new institutions is to demonstrate their worth against a backdrop of growing complexity and upheaval in UK governance. Not only did new regional arrangements have to 'bed in' and take their place among the plethora of bodies that constitute the landscape of governance, but they had to account for the changing nature of the landscape itself. Nevertheless, as many of the actors within governance arrangements started to discover, the promotion of regional spatial planning and participatory governance within each scale may be a goal worth pursuing, but still requires a form of strategic direction to set some sort of political vision if agreement by lowest common denominator is to be avoided, balanced against a central state still eager to set some of the agenda. What regional governance within spatial strategy-making seemed to be creating was greater discretion and autonomy within particular scales and across particular territories. Such moves within planning may have served a useful role to provide a perspective that was reflective of the disparate interests with regard to the economy, transport and housing. But if the new forms of regional spatial planning and coordination were to stand any chance of success, they would require a great deal of commitment and vision to ensure that all vested interests bought in to the process. This was part of the problem: so long as the central state continued to rearrange the parameters of working, and stipulated desired outcomes of regionalism in the national interest, so the agencies negotiating within the regional governance arrangements became more protective of their own positions and agendas, and less committed to the new institutional processes. Without a firm commitment and buy-in from all the governance actors, keeping the spatial planning exercise alive and relevant was always going to be an uphill task.

Chapter 7

Sub-Regionalism and City-regions

In the absence of a designated tier of regional government, the strength of regional working has largely depended on an ability to transcend the complexity and organisational framework of sub-national government by developing 'bottom-up' mechanisms for joint working. (While 1999: 5–6)

Generally, and in Britain especially, the urban problem has been largely defined in terms of particular towns or cities. Rarely in the last quarter of the twentieth century has the reality that most large towns and cities are clustered close to together and form effective metropolitan or city-regions ... More recently, however, thinking has begun to change. (Roberts, Thomas and Williams, 1999: 11)

Chapters 5 and 6 demonstrated the problems of attempting to define the extent of territorial management institutionally and what constitutes the national interest and regional autonomy, respectively. These two scales of government and planning relate, in part, to what are perceived to be more top-down attempts to control and fix territories, usually by the central state. While these debates have come and gone politically in England, led by and argued between the two main political parties, the question of our largest cities has also been accompanied by an intense debate on their structure and organization. Some of these cities are regarded as metropolitan, stemming from their historical roles as statutorily defined metropolitan areas, but also in deference to their standing as the largest cities by population in the UK. Outside London, in England these comprise Sheffield, Leeds and Bradford, Newcastle and Sunderland, Birmingham, Manchester and Liverpool. Glasgow in Scotland could also be regarded as a metropolitan area. They are some of the largest urban conglomerations in the UK, but have had a chequered governmental structure. The English examples, until the mid-1980s, possessed a unique institutional arrangement, with a higher strategic metropolitan county authority dealing with cross-metropolitan issues, and a number of metropolitan boroughs at the lower scale within each city dealing with more localized concerns. The Thatcher government abolished London's metropolitan council, the Greater London Council (GLC), and the six 'mets', as they were referred to, in

1986 partly for cost savings but also ideologically, because they were seen as Labour power bases. Higher-tier strategic functions were then transferred to the remaining lower-tier boroughs with the encouragement of rudimentary cross-borough collaboration to deal with matters of more than local interest.

Outside London and the metropolitan areas, the remaining urban centres have often been dubbed as provincial cities, but they contain cities and boroughs that are large geographically and in population size, and perhaps – more significantly – economically significant, or at least have the potential to be. Since the early 1990s, central government has embarked on a continuous process of creating unitary local government in these places (Clotworthy and Harris 1996; Hall and Tewdwr-Jones 2011), and also encouraging the creation of directly elected mayors. In London, the new governance arrangements were initiated as part of Labour's devolution programme, with the creation of a directly elected Mayor of London, a Greater London Authority (GLA) to support the mayor's work, and an elected London Assembly to hold the mayor accountable (Travers 2003; Rydin et al. 2004; Bailey 2009). Elsewhere, the economic and infrastructure relationships between individual towns and cities have also been posited as examples of sub-regional growth zones with little direct relationship to formal governmental boundaries, such as that existing between Cambridge–Milton Keynes–Oxford (e.g. While, Jonas and Gibbs 2004).

These represent 'functional urban regions' rather than administrative city-regions and the mismatch between and asymmetrical form of these two is an enduring debate within academic and policy circles (Shaw and Sykes 2005; Bianconi, Gallent and Greatbatch 2006; Lloyd and Peel 2006). Morphet (2010) states that these 'frequently represent the "functional reality", whether representing a city and its hinterland or a polycentric area' (212). Jonas and Ward (2007) have also maintained that the city-region is an economic and political territory related to spaces that stimulate trade, creativity and entrepreneurialism, while encompassing autonomously developed regulatory decision-making capacities. But there remain problems in pinning down city-regions due to unclear definitions and extent (Shaw and Greenhalgh 2011), and the lack of a precise meaning (Rodriguez-Pose 2008), leading Healey (2007: 28) to describe them as an 'imagined phenomenon', while Harrison (2007) points to the rescaling process occurring from the region to the city-region as a way of merely attempting to resolve underlying spatial disparities. As other cities have determined through a referendum to elect mayors, the question of city-region governance and planning has returned to the political agenda.

The Labour Party's victory in the 1997 general election unleashed a range of long-anticipated constitutional reforms. An ongoing process of modernization of governmental and policy processes (DETR 1998a, 1998b), the implementation of devolution within the UK (Scottish Office 1997, Welsh Office 1997), a strong interest in the regional question (DETR 1998d; HM Government 1997) and further European integration (DETR 1998e), are all important contexts to the city-region debate. After 2010, the Coalition government disliked top-down regionalism, which they viewed as being imposed by the central state over England, but has acknowledged the need for some form of strategic governmental tier, at the interim level between the defunct regions and individual local authorities. Since 2010, a new form of sub- regional governance has emerged in the shape of Local Enterprise Partnerships (LEPs), which occupy the territory partly created by the demise of RDAs. The locations of the LEPs are selective rather than total across the UK and are based on an amalgam of areas covered by certain county local authorities. Since 2010 the LEPs have been accompanied by the designation of Enterprise Zones which, unlike their 1980s counterparts, are also on a scale above that of a localized area in some cases. While all this governmental, political and administrative restructuring is occurring, it can be difficult to grasp the implications of these changes for current governmental and policy systems (see Allmendinger and Tewdwr-Jones 2000a for an overview to the millennium and Harrison (2010) for the first decade of the twenty-first century). This is related just as much to existing local systems of governance within the UK as it is to urban policy-making.

Whether it is a metropolitan area, one of the largest non-metropolitan urban areas, a new LEP, or even a non-governmental functional urban region with defined structural links beyond individual local authority boundaries, the UK city-region (see Box 7.1) is undergoing fundamental change from political and economic sources (Tewdwr-Jones and McNeill 2000; Williams 1999; Lloyd and Peel 2006; Harrison 2010). This change is at once real, in terms of institutional restructuring, or more informal arrangements resting on collaboration and partnership, but the likely implications are uncertain.

Box 7.1   A definition of city-region

'City-region' refers to a strategic and political level of administration and policy-making, extending beyond the administrative boundaries of single urban local government authorities to include urban and/or semi-urban hinterlands; this definition includes a range of institutions and agencies representing local and regional governance that possess an interest in urban and/or economic development matters that, together, form a strategic level of policy making intended to formulate or implement policies on a broader metropolitan scale.

Before going on to consider what this may mean, it is necessary to go back in time to a discussion of the Thatcherite legacy for city-region planning and governance, by considering the urban spatial focus as encapsulated by central government policies in the 1980s. The chapter then charts the development of the spatial policy focus in the early 1990s under the Major government and the almost tokenistic gesture at the time towards strategic policy-making institutional structures. The following section looks at the form of sub-regional governance style over the last ten years, first with reference to the Labour government's regional renaissance and the position of urban policy, and then to the Coalition government's economic growth agenda. The final section goes on to discuss the shifting sands of the institutional and political context for the debate, by considering three distinctive aspects of the administrative framework of policy making that have, combined, contributed towards a reconfiguration of the spatial question on a broader city-region level.

City-region governance in the UK

It should be stressed at the outset that when discussing the city-region we are dealing with *governance,* not just government. This is to recognize that structure, format and regulatory activities at a particular spatial scale involve a range of actors of varying powers and structural dependencies. As such, the discussion embraces three categories of analysis: the political and economic geography of the UK city-region; the social composition and communication cultures of the governance process, focusing on the key actors; and the institutional and regulatory framework which structure much of the governance process. This section begins, however, with an overview of the political context of the UK city-region as it developed in the 1980s in order to draw parallels with more recent events.

Thatcherism and the neo-liberal territorial project

The concept of planning at the city-region scale in the UK has had a chequered political history. Despite an enthusiastic push towards both strategic (metropolitan) and regional policy-making in the postwar period after the late 1940s, promoted essentially as a means by which economic rejuvenation could be secured, the UK consistently turned away from instigating a formal, statutory system of city-region government and planning processes (Hall and Tewdwr-Jones 2011). The perpetuation of local government administrative entities and, in turn, the planning functions operated by them, between the 1950s and the 1970s ensured that the capacity for politicians to address socioeconomic and environmental problems across the metropolitan scale was largely played down. This occurred primarily as a consequence of political decisions to divide responsibility for the administration of towns and cities and their rural hinterlands between separately elected local government units (Glasson and Marshall 2007). This was more noticeably the case in the mid-1960s to early 1970s, when the then Labour government, having already experimented with formal regional planning, considered the possibility of revising local government boundaries into larger administrative units, termed city-regions. A Royal Commission was established to consider the options (the Redcliffe–Maud Commission), and it reported in 1969 with the recommendation that England and Wales should adopt a city-region model (a separate Wheatley Commission in Scotland made a similar recommendation for north of the border). But the implementation of formal city-regionalism in Britain was compromised by the outcome of the 1970 general election: Labour lost and the Conservatives under Edward Heath took office, rejecting the findings of the Redcliffe–Maud Commission and preferring instead a revised two-tier local government structure based on counties and districts. The urban and the rural thus remained administratively separate, while strategic and local issues were similarly split between the two local governmental levels.

Academic work over the last 30 years in attempting to conceptualize urban political processes has emphasized a shift from focusing on the formal, legislatively defined functions of local government to an emphasis on *governance* (Jessop 1994; Rhodes 1995), encompassing the variety of actors that interact in any local area, often in an attempt to foster cooperation and partnership across the separately accountable political tiers to benefit urban regeneration and/or local and regional economic development (see, for example, Healey et al. 1995; Phelps and Tewdwr-Jones 1998; Raco 1998). Whether there is anything new about this form of local governance is a matter of conjecture (see Imrie and Raco 1999, for example). Nevertheless, the capacity to resolve conflicts and develop a sense of unity in any urban area is often difficult, perhaps deepened by an emphasis on quangos (quasi-autonomous non-governmental organizations), public–private partnerships, or networks.

The UK experience has been dominated by ideological issues, particularly since the advent of Thatcherite economic policy from 1979. As Peck (1995) has illustrated, the Thatcherite project involved a fundamental restructuring of the relations between the state and society that had very important implications for the governance of metropolitan areas. Central government sought to restrict the economic activities of local authorities by cutting expenditure and introducing a competitive element to bidding for resources. Furthermore, local business leaders were encouraged to play a more proactive role in newly established economic development agencies, which sat alongside the elected branches of local government. Of course, this was clothed in the rhetoric of liberating entrepreneurial activity and the 'freeing' of the market. In addition, however, 'The battle was not just about creating a space to allow untrammeled market forces to reign, but about reconstructing the institutional infrastructure through and around which these market forces would operate' (Peck 1995: 25).

And as Peck continues, the battle over the local state was 'also fought out on ideological terrain (the deployment of the language of "partnership" with the private sector, the assertion of the economic rationality of business needs, the appeal to communities of interests outside local government)' (Peck 1995: 31).

The effects of this on the existing institutions of sub-national governance and planning were marked. Primarily, this involved the abolition of the Greater London Council (GLC) and the six metropolitan county councils on 1 April 1986. The case of the GLC was, as Wannop (1995: 76–7) suggests, closely tied to electoral issues – the radically interventionist council led by the left-wing politician Ken Livingstone, subsequently to become London mayor 15 years later – that had implemented both rate rises which were unpopular with many homeowners and a series of policy proposals which ran directly counter to Conservative ideology. Across Britain – most notably in Merseyside – the metropolitan counties provided the biggest challenge to central power from within the state. Power was devolved to the boroughs within each area, and simultaneously shared out to quangos such as Training and Enterprise Councils (TECs) and UDCs. Local authority spending was 'capped' within centrally imposed limits, and funding for urban regeneration projects aimed to stimulate competition for public funding between localities. Wannop (1995: 19) points out that there were other reasons for the decline in the popularity of the 1970s–1980s regime – population growth was slowing, there was less confidence in the techniques of long-term forecasting, and it can be concluded that the decline of metropolitan planning in the 1980s was largely the result of an ideological attempt to re-regulate the local state.

Yet by the 1990s, the UK started to undergo a transition whereby strategic and regional planning matters were returning to the political agenda, partly for planning purposes *per se*, but partly for political reasons (Tewdwr-Jones 1996, 1999). As we have seen elsewhere in this book in discussion on the changing structures of government and governance in planning over time, what goes around comes around. New scales of policy making are rarely new, but are rather reinvented and given new life in subsequent periods, usually with new labels. As a result of a perceived 'regulatory deficit' in the 1990s (Peck and Tickell 1994), where the economy of the south -east of England was outgrowing its infrastructure support (particularly in relation to housing and transport), central government was again forced to consider the introduction of strategic planning measures. Although seemingly against the then ideological stance, there was a partial renaissance to strategic thinking simply because there was a practical need for it. These moves were, however, rather tentative at first, reflecting 'the ambivalence of a government torn between an ideological abhorrence of intervention in the land market, and political awareness that some interventions were needed to capture the votes of key groups of people and of key localities' (Wannop 1995: 21).

The city-region concept in the early 1990s: A grudging revival?

A lack of effective political leadership and democratic accountability at a metropolitan level by the early 1990s was evident due to a missing tier of governance following the abolition of the metropolitan counties in 1986. Ironically, it was central government that felt this vacuum as much as local government. While this was often popularly presented in terms of the latter, the growing awareness of proactive regional leadership within Europe became an issue of greater importance for the state to address (Batchler and Turok 1997). The policy agenda began to shift towards partnership and institutional networking, and as we saw in Chapter 6, led academics to conceptualize 'capacity building' and 'institutional thickness' (Amin and Thrift 1995) – in other words, assessing the ability of parts of territories to mobilize resources, think strategically rather than in an ad hoc fashion, and to form a shared discourse when addressing policy issues (Healey 1997).

There were two main challenges facing central government during this period. First, the overheating of the South-East's economy (Peck and Tickell 1994) placed added pressures on suburbs and villages in London and the Home Counties. Revolts against housing and retail developments by Conservative voters driven by the NIMBY anti-development approach to land-use planning – particularly among smaller district councils – which forced a rethink among *laissez-faire* government ministers (Newman and Thornley 1996). If all this seems familiar and exceptionally similar to the reaction against the Coalition government's abandonment of regional planning and strategic thinking in 2011 and the promotion of pro-growth and development agendas in the draft National Planning Policy Framework, it is because there are strong parallels. By 1989, the Department of the Environment (as the CLG was named in those days) began to have a change of heart, partly to placate Conservative voting opponents in the Home Counties who relied upon the planning system to oppose development proposals, and recognized the benefit of preparing some sort of strategic policy framework, and advocated the provision of non-statutory 'Regional Planning Guidance' (RPG), which was limited to land-use issues of regional importance (Roberts 1996). Interestingly, this renaissance of strategic policy was not focused on and restricted to metropolitan areas or city-regions, but rather covered the whole of England at the regional scale. From 1994, RPGs were strengthened to incorporate not only a region-wide strategy but also a sub-regional dimension, recognizing the specific needs of particular towns or cities, or new economic areas such as science parks and infrastructure hubs. With hindsight, it would appear that the preparation of these RPGs by conferences of local actors was beginning to move beyond purely land-use planning issues towards economic development, marketing and funding cooperation, areas that would be consolidated later with the establishment of both RDAs and the replacement of RPG with Regional Spatial Strategies (RSSs) following the Labour Party's election to power in 1997 (see Chapter 6; Baker 1998). So the regional and sub-regional focus of policy had commenced in government under the Conservatives at least three years prior to the Labour project.

The second major challenge to central government came from the European Union (EU) over the rise of spontaneous regional responses to the European Regional Development Funds (ERDF) available from the European Community. John (1997: 235–6) indicates a range of factors at work here: first, this brought together sub-national agencies seeking funds and European institutions seeking legitimacy; second, the regional allocation of the funds brought together a number of actors in partnership, helping to cement common interests; third, this in turn led to active lobbying activity on the part of newly formed regional interests, which included the opening of cooperatively funded regional offices in Brussels; fourth, it was convenient for the Commission's small bureaucracy to deal with geographically and politically coherent regional bodies; and fifth, political leaders found working together over Europe less problematic than over other potentially competitive issues. Thus there was an incipient Europe-driven regionalism abroad from the mid-1980s to the 1990s, which was creating *de facto* structures of sub-national and sub-regional strategy-making, leapfrogging both the then central government Eurosceptic attitudes towards Europe and the notion of European spatial development (Tewdwr-Jones and Williams, 2001), and the vacuum of formal regional government structures (Batchler and Turok 1997). This was not only driven by local authorities: the private sector was also concerned about the relative lack of a regional business infrastructure compared with some of their European competitors (Mawson and Spencer 1997b: 161).

In response to this, and in another example of a change in policy direction, in 1994 the Conservative central government established GORs, each reporting to the Secretaries of State for Employment, Transport, Environment and Industry. The rationale for such integrated offices was that business and local government needed to have a 'one-stop shop' in their search for guidance and/or funding and to institutionalize the relationship between the region and sub-regional areas. In addition, the GORs were responsible for the allocation of the newly created Single Regeneration Budget (SRB), the latter a central government initiative emphasizing the development of partnerships between private sector and public agencies as a key element of the urban-funding bidding process for specific projects. The proactivity of the GORs in actively formulating a regional policy was highly variable, and generally tentative. Nonetheless, the initiation of the SRB offered a rationale for intervention and coordination of the myriad actors which existed at a sub-regional level and which often seemed confusing and complex (Peck and Tickell 1994). Indeed, the House of Commons Trade and Industry Committee were unhappy that in some regions there appeared to be an uncoordinated use of public money: Lancashire alone, for example, possessed no fewer than 63 organizations either directly or indirectly in receipt of public funding. As a result, GORs were urged to be more proactive in the identification of funding priorities and relevant local agencies, but were stopped short by ministers of engaging in any formal debate over regional priorities (Mawson and Spencer 1997b: 173; Mawson 1997: 205). Overall, therefore, the GORs were interpreted as a means for central government to capture the regional agenda before the autonomous development of (Labour-led) regional bodies.

Simultaneous to the moves to enhance the regional aspect in national policy-making, the government also undertook local government reorganization in certain parts of the UK in the period 1996–98. The exact reasons why reorganization of the structure and administration of local government occurred at this time have been the subject of extended debate elsewhere (see Harris and Tewdwr-Jones 1995; Clotworthy and Harris 1996; Hayton 1996), but it should be noted here that the change was not underlined by a desire to create unitary city-region government per se along the lines suggested by the Redcliffe–Maud Commission in 1969. Nevertheless, in Wales, Scotland and the largest provincial cities in the UK, the government introduced unitary local government. Although the proposals did bear some resemblance to the recommendations of the late 1960s (Wannop 1995), the concept of the city-region was not taken forward on this occasion, and the largest urban areas, although becoming single-tier all-purpose authorities with the abolition of the two-tier counties and districts, remained administratively cut off from their hinterlands. The scope, therefore, for urban competition to nevertheless occur between these larger unitary authorities was still present, and there remained the politically and administratively fraught issue of how to solve urban problems on a scale wider than the immediate local area.

New Labour and the regional/sub-regional question

By the mid-1990s, the prospect of a change in government from Conservative to Labour had come to be recognized by many regional actors. Labour had taken note of the arguments emanating from its local authority members, that attempts to build capacity within cities had been hampered by a piecemeal approach to regional planning and an overly competitive funding regime. As Mawson (1997: 191–2) argued, Labour's 1995 consultation document on regional reform was strongly influenced by the arguments of the Association of Metropolitan Authorities (AMA). This represented a significant change in the attitude of big city council leaderships towards the regional question, as previously the consensus had been that regionalization was actually another form of centralization, a pertinent point made at the time and foretelling one of the criticisms of the later policy roll-out of regionalism by the Labour government after 1997. The concern prior to this time from local government was whether a new regional tier would be allowed to be the providers of strategic services outside the control of central government, but also taking up some of the functions otherwise run by local government. The AMA made reference to 'creeping executive regionalism' embodied particularly by the GORs and the unelected agencies of central government (Mawson 1997: 192). As a result, Labour proposed the establishment of regional directly elected assemblies with a reconsideration of which responsibilities should lie with central, regional and local governmental levels.

The New Labour government elected in 1997 followed through its pre-election promises for constitutional reform, including devolution for Wales and Scotland following public referenda (Welsh Office 1997; Scottish Office 1997); a streamlined government for London, with an elected mayor (again after a referendum) (DETR 1998c); plans to introduce multi-speed regionalization in England (HM Government 1997, 2002; DETR 1998d); and various initiatives to modernize both local government and the planning process (DETR 1998a, 1998b). Legislation encouraged the immediate formation of indirectly elected regional chambers, with the possibility for these to become formalized as regional assemblies later, should the regions themselves consider the move desirable. Simultaneously, RDAs were established as primarily economic-development one-stop shops for the regions, and these came into operation in April 1999 (HM Government 1997). These organizations – dubbed 'super-quangos' by critics at the time – were responsible to central government ministers and to the mayor in the case of London's. The existing GORs, however, were to remain in place. As the government at the time stated, the purpose of the RDAs were threefold: 'they have got a strategic function which is to develop the economic strategies of the regions ...; they have got an executive function in relation to regeneration and to packaging things for inward investment; and they have got an advisory, monitoring, consultative role in relation to a broad range of functions' (cited in SCETR 1998).

Their powers were concentrated in the following areas, as summarized from the *Building Partnerships for Prosperity* White Paper of November 1997 (HM Government 1997):

(i) development and implementation of regional economic strategies, developing the notion of the regional economy already carried out by the GORs;

ii) Social, physical and economic regeneration, including the administration of the SRB and the functions of English Partnerships and the Rural Development Commission;

(iii) Development of rural areas;

(iv) Taking a lead role in the European Union structural funds;

(v) Coordinating inward investment at a regional level;

(vi) Providing advice to ministers on Regional Selective Assistance;

(vii) Business support, monitoring the work of Business Links (a support service for business);

(viii) Site preparation and reclamation;

(ix) Facilitating investments, including investing public money within a private–public partnership;

(x) Marketing of the region as a business location;

(xi) Promoting technology transfer;

(xii) Improving the skills base of the region.

The Agencies consisted of a board of 12 members, with a chair chosen by ministers, and with the private sector dominant in representation. However, members were also drawn from local authorities (four members of the board were elected local councillors), voluntary organizations, and unions and education (see Jones 1999 for further discussion). It is interesting to note, however, that an urban regeneration function was also awarded to these regional institutions, but whether this move was intended to politically reconceptualize urban problems on a sub-regional or strategic basis, or simply a desire for central government to indirectly capture a fertile ground currently dominated by local authority partnerships, is difficult to ascertain.

The dilemma identified at the time of the establishment of the RDAs was how to avoid institutional contestation within agencies that possessed both a regional and sub-regional remit, and on site specific issues relating to urban projects (Tewdwr-Jones and Phelps 2000). In particular, with lines of territorial extent becoming more diverse according to different issues, there appeared to be potential conflict between the RDAs' agendas and those of other networks and partnerships, in addition to the functional relationships with central government's GORs; specific academic attention in 1998–99 was targeted at existing RPG and later RSS policies and the RDAs' own development strategies (Baker, Deas and Wong 1999; Murdoch and Tewdwr-Jones 1999; Roberts and Lloyd 1999). It took a further ten years for the

Figure 7.1 *Manchester's symbols of renaissance*

Manchester city-region, depicting the industrial legacy of the eighteenth and nineteenth centuries and the Bridgewater Canal, with the twenty-first-century focus of a service economy and the 47-storey Beetham Tower.

government to address this issue by resolving to abolish both RSS and the RDA strategies and legislate for Integrated Strategies, a move legitimized in statute but never implemented owing to the change in government in 2010. The GORs were finally wound down in 2010.

By the end of Labour's term in office, the regional issue had been legitimized but was not fulfilled to completion; the failure of the referenda to create a directly elected Regional Assembly in the first region, the north-east of England, led to the abandonment of the regional dimension, at least for the present. The RDAs had become embedded within each region to the point of fostering good relations with other public-sector partners, and in liaising with the private sector and partnerships of different organizations to enable the delivery of specific

Figure 7.2 *Bradford's fragile economy*

In the West Yorkshire conurbation, Leeds has seen improved economic growth over the last ten years or more, and is now the UK's largest centre for business, legal and financial services outside London. But Bradford, located only 8.6 miles (13.8 km) west of Leeds, has not fared so well and continues to experience housing problems, social unrest, economic deprivation and a lack of investment in the heart of the city compared to its urban neighbours.

projects at a sub-regional scale. But there were also problems relating to notions of generating sustainable development and specific spatial planning concerns and which institution and which strategy should drive change within the region: was economic development nested within spatial planning and sustainable development, or was spatial planning intended to find and promote the spatial implications of economic investment? Such a simple dichotomy revealed a greater institutional and governmental tension existing between different scales of the state and between different instrumental mechanisms.

The shifting institutional and policy context

Until now in this chapter, some of the main developments in the political parameters to city-region planning and governance at a UK level have been highlighted. It is fair to say that the governmental and planning level(s) between the nation-state and local government is one of the most turbulent, politically contentious and confusing array of political experiments and failures in the history of planning intervention. And it seems never-ending, bound up in party-political advantage, constituency interests and governmental jealousy over institutional responsibilities and freedoms. The frequency with which scales of governmental responsibility have swung from the centre to the region to the sub-region to the locale and back again militates against any attempt to embed governance processes to meet the needs of the territories themselves. No sooner has one system been implemented than a change of government creates a diametrically opposite system.

The attention will now focus on some of these issues in specific contexts. In particular, the impact of specific institutional or policy changes within localities will be examined, and we will aim to highlight how these might affect evolving forms of sub-regional governance. It was noted previously that urban policy had existed in something of an institutional vacuum between the late 1970s and the late 1990s, particularly in terms of both strategic thinking and democratic accountability. Here, therefore, the focus is on three areas which have stimulated ad hoc governance between the level of the locality and the city-region: (1) central government urban policy and funding regimes for regeneration projects; (2) the preparation of spatial strategies by local authorities; and (3) the growing significance of regional partnerships in bidding for EU funding. It is contended that all three aspects have reconfigured the urban problem onto the sub-region or metropolitan scale, even if central government has not always favoured such a move.

1 Funding regimes as stimulus to partnership

As we noted above, the 1980s and 1990s saw a gradual evolution in central government policy towards the city-region. The rhetoric and practice of partnership have now become central to any attempt to lever funding for regeneration projects and to encourage inward investment, even if below this surface of collaborative working a diversity of political action and mobilization is actually present (Phelps and Tewdwr-Jones 2000). This has been matched by a government demand for greater effi-ciency savings in the coordination and management of bids for resources, demonstrated in their requirement to demonstrate competitive bidding between different sub-regional or city-based partnerships for limited funding opportunities. The objective here is to demonstrate, first, the style of governance and the varieties of partnership that can exist, sepa-rate to formally elected tiers of government and, second, the problems which have been associated with the competitive bidding process.

Varieties of partnership

The grant coalition: as Cochrane, Peck and Tickell (1996) have shown, the 'elite localism' which existed in cities such as Manchester, which developed mainly as a result of the Conservative government's urban policy, saw the emergence of a breed of leading executives from north-west firms at the head of the policy process. Close political ties between these 'maverick entrepreneurs' and central government ministers ensured Manchester's bid for the 2000 Olympic Games, for example, would be firmly supported by government investment promises (Kitchen 1997). However, as Cochrane et al. (1996) argue, such elite localism was dedicated towards the insertion of key private-sector actors into the global circuits of capital which the Olympics attract. The Manchester 2000 Olympic partnership was thus dedicated *neither* towards freeing targeted areas for private-sector development, *nor* towards creating a strategy for sustainable growth in local businesses. Instead, it can be characterized as an inversion of the leverage of private money to help create growth, with a move to levering public money to support the private sector. Such processes have also been a hallmark of the London 2012 Olympic bid and debate about the legacy of the Games for Strat-ford, Hackney, and the surrounding areas.

By contrast, as Taussik and Smalley (1998) have described, many part-nerships are created for orthodox area-targeted regeneration. Their case study of Derby's successful City Challenge bid in the 1990s highlights the successful coalescence of no fewer than 49 groups, primarily local authorities, private sector, quangos and voluntary groups, around the consolidation and clearance of a specific site within the city. This was dedicated towards levering in private-sector and other public-sector investment on a ratio of 3.75:1:0.93 (for every pound of City Challenge funding, £3.75 of private sector money and £0.93 of other public sector funding was expected to be attracted (Taussik and Smalley 1998: 290–1)).

Finally, it should be clear that the regional arena is potentially fraught with interregional conflicts. Boddy et al.'s (1997) study of Swindon (in the South-West) highlights important tensions between contiguous tiers of government – primarily Swindon Borough Council (representing Swindon 'city', a growth pole in the boom of the 1980s) and Wiltshire County Council, covering the rural hinterland. Both represented different political groups and voters, and – in one of the most dynamic regions in Britain – were locked in battle over strategic planning and economic development issues. As such, numerous regional partnerships emerged with conflicting goals and emphases, including the Wiltshire Economic Partnership, the West of England Development Agency and the West of England Initiative.

So rather than a wholehearted embrace of any regional-level partnership, Swindon Borough Council was careful to assess (a) the time spent in person-hours in such activities and (b) actual synergies with its rural partners. Swindon Borough Council saw itself as being linked into the M4 motorway corridor, functionally integrated into the South-East and London, more than being linked into Wiltshire or the South-West (Boddy et al 1997: 128).

Competitive bidding

As several commentators have noted, competitive bidding remains a double-edged sword. The bidding process is seen as providing a means of creating a shared discourse among diverse groups and agencies, from private-sector to local-authority to voluntary-sector groups. Oatley's (1995) survey of groups that failed in City Challenge bids revealed that some proceeded with the projects regardless of the lack of funding (thus fulfilling the government's rationale), and demonstrates that new partnerships on an urban scale were formed in a response to the funding opportunities. On the downside, however, there was a longer list of problems.

First, private-sector support was hard to sustain in the absence of government subsidy. Second, there was a feeling that – rather than jump-starting new partnerships – failures in the bidding process led to demoralization and, in some cases, exacerbated divisions between partnership members. Third, some local authorities suggested that the somewhat opaque bidding process (based essentially on convincing government ministers of the merits of particular projects) was open to political manipulation. As Oatley (1995: 10) noted: 'there was an unconfirmed rumour that Bristol was on the list of winners in the [City Challenge] second round until, at the last moment, the London Borough of Brent changed from Labour to Conservative control in the local elections, and

Ministers substituted Brent for Bristol'. Feedback on the decisions taken was also considered to be insufficient, suggesting a failure of communication from the centre to the region. Fourth, the initiation of the SRB bidding process in the early 1990s concealed the fact that the actual budget for urban policy was being reduced by a quarter in real terms between 1993–94 and 1997–98 (Tilson et al. 1997: 3). Fifth, the emphasis placed on matching private-sector interest with public-sector support meant that regeneration projects were concentrated on issues of potential profitability, rather than social need. Sixth, there remained a gap between 'real' partnership and what was itemized on paper: involvement of the voluntary sector in bidding partnerships was often felt by the latter to be inadequate (Tilson et al. 1997: 11). Seventh, the huge amount of time required to prepare bids was felt to be a risk in terms of labour costs and the associated neglect of other duties.

While Taussik and Smalley's (1998) study of Derby highlights the private sector's subsidy of the bidding process (as well as a considerable degree of presentational expertise), voluntary-sector organizations noted that 'the more time we spent in partnership meetings and compiling bidding information, the less we could spend in the community' (cited in Tilson et al. 1997: 11). It has been suggested that if partnership is required, government must provide sufficient funding to ensure 'fair, representative and effective partnership' (Tilson et al. 1997: 14).

So it can be noted at a general level that both partnership and competitive bidding for government funding is by no means a straightforward process. Indeed, it may be suggested that localities are engaged in a fierce interurban competition not just for inward investment from the private sector, but also from government subsidy (Harvey 1989). To recap on what Cochrane et al. (1996) suggest in reference to Manchester, it may be appropriate to identify the replacement of American-style growth coalitions with 'grant' coalitions, with partnerships established where the key motivation is to 'top up' funds lost elsewhere in generalized cuts in government funding. In contrast to government rhetoric about building sustainable long-term local partnerships at the sub-regional level, 'the new "partners" have acted together strategically only in the sense of seeking to legitimise competitive funding bids which maximise the local "take"' (Haughton et al. 1997: 89).

Planning mechanisms: Regional spatial collaboration

An important ad hoc level of sub-regional policy-making has been the need for local authorities to consult each other and central government in the production of both Regional Planning Guidance (RPG) and Regional Spatial Strategies (RSS). Until the late 1980s, regional planning only existed in a meaningful sense in the UK in the Celtic periphery of Scotland and Wales, since government departments in these countries had been organized territorially (Paddison 1997; Tewdwr-Jones 2002). In terms of planning, prior to devolution the Scottish Office had the ability to prepare Scottish planning policy guidance and produced distinctive policy documents that attempted to emphasize Scottish spatial planning concerns (Hayton 1996). In Wales, the WO had retained similar powers of discretion, notably in terms of an ability to publish separate planning guidance documents, usually on topics that had a distinct Welsh flavour, although it did not attempt to implement a radically different policy approach to that existing in England (Jarvis 1996; Tewdwr-Jones 2002). The establishment of both a Scottish Parliament and a Welsh Assembly has since hastened the emergence of a more distinctive spatial planning process in both Scotland and Wales, although it is interesting to note that the new spatial planning policy processes for these countries would in future be referred to as 'national spatial strategies'. Since the early 2000s, city-region issues have been promoted as part of the Scottish spatial framework based on the largest urban conurbations (Lloyd and Peel 2006), while the Welsh government has worked only in a limited way to date on issues below the all-Wales level (Harris and Hooper 2006).

The regional planning powers allocated to Scotland and Wales were traditionally present to a much less significant extent in England (Murdoch and Tewdwr-Jones 1999). While local planning authorities had been cooperating voluntarily at a regional level for many years, as we noted earlier in the chapter it was only after the early 1990s that central government gave any real encouragement to this activity. According to Baker (1998: 154), 'the period from the late 1970s through to the early 1990s can be identified as almost totally barren in terms of regional and even strategic (sub-regional) planning policy in the UK'. By the late 1980s, however, increasing concerns in the south-east of England over the impact of development on the mostly rural environment led to a renewed interest in strategic planning at a sub-regional level. The government emphasized that local authorities should form conferences or partnerships in order to progress preparation of this policy guidance and these forums would not receive statutory status. The possibility of the frameworks and the policies becoming the type of city-region institutional mechanisms intended within the recommendations of the Redcliffe–Maud and Wheatley Commissions of the early 1970s was therefore already removed. The new spatial policy process at the regional level would be an advisory system to enable local government within the regions to produce local development plans (Roberts 1996).

As part of the new regional planning framework initiated in the early 1990s, consortia of local authorities prepared regional planning guidance in each region so that a regional policy framework existed for each part of Britain from the mid-1990s, a process strengthened in a second round by late 2000s. There were also some notable failures, however, on the part of strategic spatial planning and the role of the GORs to truly address the strategic needs of large conurbations. For example, the RPG for the Northern Region, originally issued in 1993, contained broad strategic statements for the region covering the counties of Northumberland, Durham and Cumbria, but failed to encompass the largest city in the area, Newcastle upon Tyne, which had been the subject of a separate Strategic Planning Guidance note in 1989. As a consequence, effective strategic coordination could not be achieved since regional planning in the North comprised a 'polo-mint', with the principal urban area a hole in the centre, politically divorced from its surrounding metropolitan area (Alden and Offord 1996).

After the emergence of a stronger form of regional spatial planning after 2001, the consortia of local authorities continued as regional chambers or regional assemblies to agree on broad policies to be contained with the RSS. These processes lasted ten years until the abolition of the consortia and RSS after 2010. There were difficulties evident here too, particularly in relation to housing growth areas, to links between economic development and sustainability, and in the planning and provision of regional infrastructure. But the style of working did engender a stronger regional–sub-regional dynamic within territories and a greater capacity of work politically and governmentally to address sub-regional problems. This was as much related to policy sectoral needs as it was about further spatial planning (Haughton et al. 2010). But any rescaling of responsibilities from one policy tier to another merely transfers problems, and the difficulty of resolving them, to other institutions and agencies without any degree of guarantee of finding easier workable solutions. So we may have to consider the onset of English strategic spatial planning in the period 1997–2010 in the context of the expectations and experience of the rescaling of governmental responsibilities. The part- disappointment associated with the regional governance model during this time may say a great deal about whether the decentralized forms were regarded as genuine by the recipient territories and whether the political control was emanating from within the regions or from the centre. Spatial planning should therefore be seen more as a symptom of the changing governance turmoil rather than as a product. In fact, spatial planning became complicit with governance forms if one accepts that one of the functions of spatial planning, as rolled out by both central government and the planning profession, was to achieve integration – deliberately designed as a tool of managing governance and achieving partnership and consensus.

The incentives offered by EU funding

The regional vacuum which emerged from the end of the 1970s was accentuated by the growing importance of EU's European Regional Development Funds (ERDF) or 'Structural Funds'. These funds were made available to so-called 'lagging regions' in Europe where the GDP levels were significantly below European averages and were worth millions of pounds to support economic growth, infrastructure provision and training. While a number of areas within the UK were eligible for both Objective 1 (Merseyside, Northern Ireland and the Highlands and Islands were eligible in the 1994 round; Wales in 2000) and Objective 2 projects (particularly in the North-East, North-West, Yorkshire and Humberside and the West Midlands), to access these funds required the preparation of a Single Programming Document (SPD). As we have seen, the creation of GORs in England were partly designed to administer Structural Funds on a more strategic basis but from within the keep of central government, rather than devolving the responsibility to local authorities. So far from being purely functional mechanisms to fulfill administrative requirements, the GORs were part of an ideological battle 'being fought out [between neo-Liberals, neo-corporatists, and neo-statists] not just at Maastricht, the council of ministers and in the national assemblies ... of the Member States but also in the partnerships, monitoring committees and technical panels of the peripheral English regions' (Lloyd and Meegan 1996: 58).

Nonetheless, for a number of reasons (for example, as a scarce funding source at a time of fiscal stringency, awareness of the effects of an emerging single European market on peripheral and/or lagging regions, and the increasing culture of partnership emerging in many regions) most local authorities were enthusiastic participants in these regional partnerships. The European Commission was active in bypassing central government and encouraging local authorities and regional 'partners' to develop their own strategy documents. The creation of the GORs was designed to rein in this autonomy. As Lloyd and Meegan (1996: 72–5) describe, the scramble for seats on the board of the monitoring committee for Merseyside's programme reflected a clear hierarchy with the Senior Regional Director of the GOR (nicknamed the 'regional viceroy' in the press) wielding significant power, followed by private sector, quangos, voluntary sector and local authorities and with '[no representation] whatsoever to local trades unions' (1996: 73). As a number of commentators remarked, however, the partnership process augmented other aspects of UK urban policy such as City Challenge or SRB bids (Mawson 1997), although the submission dates for UK and European bids were not synchronized (Tilson et al. 1997: 12). Generally, the success and quality of such bids reflected prior relationships in the region (John

1997: 239). In areas of political homogeneity such as Strathclyde in south-west Scotland and the north-east of England, these tended to be most successful, whereas intra-regional rivalry in the North-West and Yorkshire and Humberside proved to be an obstacle.

It is clear, nonetheless, that the European Commission's demand for a regional spatial framework as the basis for structural funding after the early 1990s has been an important catalyst for regional and sub-regional cooperation beyond the traditional administrative and political bound-aries of local government and an influence on the style of planning itself (Tewdwr-Jones and Williams, 2001; see Chapter 3). However, as Shutt and Colwell (1998) noted, the English regions in particular had prob-lems in efficiently accessing these funds. They highlighted a range of issues, among the most important being:

- poor understanding of local economies and labour markets on a regional level;
- GORs having insufficient sub-regional analysis and local knowledge;
- too many agencies operating at a sub-regional or regional level, leading to confusion of roles;
- private-sector and voluntary bodies unable to cope with the complexity of the process at a regional level;
- a need for regional bodies to 'learn' from their experiences through constant monitoring and development of shared goals.

After 1999, the preparation of bids for European funding fell within the ambit of the RDAs in England and the elected governments in Scot-land, Wales and Northern Ireland. The European Commission recog-nized that with the ending of the then programme of structural funding on 31 December 1999, the RDAs were ideally placed to come forward with new development programmes to 'move into a more central role, be deciding on the allocation of funding and which projects and actions are to be co-financed with European regional policy money' (cited in SCETR 1998). They were expected to work with the Committee of the Regions (although representation on this body would continue to be drawn from local authorities). The European influence therefore provided a catalyst to new forms of regional and sub-regional gover-nance working, even if attitudes at the central government level were often passive.

The growing interest in city-regions

As we have seen in this chapter, there has certainly been an ongoing interest in the possibilities and desirability for sub-national forms of governance over the last 20 years, both academically and politically (Herrschel and Newman 2002). This has ranged from ongoing discussion of world cities (Friedmann 1995; Beaverstock, Smith and Taylor 1999), to arguments about the effects of the internationalization of capital on cities (Hirst and Thompson 1999), to the success of some cities more than others (Parkinson et al. 1992), and to the changing geographies of regulation (Painter and Goodwin 1996). But the 1990s trends and the 2000s ongoing processes of political restructuring should be viewed partly within the context of a push towards local and regional economic development (Goodwin and Duncan 1986; Jessop 1997a). A key focus within academic debate has been the differences between functional/economic and administrative boundaries (Bennett 1997; While, Jonas and Gibbs 2004), and how local organizations and institutions can contribute towards local economic development (Evans and Harding 1997). This has been viewed as essential in the context of the global economy and the interests of multinational companies to respond to restructuring processes outside the UK and Europe (Hall 1993), to take into account the 'generational change' (Harding 1996) within institutional and political restructuring and to embed companies into localities through a process of 'institutional capacity building' (Amin and Thrift 1995). Local processes of governance have assumed enhanced importance within emerging systems of multilevel governance (1998; Marks, Hooghe and Blank 1996; Jones 1998), while Jessop (1997b) is of the opinion that unique forms of sub-national governance are a by-product of the decomposition of and devolution of powers and responsibilities from central government. It is important to recognize that when we discuss local systems of governance, we are referring 'not just to the formal agencies of elected local political institutions which exert influence over the pattern of life and economic make-up of local areas' (Painter and Goodwin 1996: 636), but additionally to a wide range other agents including central government, supranational institutions and quasi-governmental, voluntary and private-sector organizations. Together, these agents can form unique systems of local governance (Rhodes, 1995).

Local Enterprise Partnerships

The partnership ethos has emerged more lately to address city-regions and functional urban regions in the guises of Local Enterprise Partnerships (LEPs). LEPs were announced by the Coalition government in the June 2010 Budget with an invitation to local authority and business leaders to submit proposals for replacements to the Regional RDAs. By September 2010, 56 bids were submitted to the government and the details selecting the first 24 occurred within the Local Growth White Paper published on 28 October 2010 (see Figure 7.3). The Paper set out the government's proposals and justification for a new strategic policy level:

By shifting power to the right levels we will increase democratic accountability and transparency, and ensure that public expenditure is more responsive to the needs of business and people. By abolishing the RDAs and agreeing to the establishment of the first phase of 24 local enterprise partnerships we will encourage a responsive approach to the needs of local business, and people by:

- supporting local authorities' existing role in fostering and sustaining growth;
- putting local business leadership at the helm of bodies that represent real economic geographies;
- continuing to support the Capital's role as we rebalance our national economy; and
- managing the winding-down and closure of the RDAs to maximize value and take opportunity to look again at key European funding for economic development. (HM Government 2011: para.2.1)

There are now 38 LEPs covering all regions of England, some equating to a single local authority boundary, others incorporating amalgams of several neighbouring local authorities. Of these, 8 are within the Greater South-East, incorporating London, and the standard regions of the South-East and East of England. They are intended to cover functional urban regions, linked to the economic growth areas of England, but are still established along local authority boundaries.

Among the functions allocated to the LEPs are the coordination of key investment projects, the designation and development of growth hubs, and the promotion of consortia to run them. They do not have a significant amount of resources attached to them but there is scope for their funding, and indeed their duties, to increase in the future. In October 2011, the government announced that LEPs would play a key role in administering new local infrastructure funds intended to restart work on stalled developments as a consequence of the economic recession. The £500 million Growing Places fund would be made available to LEPs to determine priorities for investment. Interestingly, this allows LEPs to potentially fill a gap previously occupied by RDAs.

Embedding functional urban regions with spatial planning

In the UK urban context, a focus throughout the 1980s and 1990s was on central government shifting the state's interventionist role from regulation to partnership (Blackman 1997), by encouraging alternative institutional mechanisms to regenerate areas through a range of policy and financial initiatives based on local partnerships. These alternative mechanisms extended over somewhat different geographical territories to the fixed administrative boundaries of formal tiers of government. They

Figure 7.3 *Local Enterprise Partnership (LEP) locations*

The patchwork quilt of 38 initiatives across England, and the various sizes of LEPs, some based on single counties and others in collaborative arrangements. Some areas are in more than one.

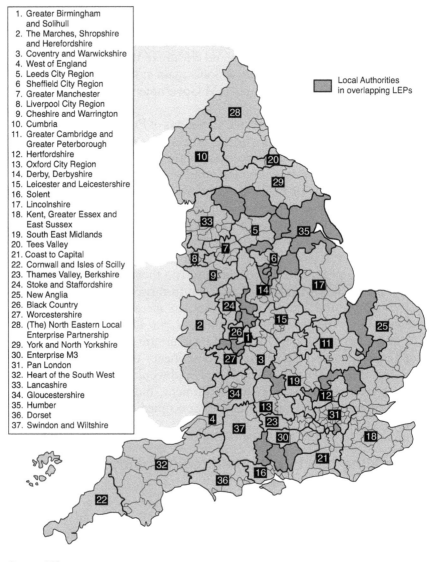

1. Greater Birmingham and Solihull
2. The Marches, Shropshire and Herefordshire
3. Coventry and Warwickshire
4. West of England
5. Leeds City Region
6. Sheffield City Region
7. Greater Manchester
8. Liverpool City Region
9. Cheshire and Warrington
10. Cumbria
11. Greater Cambridge and Greater Peterborough
12. Hertfordshire
13. Oxford City Region
14. Derby, Derbyshire
15. Leicester and Leicestershire
16. Solent
17. Lincolnshire
18. Kent, Greater Essex and East Sussex
19. South East Midlands
20. Tees Valley
21. Coast to Capital
22. Cornwall and Isles of Scilly
23. Thames Valley, Berkshire
24. Stoke and Staffordshire
25. New Anglia
26. Black Country
27. Worcestershire
28. (The) North Eastern Local Enterprise Partnership
29. York and North Yorkshire
30. Enterprise M3
31. Pan London
32. Heart of the South West
33. Lancashire
34. Gloucestershire
35. Humber
36. Dorset
37. Swindon and Wiltshire

Local Authorities in overlapping LEPs

Source: BIS.

also represented in some cases an alternative to the planning system and a reliance on spatial strategies, the latter often grafted onto the boundaried extent of the administrative territories. From this perspective, the range of partnerships and networks, each possessing their own geographical focus and institutional remit, had an advantage over formal elected governmental tiers: there were more fluid, ad hoc and malleable, unconstrained by the unsuitability of traditional governmental boundaries or by pre-existing planning approaches. To some, they were a threat to *governmental planning*, performing shadow or alternative planning roles but without the legitimacy provided by the central state and by a one-size-fits-all planning system. To others, they represent an extension of planning outwith those traditional silos and into *governance planning*. Whichever view one subscribes to, there is one undeniable fact: the dual existence of traditional governmental tiers and planning, and the newer, more flexible, responsive style of territorial governance partnerships created a legacy for the style of working existing today both in the type of instruments parachuted in to territories by the central state, in the arrangements for collaboration between different actors and institutions, and in the degree to which local partnerships come together and are legitimized as strategic bodies. It even had an influence over the emergence of spatial planning in the 2000s as an alternative to land-use planning.

Among the various policy measures introduced as alternatives to direct local government intervention, the most prominent over the last 30 years have been UDCs (Imrie and Thomas 1993), City Challenge (Oatley, 1995), the SRB (Ward 1997), the Sustainable Community growth areas (Gallent and Tewdwr-Jones 2007), Housing Market Renewal Pathfinder schemes (Allen 2008) and, more recently, eco towns, Enterprise Zones and LEPs. This focus has been made distinctly in terms of the city and the urban–regional dynamic specific: initially large areas of derelict or underdeveloped land within inner-city areas in need of regeneration and latterly to coordinate investment, housing development and economic potential over a much larger territory, accompanied lately by more localized schemes over smaller territories. As we noted in Chapter 6, the political changes put into place by the Blair and Brown governments contributed to a reconceptualization of the urban problem at the level of the region, by focusing on institutional capacity-building and the development of local systems of governance through an enhanced regional level of political administration with greater entrepreneurial approaches (cf. Healey 1992b; Stoker and Young 1993). The regional focus in the period 1997–2010 has since been replaced with a more ad hoc, incremental policy concentrating on particular areas, very much a return to the style of split government–governance approaches favoured by the last Conservative government. Commentators are starting to recognize that the promotion of partnerships on the urban local scale in the latter 1980s and early 1990s (Duncan and Goodwin 1988; Cooke 1989) are now being mirrored once again in the second decade of the twenty-first century through LEPs. The establishment of, first, regional institutions and policy agendas, and then secondly, LEPs, either required new forms of governance or new, academic ways of interpretation (Keating 1997; Storper 1997; Lovering 1999; Swyngedouw 2005). The institutional space between central government and local government (which are, incidentally, the two tiers least vulnerable to radical and structural institutional change) is in a constant state of flux. The local has always impacted on the regional, and vice versa, and both have been influenced and shaped by central agendas that have changed directions several times. But it remains a problematic exercise to assess how each tier or scale influences others or whether each new tier gives rise to new experimental forms of governance working and spatial planning.

In order to assess the current and possible future position in the UK in relation to the city-region, it is vital to identify and understand the historical context for governance between the nation and the locale. The changing nature of the policy-making parameters within the UK raises many questions, not only in relation to the future of regions and cities, but also about the nation-state, national remit over and within regional and sub-regional policy-making and government, and the tensions inherent within the nation-state and devolved forms of governance (Jessop 1995; Jones and MacLeod 1999). The unfreezing of the locale through new forms of partnership in governance has not commenced with the Coalition's localism agenda after 2010; it commenced in 1997 after an ideological offensive lasting 18 years, which sought in many cases to limit the autonomy of elected sub-national government, particularly in the field of planning (Thornley 1991; Allmendinger and Tewdwr-Jones 1997; Allmendinger and Thomas 1998). In fact, one could argue that elements of the localism agenda go back much further, to the introduction of municipal government in the UK in the nineteenth century. Given the ongoing political and institutional context in the UK, and in keeping with a theme developed throughout this book, perhaps we should see this faltering and patchy approach to sub-regional forms of governance and planning as something of an ongoing *search* for city-region planning and governance. A key debate at present is about *whether* a capacity for such governance can be created and, indeed, sustained, and whether new institutional arrangements can be embedded into unique cultural and political territories, a key problem with the imposition of regionalism, as we saw in Chapter 6.

So where is planning in this complex and confusing myriad of governance arrangements? Spatial and land-use planning will sit within and across a new political structure comprising a web of formal administrative and governmental actors and more ad hoc partnership bodies that are more temporal and fluid but nevertheless statutorily recognized. This structure will yield new sets of expectations and tensions as spatial planning at the sub-regional scale is stretched to deliver in territorial, social, sectoral and substantive ways. The key issue for policy makers will be how to reconcile the apparently irreconcilable tensions inherent within the new governance of planning through this 'rescaling' of governance (Jones and MacLeod 1999; MacLeod, 1999) and how to meet the perceived high expectations from a range of government tiers, agencies, organizations, businesses and the public on what this revised policy-making process is expected to achieve, both at the sub-regional level and its relationship to the urban level. More fundamentally, we need to consider for whom this revised governance framework is being established. The more conceptual issue to relate this point to is over the future definition of how one exactly defines both 'sub-regional' and 'the state' within a supposedly decentralized policy framework. The UK has witnessed a continuous decentralization of power from the central state to a range of different sub-central state entities, assemblies, institutions, partnerships and agencies over the last 30 years. The post-2010 changes are merely the latest wave in an ongoing chain of events. Each of these entities possesses a different remit, different powers and very different relationships to central government. But each of these entities also represents a compromise between full decentralization and the retention of a degree of central government functioning. The tensions within these compromises reflect not only the dilemmas of individual ministers and the government, but also the very nature of the state itself, compromises in policy-formulation processes, and the outcomes of different policy-making decisions. Different arms of the state will always possess different agendas, and different claims of legitimacy. This could well be true in the context of the emergence of the sub-regional tier in its structure and working in delivering national policies as much as it had been in the 1990s and 2000s with regionalism (Jones and MacLeod 1999).

Conclusions

In conclusion, it should be noted that there have been and continue to be shifts in the perception of the government and other agencies towards cities, the regions and city-regions. The proposals for formal regulatory mechanisms inherent within unitary and statutory city-region local government in the 1960s were displaced with a strategic vacuum throughout the 1970s and 1980s, not assisted by the Conservatives' abolition of the metropolitan counties in 1986. The 1980s also witnessed the development of Thatcherite policies in favour of urban policy and competitive urban local bidding. The 1990s witnessed, first, the development of a regional interest in national political circles and, secondly, a regional renaissance under the New Labour government, with a focus on the urban *within* a regional context. The difference between the policies of the latter 1990s compared to the latter 1960s relate essentially to the notion of statutory responsibility. We moved from a period of mandatory regulation of our larger urban areas, to one of voluntary cooperation and partnership. In the 2000s the regional and sub-regional relationship was emphasized further with the assistance of the RDAs and in the devolved countries by their governments. This had the effect of prioritizing working on site-specific projects within the region but also led to consideration of spatial differences between different parts of the region, city to city, but also city to countryside. The removal of the regional level governmental paraphernalia after 2010 seemed to threaten the experience and benefits of this sub-regional focus, but the establishment of an RDA replacement sub-regional policy tier, the LEPs, potentially enhances the city-region and sub-regional issues to be addressed more prominently in future, albeit within what is currently a weaker institutional arrangement and where spatial planning is either absent or less conspicuous.

A notable outcome of this fluid form of sub-national governance arrangements in the UK is the variety of partnerships, agencies of governance and forms of urban networking that have occurred within different territories and for a variety of purposes. It is possible to suggest, for instance, that the unique forms of sub-regional and urban governance existing within each of the three countries of Britain amount to a kaleidoscopic policy-making structure, partly initiated by political commitments toward devolution and decentralization, but also as a consequence of a range of policy initiatives emanating from central government and the EU that have been seized upon proactively in different ways by the agencies of governance. In the 2000s, the establishment of more formal institutional policy-making mechanisms at the regional level through the government's political commitments could perhaps be viewed with hindsight as central government attempting to internalize what were previously external forms of ad hoc urban partnership networking. This was perhaps necessary to attempt to harmonize both economic development and institutional restructuring at a time when the central state believed in a harmonizing role. With similar partnership arrangements potentially now emerging under the LEPs, this internalizing by the central state is unlikely to occur again given the Coalition government's insistence that their policies amount to a fundamental reconfiguring of the state and the opportunity for central government to remove itself from some of the functions with which it had previously been involved. A similar perspective could be attributed to the rise of spatial planning and strategic spatial plans, where the latter were seen as more fluid and less boundaried forms of planning documents to traditional development plans, addressed a broader suite of issues and linked space and agency together in an integrating way. Perhaps they were attempting to internalize the governance planning issues that had previously been enacted by networks and partnerships outside the formal governmental planning structures.

The enhancement of the sub-regional level of policy-making in the guise of the Labour government or that of the Coalition does raise questions over central government rescaling its functions to another tier, and to its relationship to the nation-state, national political objectives, and local capacity for collaborative governance. The emerging forms of institutionalized sub-regional governance are an imposed solution to resolving a strategic policy deficit caused, *inter alia*, by the Coalition government's policies towards localism, the abolition of the regional structures, and area-assisted urban regeneration and infrastructure funding plans. As a consequence, any new set of institutions and agencies of governance will either replace or overlap existing local and sub-regional governance capacity in particular areas that have emerged from urban locality-specific arrangements. The state has reconceptualized urban partnerships and urban governance within new sub-regional institutional and political systems. The search for city-region planning and governance within the UK must therefore be seen as a dual-tracked process, with both local and national agencies devising new mechanisms to meet different needs and differently perceived requirements. To what extent central government's designed sub-regional mechanisms are able to be integrated with or sit alongside the locally designed urban partnerships, or whether conflict or convergence will occur at this enhanced tier of governance, will only be realized after assessment of the new practices. The key determinants to this restructuring process are set not only within political preferences at each of the tiers, but also the funding, European, and strategic opportunities and deficits on offer to resolve the socioeconomic and environmental problems that these institutions of governance themselves were designed to resolve.

Chapter 8

Localism, Local Planning and Reform

Chapters 6 and 7 highlighted the form and implications of the move towards regionalism and city regionalism in the UK during the 1990s and 2000s, and there has been a great deal of academic analysis and speculation concerning the various changes to spatial planning and government at those scales in the period since (Amin, Massey and Thrift 2003; Counsell and Haughton 2003; Davoudi and Strange 2009; Allmendinger, 2010; Haughton et al. 2010). But, whereas this focus has tended to occur at the regional and sub-regional or strategic scale, the implications of these changes at the local level within the UK have been discussed from a governance perspective only briefly (Stoker 2004b; Morphet 2010). Similarly, analyses of the trajectories of change, how they relate to past approaches and debates, how and whether they constitute aspects of 'localism', and their impacts on planning, have been slow to materialize.

Without such a local-level analysis, the full implications and significance of such changes to spatial planning, to government and governance, within an increasingly fragmented nation-state, are lost. Aspects of the relationship between development planning and local government and governance have been discussed elsewhere (see, for example, Vigar et al. 2000; Allmendinger, Morphet and Tewdwr-Jones 2005; Tewdwr-Jones, Morphet and Allmendinger 2006). Since 1997, local government reforms under the 'modernization' banner (as described by the Labour government in terms of practical policies) and under the 'localism' banner (as described, initially, by academics in conceptual assessment in the 2000s and, lately, by the Coalition government to describe its legislative and policy focus on the locale after 2010) have had a significant impact on the operation of planning in every part of the UK. Such changes, or themes, include a rescaling of development planning, the integration and submergence of development plans within other strategies and plans, and the continued marketization of development plans and planning (see Le Grand and Bartlett, 1993 for a context). The reform of the planning system has been continuing over a period of years since the Blair government was elected to office in 1997, stemming from a Green Paper on planning published in late 2001, the implementation of the Planning and Compulsory Purchase Act of 2004, various drafts of national planning policies, the Planning Act of 2008 and the Localism Act 2011. And these relate only to the planning reforms. An equal, if not greater, amount of reform has occurred within the local state, to local government structures and new public management, all of which has impacted upon the context and operation of local planning. This has led to planners being highly concerned about the volume, speed and scale of change within their own immediate operational sphere and has meant that the local planning institutional framework has been constantly in turmoil during a rapid period of legislative turbulence.

While analysis of these changes has not been drawn out fully from a local-level perspective, none of these changes can be fully comprehended or understood outside broader and interrelated debates on state theory, multi-scalar governance and the shift under towards what might be termed 'neo-corporatism'. One of the key reasons to consider the local level is because it serves as the practical implications of the effects of higher levels of planning and government policy-making; it is the phys-ical manifestation of contentious policy concerns and the theatre within which actors supporting and opposing projects of varying degrees lock horns about land-use change. But the locale should not be seen as a theatrical set, and local government is not merely the delivery conduit of higher levels of government and their planning policies. The local level is democratically elected separately, forms its own plans and policies to manage change, is set within unique places, and devises the means by which a range of services can be delivered at a level closest to the people. If anything, this makes the local level of planning and governance the most interesting but also potentially the most controversial, and lately the most complex, scale of spatial change. The local level of planning is at the crossroads of the delivery of national, regional and sub-regional projects and policies, with more localized, grounded and politically contested choices. When the debates come down to unique parts of a town, or to specific parcels of land, all those high policy expectations about change, growth, protection, responsibilities, needs and the future are thrown into sharp relief. There is an inverse relationship between the policy and planning ladder and public involvement in spatial planning: the more you focus down at the very small geographical scale, the greater the appetite for people to get involved or express an opinion about physical change. It is no accident that members of the public appear to recognize planning to be first and foremost an activity that affects indi-vidual properties and the desire for development and personal gain.

The context for this localized debate about change is not a static one. Perhaps to the public, the opportunities to get involved in local planning disputes and plan making appear to be relatively constant. To some extent, that is a truth, or at least has been for over 40 years. The public have been given statutorily defined opportunities to be consulted on individual development proposals and to comment on draft local planning proposals in their relationship to local government; those opportunities have become to all intents and purposes a democratic bastion. But the framework, governmentally and ideologically, within which these processes occur have been subject to continuous change. Over the last two decades at least, local government functions have diversified from direct service provision to a much broader range of activities involving regulation, leadership and enabling. In the period 1997–2010, New Labour promoted an agenda of state infrastructure revitalization, decentralization and local responsiveness, cooperation and partnership with civil society, together with social responsibility. In particular, there was an emphasis on what was termed 'local government modernization'. The planning reforms, introduced within the Planning and Compulsory Purchase Act 2004, were set within this wider context. The planning system was charged with coordinating the spatial aspects of a range of policy agendas being brought to bear at the local level, and to provide a mediation forum for various interests that were responsive locally and flexible to changing local conditions. As such, the reformed planning system was perhaps the fullest policy expression and implementation tool of New Labour's interpretation of 'new localism' (yes, it did exist prior to the Coalition). As we shall see later in the chapter, the transition from development plans to LDFs and Community Strategies (later, Sustainable Community Strategies, SCS) provided optimism for a positive local planning process.

After 2010, the Coalition government also embarked on a radical programme of 'localism' with a commitment to enhancing participation within policy and decision making and the transfer of powers to neighbourhoods and citizens away from regional and local governance actors and government agencies. The difference between the two versions of localism relate to whether elected local government is the level through which some of these measures are delivered, or whether local government is bypassed in favour of direct involvement and decision making by citizens, neighbourhoods and community groups. The planning processes, especially at the local level, have all been subjected to an intense period of ongoing reform, and there is every likelihood that these changes will continue in the years ahead.

The debate here is intended to illustrate the wider trajectory of planning in the modernization and governance agendas at the local level within the UK at the present time. Although this is resulting in new participatory processes and greater contestation on the form and trajectory of local plan-making, it is nevertheless occurring within a planning legislative framework whose legacy remains firmly rooted within established local governmental and professional planning duties. Here, the tension surrounding the form of planning occurs at the level of the local state between the broader form of and relationship between governance and government. In essence, and the key question is, when new styles of planning occur within broader participatory governance, what happens to older styles of government working and practice, which remain *in situ* alongside new governance models but have been used to very different forms of working?

The focus of this chapter, then, is on the emerging system of local development planning, in the context of the planning reforms, at local authority level. It encompasses issues in relation to the processes of plan preparation, content and implementation, in addition to the management and delivery of the local planning process. The key aim in initiating a discussion on planning reform since 2004 is to identify the major themes of change within which local planning operates, and to identify the extent to which there appears to be a shared understanding between the trajectory of planning and ongoing government agendas relating to who has responsibility for managing change locally. This includes discussion as to whether the LDFs can begin to make a distinct departure from previous development plans, partly to aid development delivery, partly to initiate localism in practice, but also to galvanize a culture change more broadly within local planning at the start of the twenty-first century.

From local to spatial and back again: Turbulent local planning reform

Chapters 1 and 5 both demonstrated that the planning system in the UK has been kicked around as a political football ever since its statutory enshrinement in the Town and Country Planning Act 1947 (Cullingworth 1999). It has accommodated the agendas of divergent political administrations, as well as major shifts in the national and international economy since the post-war period (Hall and Tewdwr-Jones 2011). Emerging from roots in social reformism, the planning system has yielded important successes in policy terms (Bruton 1974). However, the system and its administration is beset by trade-offs – between participation and resources, participation and speed, and resources and speed (Reade 1987). Politicians, developers and the public have all criticized planning locally for its failure to realize development speedily, or for its perceived block on development opportunities, a set of criticisms that emerged in the 1980s but which are still apparent today (Thornley 1991; Allmendinger 2001; Conservative Party 2010).

Key criticisms of the local plan preparation system over the last two decades of the twentieth century and first decade of the twenty-first century as advanced by government, representatives of the private sector and other users of planning, are remarkably constant. They relate to the speed of plan preparation and an accusation that planning is overly bureaucratic and a constraint on business and growth, that it possesses a narrow focus on land-use matters concerning the physical development of land and is unable to integrate with strategies of various organizations, that the quality and quantity of stakeholder involvement is poor and that the public feel remote from planning decision-making (McKinsey Institute 1998; Arup Planning 2004; Conservative Party 2010). Some of these criticisms are indeed genuine and relevant issues of concern, but some are repeated as assertions with little in the way of evidence to back them up. The RTPI, among others, has been proactively attempting to debunk some of these myths in order to defend local planning, but it has proved to be an uphill struggle, since the task requires not only finding any relevant evidence to make counter-claims but actually involves direct challenges to parts of government and the property development and real-estate sectors, the very agencies perpetuating the myths.

One of the latest waves of criticism directed at local planning came in the Conservative Party's Open Source planning Green Paper in March 2010. This stated:

> The planning system is vital for a strong economy, for an attractive and sustainable environment, and for a successful democracy. At present, the planning system in England achieves none of these goals. It is broken.
>
> ... we need a planning system that enables local people to shape their surroundings in a way that ... is also sensitive to the history and character of a given location ...
>
> Our conception of local planning is rooted in civic engagement and collaborative democracy as the means of reconciling economic development with quality of life ... the planning system can play a major role in decentralising power and strengthening society. (Conservative Party 2010)

Although there is merit in some of these ideas, not least the idea of encouraging direct civic engagement and linking planning to issues of place and cultural identity (both commitments that the Conservatives labelled 'localism'), the criticisms towards a broken planning system seem a politically expedient viewpoint to justify further radical ideological reform without an adequate case being made for the necessity for change. The Chancellor of the Exchequer, in his Budget Statement of March 2011, went further, stating: 'We are going to tackle what every government has identified as a chronic obstacle to economic growth in Britain, and no government has done anything about: the planning system' (Osborne 2011).

There seems to be sleight of hand here, in part because such statements have become so routine. Michael Heseltine, when Environment Secretary and Planning Minister in 1980, accused planners of 'locking jobs up in filing cabinets', referring to planning being an impediment to employment creation. In 2001, his successor, Lord Falconer, stated: 'The planning system is often rules-driven, reactive as opposed to pro-active, over-complex, unpredictable, lacking in adequate community engagement, under-resourced and not user friendly.' Those sentiments justified the introduction of new legislation to 'do something about the planning system'. A further White Paper in 2007, 'Planning for a Sustainable Future', and a subsequent piece of legislation, the Planning Act 2008, again promised to revise planning to ensure it was fit for purpose. A year later, a further piece of legislation amended aspects of the 2004 reforms. So the Chancellor's statement is factually incorrect: government has continuously 'done something' about the planning system, probably too much, especially since 2001. But clearly something is not working: either the local planning reforms are not delivering in the way governments are intending them to, or rather the reforms are targeting the wrong issues.

Mindful of ongoing criticisms, particularly emanating from the Treasury, economists and real-estate experts since 1998, successive planning reforms have sought to address some of these perceived inadequacies. The period since 2001 should therefore be viewed as one of the most turbulent periods for planning in England. The legislative and policy framework of planning has undergone continuous periods of reform in 2004, 2008, 2009 and 2012, intended to modernize planning as a public service for the twenty-first century. In contrast to the legislative reforms to planning during the Thatcher and Major years, when planning was reduced to nothing more than a regulatory rump (Thornley 1991; Allmendinger and Thomas 1998), reforms under the Labour government – and continued in a different vein under the Coalition government – have reinvigorated planning into both a proactive coordinating activity, intended to assist in delivering development as part of continued economic growth, and as a delivery vehicle for public and neighbourhood services (Allmendinger and Tewdwr-Jones 2000a; Morphet 2010). The Planning and Compulsory Purchase Act 2004 completely reformed the local planning policy and strategy-making function, with the old Structure Plans, Local Plans and Unitary Development Plans being replaced with LDFs, Area Action Plans and Masterplans (see Box 8.1). At the sub-local level, the Local Government Act 2000 had introduced Community Strategies, revised after 2007 as

Sustainable Community Strategies (SCS), and these were to find implementation through the revised planning system at neighbourhood level within LDFs. The Localism Act abolished aspects of the national and regional spatial planning processes (as was discussed in Chapters 5 and 6), but retained LDFs. At the neighbourhood level, new Neighbourhood Forums and Neighbourhood Plans are now to bring the citizen directly into the planning process by transferring some power away from local government to a more detailed scale.

Box 8.1 Development plans

The origin of development plans date from the 1947 Town and Country Planning Act when individual local authorities were encouraged to produce town plans. Their purpose is to set out a vision and long term agenda for change and development in individual places, highlighting specific areas where development would and would not be permitted. The plans also serve as guides in determining applications for new development.

In 1968, the UK introduced a revised planning system, and a two tier development plan system comprising strategic plans (Structure Plans) and local plans (District Plans). Following local government reorganization afterwards, county councils were charged with the task of preparing structure plans and city or borough councils charged with the task of preparing district plans. Structure Plans were mandatory but district plans were voluntary. In the 1980s, the status of development plans was watered down in favour of other considerations, most notably job creation. In 1986, following abolition of the GLC and the six metropolitan counties in England, a revised development plan system was introduced in those areas: each borough council would prepare a Unitary Development Plan, combining the functions of the Structure Plan and the Local Plan. Further changes occurred after 1991 when district or local plans became a mandatory requirement of all district or borough councils and where the plan was given priority status in determining planning applications, the so-called 'presumption in favour of development that accords with the plan'. The intention was to have completed local plan coverage of the country within five years. This did not occur.

After 2004, the system was changed again, with all Structure Plans, Local Plans and Unitary Development Plans gradually being replaced with LDFs comprising local development documents and action plans. After 2010, LDFs are retained but the priority given to the plan as the key determining factor in determining planning applications for new development has been replaced with a 'presumption in favour of sustainable development'. Complete local plan/LDF coverage of England remains an illusive goal.

Neighbourhood Plans are the newest form of development plan, to be formulated and owned by the new Neighbourhood Forums. It is intended that these should dovetail, as much as possible, with LDFs. SCSs, devised after 2007, are not technically planning documents but do possess a strong relationship to LDFs and require some degree of harmonization.

LDFs will be required to conform to the provisions of the newly released NPPF that sets out the key issues and principles for the planning process to address (see Chapter 5). But they will also be required as an integrative tool on a range of strategic local matters and will continue to act as a way through which other non-planning bodies can be brought into the policy-making process. An objective of the planning reforms since 2004 has been to 'front-load' the planning system by introducing more upstream public consultation within planning policy-making (ODPM 2005). Despite the political commitment to enhance the neighbourhood level after 2010 alongside local government practices, front-loading for policy development will still be required. The Coalition government believes that it has set clear objectives to ensure faster, more inclusive and better-quality local plan-making in future.

The key themes embodied in the shift from development plans to LDDs within broader LDFs in 2004 were an emphasis on spatial rather than land-use planning; a focus on managing the planning process and development management, rather than development control; and the generation of wider ownership in strategy preparation, rather than the by local planning authority alone (Morphet 2006; Tewdwr-Jones et al. 2006). The LDFs were specifically intended to deliver:

- a simple hierarchy of plans;
- shorter, more focused plans locally;
- more streamlined plan-preparation processes;
- better community engagement; and
- better integration of development documents with other strategies. (ODPM, 2005)

And, of course, many of these themes are identical to the principles for planning under localism set out by the Conservatives in 2010. It has been debatable whether planning at the local level, and indeed the focus of local planning reforms, especially in England since 2004, add up to or have delivered 'spatial planning' (cf. Albrechts 2004; Allmendinger 2010; Haughton et al. 2010; Morphet 2010). Morphet (2010) has considered spatial planning to be about the delivery of planning and the relationship between planning and other public-sector concerns, a somewhat different interpretation of spatial planning compared to both the European origin of the phrase and its regional and sub-regional focus (see Chapters 3 and 4). And there was little sign in 2001 as the first spatial strategies were being developed across the UK (in Wales, Scotland, Wales and, later, the English regions), that spatial planning occurred at any level other than the strategic scale. But, as the 2004 planning reforms were being rolled out by government, its revised national PPS1 of 2005 stated:

The new system of regional spatial strategies and local development documents should take a spatial planning approach. Spatial planning goes beyond traditional land-use planning to bring together and integrate policies for the development and use of land with other policies and programmes which influence the nature of places and how they can function. (ODPM 2005: para.30)

This interpretation of spatial planning (as outlined in Chapter 3) is not without its critics (eg. Allmendinger and Haughton 2009; Allmendinger, 2010), but is potentially at variance with some academic views of what spatial planning could mean, with its focus on strategic matters as well as slightly divorced from its European roots. So spatial planning as a phrase seems to have been appropriated by the UK government and the RTPI into a local integration and delivery framework for public policies which are not necessarily planning in style and substance. This has been the challenge for local planning over the last eight years. The Planning and Compulsory Purchase Act 2004 and its attendant regulatory and policy components emerged as part of a wider pragmatic agenda then termed 'new localism' (Morphet 2006). Since 2010, the Coalition government has, in turn, appropriated the localism label to signify its own agenda of recalling power from the regional and local levels of governance to neighbourhoods and citizens.

The (re)emergence of localism

The political-philosophical principle of 'localism' or 'new localism' has been at the heart of a growing debate in central and local government, and academically, since at least 2001 (Stoker 2004a, 2004b). Its origins derived from pressures on government to consider whether it should divest more central power to the local level. The principles of 'smaller government' (Osborne and Gaebler 1993) continue to generate contested space, leading to debates about both the most effective size of nations from an economic perspective (Alesina and Spolaore 2003), for example, which relates efficiency, effectiveness and performance to size and social capital (Putnam 2000). Devolution within the UK has enabled these principles to be tested out uniquely within each part of the country in the new relationship between the central, devolved and local states (Allmendinger et al. 2005), with localism currently forming a core approach for England but not for the rest of the UK.

Local government and its functions have changed dramatically since the late 1990s, with a shift away from direct service provision to a much broader range of activities involving regulation, leadership and enabling (Corry and Stoker 2002). Integral to the widely perceived government–

governance modal change, the state is now but one actor in a 'heterarchy' of governance actors, often in an array of partnerships focused on delivering services and linking together policy communities which operated separately (Wilson and Game 2002; Imrie and Raco 1999). In this context, the language of enabling has become established in the public sector. New Labour promoted an agenda of local government modernization. After 2010, similar debates are apparent but now with the added of complexity of a new dynamic occurring between the local and the neighbourhood scales.

The new localism is understood as a main organizing principle of sub-national governance in England. If local government privileges the local level with 'freedom from' the centre, then new localism is seen to afford the local tier 'freedom to' respond locally through enabling-style local/supra-local/neighbourhood relationships (Pratchett, 2004). Rationales for adoption of the principle include modern social, economic and cultural complexity, the need for new forms of democracy, and the imperative on social capacity-building (O'Riordan 2004; Stoker 2004b). It is seen as a means of improving democratic accountability, providing a local mandate and producing collaborative approaches to localities. The notion of 'new localism' is, as Mulgan (2004) contests, often a confused one, or even a term used promiscuously (Corry et al. 2004). But it is possible to see how a combination of drivers is pushing a reassessment of what should be undertaken locally, by whom, in relation to local decision-making and effective service delivery. The planning reforms of both the 2004 and 2011 periods are set and must be viewed within this wider perspective.

The reformed planning system is charged with coordinating and delivering on the spatial aspects of a range of policy agendas being brought to bear at the local or sub-local level, and with providing a mediation forum for various interests that is locally responsive and flexible to changing local conditions. The former Prime Minister, Gordon Brown, speaking as Chancellor of the Exchequer in 2002, described:

> a new localism where there is flexibility and resources in return for reform and delivery ... a new era – an age of active citizenship and an enabling state – is within our grasp. And at its core is a renewal of civic society where the rights to decent services and the responsibilities of citizenship go together. (Rt Hon Gordon Brown MP, speech to New Deal for Communities Project, Hull, 2002)

Interestingly, this language is not so far removed from the Conservatives' policy towards localism, decentralization and neighbourhoods, with an increased emphasis on transferring duties from the state to the citizen.

The changing nature of governance and the implications of local change

Issues such as coordination, integration and better regulation were key themes of New Labour's approach to the modernization of governance in the period 1997–2010. In the view of some, this emphasis amounted to a 'neo-corporatism' (Allmendinger and Tewdwr-Jones 2000a; Allmendinger, 2003) with its emphasis upon 'win–win–win' solutions or the 'triple bottom-line' approach (Counsell et al. 2003), that sought, for example, to avoid trade-offs between economic growth and environmental protection and include a broad range of voices and inputs into policy processes and outcomes. Key to achieving this approach was greater policy integration across and between public and private bodies and a renewed emphasis on partnerships (Newman 2001). Since 2010, this emphasis has been less prominent, with a concentration instead on achieving cost savings, and allowing local authorities greater freedom and responsibility across a range of services. Nevertheless, although the Coalition has attempted to emphasize its commitment to reducing big government and prioritizing the local level as part of its ideological commitment to localism, the need for integration, coordination in partnership and efficient regulation remains ever present. Part of the reason for this need relates to the fragmented nature of the state itself, and how it has diversified over the last 20 years with the allocation of responsibilities for goods and services between different actors and institutions. Partly, it is to ensure a spatial or geographical focus to many of these institutions' policies and decisions.

These driving forces of state restructuring, multi-level governance and central government policy have led to a heady mix of policy initiative across government to which planning, and spatial planning especially, has been directly and indirectly subjected. Most significantly, legislative bills relating to planning reform have progressed through both the Westminster and Scottish parliaments. But the reforms to planning have been set within much broader reforms to local government, including new provisions to change the structures, objectives and internal management of local government that have completely transformed not only the practice but also the image of local government (Newman 2001; Stoker 2004a; Morphet 2010). Immediately following the general election in 1997, the government had clearly signalled an intention to 'modernise government' (Cabinet Office 1999). For local government, the first priority was to improve performance, which was thought to be the main source of the lack of public confidence (DETR 1998a). This was to be achieved first through the introduction of the Best Value regime of local performance indicators, followed by the introduction of Comprehensive Performance Assessment (CPA) in 2002 (Martin 2003). Following the implementation of devolution, the four administrations in England,

Scotland, Wales and Northern Ireland also signalled a strong encouragement to involve the public in decision making and setting service standards (a requirement of the Local Government Act 1999). In terms of more general decision-making, the government published guidance that signalled a more thorough and systematic approach to taking and using citizen views as part of decision making (DETR 1998a). It was the start of a long process, still occurring, to enhance the opportunities for citizen involvement in public-policy realms but also to transfer responsibility in some key areas away from elected government and directly to neighbourhoods. Other drivers for change across the UK include a commitment to more transparency and the application of a code of conduct for all elected members, including the ways in which they treat officers (IdeA 2001). Overall, the modernization of public services under way since 1997 is intended to ensure that public bodies deliver services to the public in an efficient, effective and public-orientated fashion. In England and Wales, these changes were encapsulated in two Local Government Acts, in 1998 and 2000, the Local Government and Public Involvement in Health Act 2007, and the Local Democracy, etc. Act 2008. These reforms are set to continue with the implementation of the Localism Act and another Local Government Bill after 2012.

Not only has there been a frenetic pace of local government modernization and restructuring over this time, but there has also been the regrettable onset of institutional alphabet soup. The key legislation to date has been the 2000 Act, prompting – but not *requiring* in all locations – the introduction of 'Local Strategic Partnerships' (LSPs), which were subsequently charged with the production of 'Community Strategies', delivering their objectives through PSAs (Public Service Agreements) and then Local Area Ageements (LAAs, which essentially became the delivery plans for community strategies). LSPs are multi-agency partnerships matching local authority boundaries, and which have brought together at a local level 'the different parts of the public, private, community and voluntary sectors; allowing different initiatives and services to support one another so that they can work together more effectively' (CLG 2007c). They are also not statutory bodies emerging directly from legislation: rather, their creation was only mandatory, after 2000, in 88 Neighbourhood Renewal Fund areas. After that time, the LSP model was more widely adopted and government later highlighted the need for planning to work closely with the LSP to ensure 'informed engagement with the planning process' (CLG 2007c: 10). The White Paper of 2006 (and the subsequent Local Government and Public Involvement in Health Act 2007) consolidated previous legislation, assigning a formal role to LSPs in the production of community strategies (these were rebranded SCSs following the Sustainable Communities Act 2007) and defining – in broad terms – the relationship between SCS and local planning (CLG 2006: Para 5.63), calling for the integration of LDF core strategies with the SCS. These SCSs – which all local authorities had a *statutory* duty to produce – were 'long-term, sustainable visions' that set an agenda for local priorities, subsequently written into an LAA (which the LSP partners sign up to). In government guidance on the relationship between the SCS and statutory planning activities and policies set out in an LDF (CLG 2007a: 14), these two strategies were depicted as fully integrated, with the SCS being a product of shared inputs (and community engagement), linking to the LDF core strategy which was then connected to delivery mechanisms (including planning decisions) through the LAA, and ultimately delivering the outcomes of the community strategy. The link between LSPs and SCS preparation (indicating that partners, or 'such persons as the authority consider appropriate', should play a role in the preparation of these strategies) was set out in the Local Government and Public Involvement in Health Act 2007. Government reaffirmed its commitment to aligning LDF Core Strategies with SCS (the 'overarching plan') in a further consultation issued by the CLG (2007b: 31) in November 2007; however, it called on local authorities to share their experience on how this could actually be achieved (2007b: 32) without offering any prescriptive guidance. But technicalities aside, the new local planning system appeared – in principle – after 2007 to be subservient to the wider community, and dedicated to achieving its choices and objectives (see Figure 8.1). Since 2010, LAAs have been scrapped but LSPs remain in place for most areas, even though some of their functions have been lost as a result of policy change. The opportunities emerging from planning and local government reform appeared to attach new importance to participative community planning, assigning parish plans (and other community-led plans) a bigger role in England's new approach to local planning.

Greater public accountability and scrutiny of local government have been enduring themes. There were concerns in government about democratic engagement with lower participation rates in elections and particularly low involvement from young people. With this context, the establishment of Community Strategies may illustrate the enhancing of neighbourhood partnerships and development of community voices in local government policy- and decision-making at a time when the traditional approach and reliance on local government alone has been questioned. SCSs, first introduced under the Local Government Act 2000, were intended to provide a more robust assessment of the social and economic problems facing individual communities. And so the Coalition government's commitments towards localism, greater neighbourhood planning and the introduction of what it termed collaborative planning (Conservative Party 2010) has to be seen in the context of a move in that direction that had been going on for more than ten years.

Figure 8.1   *The localism relationship between LSPs, SCSs and LDFs*

Overcoming the alphabet soup of local governance acronyms. Until 2011, this was the relationship between various initiatives, where the LSP set the direction for future local delivery and the content of the SCS, utilizing evidence bases of change and need and results from the community consultation. This then led to the formation of an LAA and the LDF within the local authority as a spatial strategy for local service delivery.

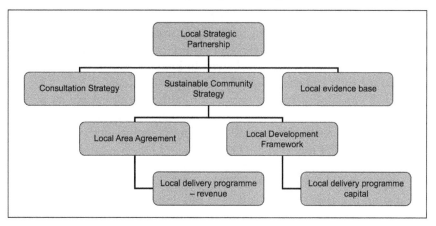

Source: Morphet et al. 2007, reproduced with permission of the Royal Town Planning Institute.

Sustainable Community Strategies, neighbourhoods and participation

Sustainable Community Strategies

Sustainable Community Strategies (SCSs) have formed an important feature of the recent structure of local government. Their preparation has become a duty for the whole council of the local authority. SCSs are meant to be the 'plan of plans' or overarching policy statements for each council. The purpose of the plan is to provide a coordinated approach to the social, economic and environmental well-being of the authority area. As such, they have provided an opportunity for a programmed approach and one where public-sector and external funding can be targeted. The strategy also helps ensure that sub-authority issues across the public, private and voluntary sectors are tackled in an integrated way.

SCSs are also seen as a key component in the commitment towards the reduction in the requirement on local authorities to submit so many plans to government as part of the 'audit culture' (DTLR 2001). In their role as the 'plan of plans', SCSs may also be seen to take precedence over all of the other policies and strategies produced by a council. The relationship between the SCSs and other required plans – including LDFs – are currently being worked through.

Since the implementation of the Local Government Act 2000, a high percentage of local authorities have now prepared SCSs. This represents very rapid implementation of the new requirements and represents the degree of importance attached to the new strategies within local government as both overarching documents and, indirectly, financial frameworks. The speed of implementation of the SCS preparation at the local level is in stark contrast with reforms to albeit complex established systems. Nevertheless, it is an inevitable consideration that once LDFs are introduced in a more widespread fashion, this will create an entirely changed plan context at the local level. In England, the new relationship between the SCS and the revised LDF process is radical.

An SCS can have a spatial expression, although of course an SCS is not technically or legislatively a formal planning document (ODPM 2003a, 2003b; ODPM/Arup 2003). The Planning and Compulsory Purchase Act 2004 initiated the possibility of LDFs becoming the spatial expression of SCSs. Even as early as the planning Green Paper of 2001, the relationship between the (S)CS and local planning was discussed, advocating a major role for this new relationship: 'Community strategies will play a key role in informing the preparation of LDFs. In turn, the Framework must assist in delivering the policies in the Community Strategy' (DTLR 2001: para. 4.7).

Traditional development plans have tended to focus on land-use policies, narrowly defined to what happens on the ground, literally, but the form of the SCS document was innovative and groundbreaking: it was essentially a vision and action plan for improvements in the district that local people needed and wanted. It was not restricted to land-use planning, or 'just housing' or 'just environment'; it could cover any topic. Responsible for the preparation of the Strategy, were not professional planners alone but the LSP, which had been seen as 'the key to our strategy to deliver better towns and cities' (DETR 2000a: 34) by bringing together the public and voluntary organizations to identify and take action on local priorities. Extending the enterprise-led urban regeneration process, the SCS is therefore more of a comprehensive and strategic multi-agency scheme. Local planning authorities, as the service providers in the local authority and as one partner within the LSP, are to cooperate and contribute to the preparation and implementation of the Strategy. According to the aim of government, the role of planning is viewed to be 'at the heart of the Community Plan' (ODPM 2003a). This role of planning in the Strategy or the strategic partnership may therefore be described as 'Supporting communities that: are economically prosperous; have decent homes at affordable prices; safeguard the countryside; enjoy a well designed, accessible and pleasant living and working environment; and are effectively and fairly governed with a strong sense of community' (ODPM 2003a, Planning Division).

Therefore, although the local authority has had a legislative duty to prepare the SCS, the ownership of the Strategy rests with the LSP where one exists. The LSP's partnership working will provide a considerable input from other public agencies, the voluntary sector and the business community and, as a result, the Strategy should not only be developed in conjunction with the LSP but should also focus and shape the activity of local organizations, including those in the public sector, of which the council's actions should be part. The degree of importance attached to the SCS, as a coordinating and shaping governance tool owned by non-local authority agencies, and the way by which it may control planning within local government, becomes immediately apparent.

The government therefore viewed the relationship between LDFs, LSPs and SCSs as one that amounted to spatial planning. That was why the national planning statement PPS1 of 2005 suggested that spatial planning went beyond land-use planning and the traditional role of development plans to bring together and integrate policies for the development and use of land *'with other policies and programmes which influence the nature of places and how they can function'* (ODPM 2005: para. 30; emphasis added). To some commentators, this extension of spatial planning beyond more regional and strategic concerns into, essentially, local government management and local governance integration, promoted by Morphet (2010), among others, was not welcome and should not have happened (Allmendinger 2011). And it certainly has comprised a distinct interpretation of spatial planning compared to most other countries that have tended to focus on spatial planning at a regional or strategic scale.

Neighbourhoods

The Coalition government's enthusiasm towards localism takes the interpretation of the locale more towards neighbourhoods, that is, at a spatial scale below the local authority level. As was mentioned in Chapter 5, this agenda promises to involve citizens directly in decision making on planning and development issues by the possibility of groups of citizens organizing themselves as Neighbourhood Forums, preparing Neighbourhood Plans (a new statutory plan unseen in the UK previously) and taking decisions on projects through the use of referenda, incentives and area development Neighbourhood Orders. These provisions allow the local authority to be bypassed, the first time the link between local planning and local authorities serving as the democratic conduit for development choices has been severed. Much of these new provisions have occupied the time of both Parliament in its deliberations of the Localism Bill and opponents to the planning reforms. Criticisms have been directed in particular at who will be able to establish Neighbourhood Forums, whether they will have to reside in the neighbour-hood concerned, and what legitimacy they will have to take decisions for a larger constituency when they will not be an elected body. There has also been concern at how any deliberations of a Forum, or the contents of a Neighbourhood Plan, will dovetail with the local authori-ty's LDF, or the SCS and its local governance partners.

There is also a question regarding the strategic relationships between these new neighbourhood arrangements, the local authority, and LEPs (see Chapter 7) in terms of who has the vision and direction to initiate debates about growth and change that have localized implications. This is particularly pertinent since the introduction of the Localism Bill was heralded by ministers claiming that the neighbourhood and citizen focus amounted to a fundamental shift in democratic power direct to people rather than their elected representatives. But, as we saw in Chapter 5, the introduction of the new NPPF with a new presumption in favour of sustainable development – where sustainable development is interpreted as economic growth – effectively predetermines the agenda at the LEP, local authority and neighbourhood levels even before the neighbour-hoods have had any opportunity to commence work. This is as a conse-quence of ministers insisting that the contents of the NPPF de facto takes priority at the local and neighbourhood scales where there is no up-to-date and relevant plan in place; recent planning history has shown that this provision makes it inordinately difficult for non-national inter-ests in planning to take priority even on localized decision matters (Tewdwr-Jones 2002). Little wonder, then, that the apparent different agendas as represented by the Localism Bill and the NPPF have been subjected to an intense debate and public campaigning by amenity groups, professional institutes, and journalists all against the proposals (see, for example, Jenkins 2011a, 2011b; Monbiot 2011a, 2011b).

Ironically enough, the NPPF's presumption in favour of sustainable development provision is nothing more than the imposition of a central-ized agenda, something that the Coalition's proposals were reacting against and at the heart of the localized ideological focus. Similar to the deregulatory proposals of the then Conservative government in the 1980s, which also precipitated a reaction from Conservative-voting rural residents, the pro-growth agenda when applied to the planning system in areas other than inner-city locations necessitates centraliza-tion tendencies on the part of central government to have the unpopular policies enacted locally. There is clearly the potential for little local difficulties in the years ahead, but also a test of whether this new governance and planning structure does realize in benefits compared to historic approaches to planning decision making through democrati-cally elected government.

Participation

One of the other elements of localism and neighbourhood planning is intended to be the introduction of much broader public participation approaches in the formulation of local and neighbourhood strategies. Traditionally, following the introduction of public consultation processes in the British planning system after the findings of the Skeffington Report of 1969, local development plan preparation has incorporated formal opportunities to consult the public on draft proposals. Over the decades, much of this consultation technique appeared almost tokenistic (Thomas 1998); the local authority would devise its own plan, invite the public to comment, and then prepare a revised draft plan later prior to an inquiry and adoption. Agendas and policies had been already determined by the time draft plans were viewed by the public. Some local authorities, however, attempted more than the bare minimum with public consultation, by utilizing a range of other techniques to publicize the contents of the plan and proposed changes locally and encourage active citizen participation (see Box 8.2).

In the 1980s and 1990s, academic debate within planning theory started to address issues of more innovative forms of public involvement in planning, through the development of communicative or collaborative planning (Forester 1989; Healey 1992a, 1997). According to a number of authors over the years there is a consensus that the communicative or collaborative turn has been the paradigm that dominates urban planning theory (e.g. Innes 1995; Mandelbaum 1996; Alexander 1997; Umento 2001). The communicative turn has certainly dominated theoretical discourse and has begun to spurn a number of interpretations and investigations beyond the original core proponents. But it has also undergone a number of mutations as 'planning through debate' (Healey 1992a), 'communicative planning' (Healey, 1993; Innes 1995), 'argumentative planning' (Fischer and Forester 1993), 'collaborative planning' (Healey 1997) and 'deliberative planning' (Forester 1999). It has also developed in different directions as a consequence of stemming from various intellectual schools of thought that have intertwined with the communicative approach, including neo-pragmatics (Harper and Stein 1995), critical theory (Forester 1993), Foucauldian perspectives (Flyvbjerg 1998) and planning practice (Hoch 1994). It has also overlapped academic concern relating to governance processes and policy ideas and institutional structures that have attempted to pin down, after Giddens, a 'new institutionalism' (Amin and Thrift 1995; Painter and Goodwin 1996; Amin and Hausner 1997).

In its latest manifestations, the communicative turn has been referred to as 'collaborative planning' in the UK literature (Healey 1997) and 'deliberative planning' in the US literature (Forester 1999). In the UK it

---

Box 8.2 Innovative collaborative participation: A case study of the Brecon Beacons

Brecon Beacons National Park (BBNP) Authority was one of the first authorities in the UK to embark on an innovative public participation scheme in the style of collaborative planning in the mid-1990s, some 15 years before the push towards localism and neighbourhood planning. The park covers an area of 518 mi2 and incorporates parts of 4 counties, and 49 communities. The core of the park authority's public participation on the emerging park-wide local plan amounted to two rounds of 34 meetings with local communities. Brecon planners approached the process by taking the plan out to the people in an exhaustive programme using a variant of the Neighbourhood Initiatives Foundation's 'planning for real' (PFR) exercise. The aim of the park planners was to move away from a reliance on the 'traditional' focus of exhibitions, public meetings, and written comments – which in the past have favoured the articulate, confident, and professional public – and develop a new public participation programme.

The public was encouraged to develop ideas from a series of posters placed around the walls of the meeting hall, each depicting topics and questions, and were then 'let loose' to develop questions, choose land uses for particular sites, and mark these by inserting appropriately coloured pins into a large map. The public set the agenda; the officers merely provided the coordination. Discussion was not restricted to 'normal' plan topics but covered any subject affecting the community. In this way, each meeting acted as a focus for community discussion on a wide range of social, economic, and environmental issues. Once topics had been identified and a degree of discussion taken place, assessment questionnaires were given out to allow individuals the opportunity to record their preferences more fully. This also allowed those people who were reluctant to speak at the meeting to express their opinions and record any grievances. Action sheets were prepared by officers to record issues which were outside the remit of the local plan, for example, those involving highways and utility services. On the morning following the meeting, officers at BBNP headquarters usually undertook a briefing session at which issues raised would be related to land-use planning policies. Within seven months a draft local plan, based on traditional bilateral consultation with various organizations in addition to the PFR exercise, had been completed (see Tewdwr-Jones and Thomas 1998).

---

has overlapped with notions of a 'third way', trumpeted as the ideological underpinnings of the New Labour government (Giddens 1998, 2000), echoing concerns over participation, empowerment and partnership, and more recently the phrase 'collaborative planning' has been used by the Coalition government to reflect its commitment to enhanced public involvement in the planning system, as part of its 'Big Society', but it is debatable whether the government has based its policies on this academic body of work. This theoretical concentration is occurring as part of 'a wave of intellectual reformulation which is sweeping across the social sciences in general' (Healey 1992b). This wave has moved on from earlier views that saw it viewed explicitly as a means of assessing the personal dilemmas of the individual in day-to-day urban planning contexts by promoting debate (Forester 1989; Healey 1992a; Innes 1992) and as a way of promoting social justice and environmental sustainability (Healey 1992b). What we today refer to as the communicative or collaborative turn in urban planning is in actuality a range of different theoretical pulses allied together by Habermasian and/or Giddensian thinking (Tewdwr-Jones and Allmendinger 1998; Allmendinger and Tewdwr-Jones 2002a, 2002b).

The Coalition's push towards collaborative planning was part of what Prime Minister David Cameron saw as the 'biggest shift in power for decades' (Cameron 2011), the essence of which was in the promotion of the neighbourhood and neighbourhood planning within the Localism Bill: 'Communities will be able to come together to decide what their area should look like, where new shops, offices or homes should go and what green spaces should be protected. Parish councils and new neighbourhood forums of local people – rather than town hall officials – will lead the way in shaping their community' (CLG 2010).

This is not the place to debate the merits or otherwise of collaborative planning theory. But whether the Coalition government's rolling out of collaborative planning as more public participation techniques in plan making will lead to greater innovation in the styles of citizen engagement with planning and governance, only time will tell. Despite a time of major uncertainty in public sector expenditure and local authority finances, there does seem to be a degree of enthusiasm on the part of some authorities to adopt more participatory techniques.

Contested spaces or new hierarchies?

If we return again to the implications of localism for local planning, we can see that the transition from development plans to a mix of LDFs and Neighbourhood Plans provides optimism for a positive planning process at the local level. But questions remain concerning the potential for the planning profession to fully embrace the culture change necessary for the optimum implementation of services in the interests of localities (Tewdwr-Jones et al. 2006), since they could be thought of as essential rule-intermediaries. There is also uncertainty about the ease with which the twin processes of reform – the application of the principles of localism and the overhaul of the hard infrastructure of development delivery – are likely to be achieved quickly within planning.

It has been stated that 'Bright new models of governing ... still come up against old attitudes, power relations and management structures ... We must all be alert to "old order" framings and "new order" institutional design. This coupling will provide the centre ground of the new localism' (O'Riordan 2004: 245). There is recognition in government that the hard infrastructure of policy procedures cannot, on their own, meet the aims of the planning reforms (LGA 2000). Instead, a subtle yet concerted change in the soft infrastructure of working practices or cultures is demanded as a necessary complement to bring about change. Local-planning cultural change is a microcosm of governance culture shift sought through the overarching localism agenda. In the current situation, however, allusion to localism or previously to the wider local government modernization agenda is now integral to the planning reforms debate.

Although SCSs and LSPs stemming from the reforms of the Local Government Acts of 2000 and 2007 have started to take effect, it is clear that – to date – links in practice between these new inclusive broader governance processes and the existing governmental planning tools as utilized by the planning profession may take some time to work through (Morphet 2010). Perhaps one reason for this is the lack of skills and woeful inadequacy of planners to address issues relating to public participation and involvement, as much as it is to issues concerning community and social inclusion. Partnership, within which community engagement is one of the key themes, is a concept or framework that builds upon different theoretical researches, such as Healey's (1997) collaborative planning, the more political concept of Giddens's (1998) structuration approach, and Habermas's community rationality (1984). These present a model of planning in which stakeholders are brought together to 'shape places' jointly and build a consensus for local planning (Rydin 1999). Partnership is the most achievable approach towards the first stage in the ladder of citizen participation (Arnstein 1969). Community engagement within the planning reform agendas, we may argue, reflects the government's attention to a more partnership-type approach in the planning system. The sense of partnership that is explicitly related to planning is twofold: community empowerment and the 'community institution'.

Given these political developments, the potential tensions, and the implementation of the Planning and Compulsory Purchase Act 2004 and the Localism Act 2011, it will be interesting to see how the SCSs, the new LDFs and the new Neighbourhood Plans are used together in a more proactive way. With a new sense of partnership, the traditional consultation process will be transformed to a more advanced form that 'is indispensable to the development of a professional comprehension of how and why society functions', but focuses 'on production without any preoccupation about what we are producing, who it benefits, who it hurts' (Freire 1998). The independent community, here, including the local business, neighbourhood and voluntary sectors, act together and collectively within the framework of planning, not to change each other, but to transform the oppressive aspects within the plan that block the fulfilment of their own potential (Byrne 2001). Such a vision is highly ambitious but is feasible if the will of these sectors is apparent. Clearly, the opportunities are now there for the taking within local planning; but it would be ironic if planners themselves who have long complained about their lack of influence on issues concerning community action – rather than the government, the people, the market, or environmental principles – prove to be the barrier to such innovation.

Conclusions

In reviewing the relationship between SCSs, LDFs and Neighbourhood Plans, it is clear that a number of key issues emerge. The first is related to timing. The duty to prepare a LDF preceded the SCS and the Neighbourhood Plan, thus giving it a head start. Although the guidance indicated that there should be a link with the development plan and that the Community Strategy should have a spatial expression, it is also clear that the linkages would have to be made at the local level and in an informal way initially, in the absence of any central guidance on a more formal relationship. The leadership for the development of the Neighbourhood Plan in each locality will vary. The government has put into place procedures to ensure the new plans will be formulated and adopted in an appropriate manner, although even here the desire for legitimacy and statutory certainty nationally may derail any attempt to allow flexibility and differentiation in plan preparation, neighbourhood by neighbourhood.

An additional issue relates to contestation over the ownership of the various plans and strategies. Each local authority owns the formal LDF. The Local Government Acts of 2000 and 2007 formally gave the responsibility to the whole council for the adoption of SCSs, even though their content was shaped and led by LSPs. Neighbourhood Plans, in contrast, will be prepared and owned by the Neighbourhood Forum. So under this localism agenda the preparation of each of the plans will be led by one agency but has to be undertaken in consultation with the other agencies, and these partners do not formally own the plan.

The emerging function of local governance across different parts of the UK appears to be reliant on both formal and informal structures of policy making. In the absence of strict codes and institutional, statutory and political parameters provided by central government for the establishment of the more ad hoc, informal and partnership bodies, governance in different parts of the UK appears to be a diverse picture which reflects local requirements increasingly over central direction. Partnership organizations may take responsibility for the continuation of the new governance structures and the feeding in of any output, recommendations, advice and policy in to more formal government mechanisms in due course (Corry et al. 2004).

But some tensions are emanating at an early stage of new planning practices from differing government objectives for more open policy making to a larger group of stakeholders and the expectations this then places on emergent and more formal processes. In short, there may be an emergent distinction between new governance structures, expected by central and local government, that are intended to act as a leading group to formal processes, and the expectations on the processes which contribute to them. Actors – both participants and professional officers – within new structures of governance may be uncertain over what role they perform, for what purpose, and how their outcomes are to be filtered through existing formal or informal governmental processes. These processes may reveal differences in opinion, expectations and commitments between different individuals and government departments towards new governance processes and delivery as different contributors to the new system come (perhaps slowly) to appreciate their changed roles. The new relationship between the LDF as part of its delivery mechanism and the Neighbourhood Plan may bring this difference to the surface very rapidly in some areas, whilst other tensions may otherwise remain hidden beneath the surface.

Turning briefly to the more conceptual issues that arise from this review, we can identify problems relating to the emerging forms of multi-level governance/government mix that require attention. The Coalition government's approach to dealing with local policy delivery rests on a mixture of existing formal governmental frameworks, some of which are set within local authorities, others of which are reliant on the ongoing rolling-out of new neighbourhood processes and more open forms of participation. Other aspects of the localism process require participatory processes, resting on forms of governance that are not structured or organizationally determined, and where actions and outcomes emanate from users of services rather than from local authority personnel.

Such a diverse mix of governance styles within formal governmental processes may also undermine delivery outcomes, as most of the focus for personnel is taken up with the desire to ensure compatibility and integration between government and governance processes, even within the same public service organization. Within the evolving forms of government now existing not only at local, but strategic and national scales, and in discussing the apparent shift from government to governance, it is easy to forget that government still exists alongside new governance processes, and those formal government requirements cause a legacy that impinges upon or influences the shape, form and outcome of new governance activities. Within a public service activity such as planning, there will invariably be difficulty in reconciling ongoing commitments to neo-liberal regulatory frameworks, while also governing through communities to increase participation and democracy. Such problems only serve to emphasize the more general problem of extending partnerships at the local level within a government process such as planning. However one may support the principles of more open and collaborative forms of planning within the new spatial planning activities of British governance, there remain fundamental barriers to achieving outright governance transformation success.

The overwhelming conclusion emanating from this chapter is that further discussion is warranted on whether neighbourhoods and citizens in their interaction with those individuals working within local planning understand their role within the bigger picture of local service delivery. Localism and neighbourhood planning will require a fundamental shift in the way that government at all levels and planners think. There is no doubt about that. And I contend that localism and neighbourhood planning, if they are really going to take hold, will also require a fundamental shift in the way that neighbourhoods and communities think and act. Actors within the governance arena probably do recognize the value of integration, the relationship between various strategies inside and outside government, and the need to relate policy to resources, many features of planning promoted by both the former Labour and Coalition governments. Localism needs to find expression in institutions (Stoker 2004b); but moreover, the planning reforms conversely need to draw on the localism ideology for success in the government's terms. Certainly, there is no obligation to accept unreservedly the current version of localism. But we should at least debate and challenge the wider expectations of why planning exists locally, what and whom it serves, and what shape it performs in assisting in the development of places.

Chapter 9

Spatial Planning, Governance and the State

The previous chapters demonstrated the ways in which spatial planning has been presented, embedded and appropriated within governance processes across the UK since the mid-1940s. During this time, the UK has witnessed the institutional framework of planning lurch from one -ism to another. Centralism agendas under the welfare-state model of planning were balanced by a failed attempt by the then Labour government at regionalism in the 1960s. In the late 1960s, city-regionalism emerged as a preferential conduit for planning issues but it never took off politically and, as we limped into the 1970s under a Conservative government, centralism agendas were matched by growing localism agendas until the end of the decade. Then, in the Thatcher years of the 1980s, alongside a new role for the market in and over planning, centralism returned in order to create the necessary institutional, political and legal conditions for neo-liberal thinking to infuse planning. As the centralism–market axis started to become democratically unpopular in the late 1980s, particularly with Conservative voters, a U-turn occurred, with localism promoted by the Conservative government and being labelled 'local choice'. As we headed into the 1990s, and with support switching to Labour again, the regionalism agenda re-emerged and finally was instigated in the latter 1990s and early 2000s as commitments to devolution and new regionalism, but English regionalism was never fully publicly embraced; ironically it was Labour's own voters who instigated the fall of regionalism in 2004. As politicians backed away from being associated with aspects of the regionalism agenda, so city-regionalism and a new localism re-emerged, promoted by metropolitan and provincial local government eager to fill the post-regional vacuum but also to demonstrate their ability to run services and think strategically themselves. After 2010, and the election of a Conservative-dominated coalition government, regionalism was abandoned in favour of a new commitment to localism but promoted and instigated by central government. Localism is partly about the central state relinquishing duties to the local level but it is two-pronged: the other element is a rescaling of functions and decision making from the local to the neighbourhood level. This has since been accompanied by new commitments in favour of more informal city-regionalism. Over the last 20 years, alongside the formal structures of government, governance has emerged more prominently, involving partnerships and networks of government and non-government agencies sitting vertically and horizontally across the formal tiers of government, and possessing some policy- and decision-making powers. This has led to a growing desire, and necessity, for strategy and policy integration. And of course every time the government and governance structures have changed, so too has the planning process, directly or indirectly. As we begin the end of our journey through this tangled, time-dependent web of political, institutional and spatial change, one cannot help but think, 'how on earth did we end up with this mess?'

All these institutional changes demonstrate a heavy political hand in the type of scalar politics desirable in the UK and complete disagreement politically on the appropriate governmental structure to deal with sub-national issues. The different preferences reveal internal UK debates on the ongoing relationships between different political tiers of the state, but are also affected by global governance trends. It is clear that spatial planning, as one of the latest manifestations of the fluid, changing and changeable forms of land-use planning and spatial development, remains a deeply contested process. It is stretched vertically and horizontally across the various political axes of the state and attempts to mediate between different interest groups and address sectoral policy concerns that often pull in opposite directions. As the governmental and institutional structures are amended politically, so too is spatial planning as an instrument of those structures. In order to make sense of this spatial complexity, it is vital to understand some of the deeper components of the governance frame within which spatial planning is set. The governance frame itself is not a static construct, even though it comprises layers of institutions possessing differential roles and power. The political process constantly re-layers governance, removes discretion from some governmental scales, adds to others, and changes the balance of relationships between the institutions. These changes are as much affected by forces outside the UK as inside, with global economic ebbs and flows and climate change, demographics and migration, and mobility all driving the need for change and state reaction. Spatial planning, by implication, is utilized by the state, and by different layers of the state, to recognize the forces of change, their implications for the status quo, and to manage tensions and expectations. It is a delicate balancing act, with no guarantee of certainty of outcome or results to meet all those expectations.

This chapter is set within the conceptual framework provided by Jessop (2000) in his contribution on the shifting scales of power of the state, by Agnew's (1999) analysis of the jostling of power between divergent forms of the state, and by Martin, Scherr and City (2010) in their analyses of rule-intermediaries. It is combined with the book's previous discussions of the changing and appropriated form of spatial planning. It is contended that aspects of the ongoing and emerging relationships between pre-existing and new scalar politics of the state (MacKinnon 2011), with responsibility for spatial planning, form a contested and malleable framework of territorial governance and management (Haughton et al. 2010). Within this understanding of territorial governance, different levels of government and new forms of governance 'flex their muscles' and claim ownership of responsibility for spatial planning and strategic coordination across and within government, or sometimes even temporarily abandon it. The overall determinant in the bedding-down of power and responsibility between scales, and between government and governance is the desire for integration and strategic development to serve particular political ends. This chapter considers conceptual developments in sub-national spatial governance and deconstructs the key determinants of the form of territorial governance and management. These relate to a deeper understanding of spatial planning and a consideration of the emerging form of sub-national governance and spatial strategy-making, the permeability and durability of partnership arrangements, the complex nature of governance processes, difficulties in expectations on new governance processes between different scales of government, and the relationship between process and delivery.

As discussed in Chapters 3, 6 and 8, there have been several theoretical developments over the last 25 years surrounding the significance of regional, devolved and local territories within broader processes of globalization, European integration and the changing form of the nation and local states. Initially, academic interest focused on agglomeration (Scott 1983, 1986), closely followed by analysis of local outcomes of and responses to global processes of restructuring on localities (Cooke 1989). During the 1990s, theoretical development centred on assessing the 'new regionalism' and the rescaling of political processes (Jessop 1996; Keating 1997), alongside academic debate concerning the prospect and form of institutional capacity-building in territories to organize for economic growth and development (Amin and Thrift 1992, 1995). Theories of 'associative democracy' (Hirst 1994), 'relational assets' in regional development (Storper (1997) and 'institutional thickness' and 'interactive governance' (Amin and Hausner 1997) were among some of the most influential within the field of urban and regional development. Hirst's (1994) theory of associative democracy sees a collective communicative rationality or normatively regulated action overcoming distortion in social action and interaction. The work of Amin (1996), Amin and Thrift (1992, 1995), Amin and Hausner (1997) and Phelps and

Tewdwr-Jones (2000, 2004), by contrast, identifies regional capacity-building with notions of diversity in social action in the institutions underpinning local development.

Within the planning discipline, too, there have been several related theoretical developments, each attempting to understand the role of spatial planning and spatial governance in emerging forms of sub-national scales that possess development, infrastructure and spatial coordination political objectives. These have been varied in substance and reflect the lack of consensus academically on the form and trajectory of spatial theory within planning. The writings include notions of collaborative planning (Healey 1997) and spatial strategy and governance (Vigar et al. 2000; Healey 2007) that emphasize aspects of spatial coordination and integration within regional and local partnerships; the planning polity (Tewdwr-Jones 2002; Tewdwr-Jones and Allmendinger 2006), where planning is viewed as a function of vested interests within the political arena of both government and governance; city-regionalism and governance (Herrschel and Newman 2002), where spatial strategy is one of the outcomes of increasing city- and metropolitan-scale reactions of European and global trends; and regional sustainable strategy-making (Haughton and Counsell 2004), that identifies the relationships, structures of and outputs from the variety of regional actors and networks in achieving more sustainable forms of spatial policy-making.

At the same time, events in the political and governmental world have also developed at a frenetic pace. The governmental and institutional structures within which spatial plan-making and the planning system reside have been continually reformed, with a push towards the 'rescaling' of governance (MacLeod and Goodwin 1999b), the development of regional government (Tomaney 2000, 2002), the promotion of governance and partnership (Raco 2000), the promotion of localism and the modernization of local government (Morphet 2004), and an enhanced European dimension to spatial strategy-making (Tewdwr-Jones and Williams 2001; Jensen and Richardson 2004; Dühr, Colomb and Nadin 2010). All of these developments impact upon the style of government, policy making and territorial capacity across and between states and scalar politics, and influence the form and content of academic analysis as well.

While there are important differences in the origin and emphasis of each of these formulations, all have – to a greater or lesser extent – concerned the building of regional or local institutional capacity within aspects of spatial governance. They have attracted the interest of both the geography and planning disciplines and, as such, there are some important similarities that may be drawn out between them (Vigar et al. 2000: 43–6), even if protagonists of each of the analyses have often, or so it seems, preferred not to draw out such relationships. Most notably, the formulations draw on and discuss a particular type of social action and interaction, drawing on Habermasian, Giddensian and inter- and intra-governmental concepts, concerning interaction, participation, policy implementation and capacity building, both below the level of the nation-state, and between the nation state and sub-national entities.

Deconstructing Emerging Governance and Planning in the UK

In an attempt to consider these matters in greater detail, 20 key problems are presented, divided into four broad categories, relating to the mix of government and governance styles, and its impact upon spatial planning in different territories (see Figure 9.1).

Figure 9.1   *Determinants of the form of territorial governance for spatial planning*

The various components that can affect governance and planning forms in any area, both intended and unintended, that give rise to unique governance models.

GOVERNING FORMS	Government and governance mix Purpose of new and remaining scales Certainty of new governance mix Modus operandi of government Varied structures, operations and roles
POLITICAL FORMS	Political–governance relationship State sponsorship of governance Structure and policy compatibility Participation form and purpose
OPERATIONAL FORMS	Intergovernmental compatibility Availability of discretion at scales Desire for rationalization within scales Definitions of institutional structures Judging success in institutional design Duplication and fatigue of structures
IMPLEMENTATION FORMS	Expectations and promises of new structures Policy turbulence Changes within the policy-making culture Appropriateness of traditional boundaries Territorial constraints

The conceptual forms that comprise the determinants of the form of territorial governance for spatial planning illustrated in Figure 9.1 are intended to be pertinent to both academic and political concerns with territorial capacity development, and are situated at the heart of debate surrounding contemporary reworkings of the state. The four categories comprise governing forms, political forms, operational forms and implementation forms:

- *Governing forms* relate to the type of government and governance mix within territories, and the types of governing agents existing in order to design, strategize and implement policies, projects and programmes.
- *Political forms* relate to the strategic purpose of the governing styles, the existence and distribution of power between agents of change, and the control of scales of governing bodies.
- *Operational forms* relate to the workability of the governing structures, the practical relationships between agents of change, and the definitions of working boundaries between them.
- *Implementation forms* relate to the factors surrounding the implementation of governing forms and their policies that could either support or inhibit desires and expectations within territories or even within governing agents.

The intention is to deconstruct the emerging forms of spatial planning and governance within the UK and to provide a critique of the confusing array of government, governance and planning forms across different territories. In outlining each of these concepts, the debate is set within a frame of reference of the shifting scales of power of the state and by the jostling of power between divergent forms of the state. It is contended that aspects of the ongoing and emerging relationships between pre-existing and new scales of the state with responsibility for spatial planning form a framework of territorial capacity which is itself constrained by institutions, constitutional roles, politics and power. Within this understanding of territorial capacity, different levels of government and new forms of governance flex their muscles and claim ownership of responsibility for spatial planning and strategic coordination. However, the power jostling between the governing agents is not restricted to factors concerning scale, relationships and power alone, as Jessop (2000) and Agnew (1999) assert. The factors determining the degree of territorial capacity development also relate to operational uncertainties and policy and project implementation factors, both within and outside the control of the governing agents, which also initiate aspects of influence on change. Each of the blocks of determinants contained within Figure 9.1 is described below.

Governing forms

The relationship between the mix of formal government and emerging structures of governance

The emerging function of governance across different parts of the UK appears to be reliant on both formal and informal structures of policy making. In the absence of strict codes and institutional, statutory and political parameters provided by central government for the establishment of the more ad hoc, informal and partnership bodies, governance in different parts of the UK appears to be a diverse picture of fragmentation and responsibility. It may be unclear, for example, who takes ownership of collaborative efforts between different organizations and who may take responsibility for the continuation of the new governance structures and the feeding in of any output, recommendations, advice and policy in to more formal governance and government mechanisms. There is particular concern that, if certain of these new fora are reliant on the commitment of and strategic direction provided by key individuals, there is no way of telling how enduring the governing form will be for a participating agent once those lead agencies divorce themselves from its operation and functions.

The purpose, desirability and permeability of new policy scale

The degree of policy entrepreneurship required between formal and informal governmental bodies, and between informal networks of partners within specific territories or within specific sectoral areas, may be unsustainable. Policy entrepreneurship requires heavy commitment from all concerned to ensure policy and strategy cross-referencing and policy integration between various arms of the state and partnership participants both within formal government and outside institutional government. Some of the policy entrepreneurship may be generated as a consequence of statutory requirement, or from teleological action on the part of central government ensuring that greater stakeholding and accountability requirements are met in new policy making. Some of the policy entrepreneurship, by comparison, may rest on goodwill of governance participants, both at the level of the institution and of the individual. A key concern rests on the distinction within the policy entrepreneurship term: to what extent does policy entrepreneurship reflect changing structures within existing government, or does it generate and create new and possibly innovative modes of governance? Does this distinction make a difference to the degree of permeability of policy entrepreneurship for given territories or policy sectors, and would this make a difference to policy outcome and achievement?

Uncertainty of strategic direction, purpose and outcome of governance processes

The impetus for the creation and operation of new governance structures varies across the UK. The enthusiasm for new fora, new arrangements and the sharing of policy-making powers varies according to place, sectoral policy issue and degree of formality or institutional presence provided by formal agencies of government. In some territories historically, it is clear that some places have experienced difficulties in establishing new fora, particularly where there is a dearth of expertise in relation to establishing wider governance structures, or where there is a lack of expertise among the individuals who would populate the new governance structures. Other territories, in comparison, may be familiar with wider consultation and participation structures as part of the strategy-forming and policy-making process. Nevertheless, a territory's familiarity or lack of familiarity for broader policy-making structures may not necessarily relate to the degree of enthusiasm for participation in new structures of governance once these are operationalized by an institutional promoter of governance. It may be unclear, however, where the impetus for new structures of governance is emerging from, together with a related uncertainty over which agency or participant is responsible for mediation in the event of institutional or policy conflict within a governance form. Governance, by its very nature, suggests degrees of openness, harmonious agendas and a desire for all concerned to progress towards agreed solutions. A lack of awareness on the part of participants on the strategic purpose and direction of governance may create difficulties or a refusal on the part of some participants towards taking collective responsibility for outcomes. Such reluctance may be indecorous to new and emerging structures of governance during the early periods of collaborations, or may be indicative of more insoluble problems that arise in creating governance processes.

The changing or non-changing modus operandi of government

Actors within new structures of governance may be uncertain over what role they perform, for what purpose, and how their outcomes are to be filtered through existing governmental processes. Related to this, there could be concern over what – if anything - has happened to the existing structures of government in the light of new governance processes being established. If little has altered within formal government in terms of its operation, strategic direction, agenda and mode of working, a cynical outlook could develop on the part of the participants within the new governance arrangements and networks towards its actual purpose.

This may also generate a possible associated belief that the new structures may not actually create any difference at the end of the day. It may also reveal differences in opinion, expectations and commitments between different individuals and government departments within the central state towards new governance processes and delivery that might otherwise have remained hidden beneath the surface.

Varied structures and operations of new governance structures

It would not be unusual for tensions to emerge within different parts of the UK relating to new governance mechanisms. This mainly reflects the diverse paths to devolution, decentralization, regionalization and localization that have emerged within the UK over the last 15 years, and the previous speeds with which government/governance change has been enacted. But it is unclear whether the shift from government to governance has occurred as a concomitant feature of devolution, decentralization, regionalization and localization by design or by accident. The different promoters of governance may be the new formal institutional, political and governmental fora established by central government in the four countries of the UK. Alternatively, widening out government to a larger constituency of policy-making and policy advisory actors may have occurred as a consequence of the opportunities identified and taken up by these broader groups in their search for roads to influence the new formal governmental arrangements. As a result, the form the wider governance groups may take and the degree to which it shapes directly or influences the policy-making agenda will vary from territory to territory. The establishment of concordat and memoranda of understanding relating to specific tasks, sectors or policy areas may be, in part, an attempt to coordinate and pull together not only specific policies that may otherwise become more diverse, but also an attempt to create symmetry and consistency to the benefit of the central state in retaining a national remit in the decentralized and devolved territories.

Political forms

Transference of power and political responsibility within governance structure

The establishment of new governance structures are normally dependent on higher executive government tiers permitting and legitimizing alternative forms of policy making involving a range of different actors. As a result, the new governance forms are required to link in to the government structure somewhere, or at least its policy-making role or financial model. This comprises an intergovernmental bargain, where the new semi-independent governance form and structure are nevertheless subject to auditing and indirect control by the pre-existing governing forms. The question may then be posed whether the new governance forms are truly independent and distinctive from the government form, or whether the new scales of governance are the mere replication of the government form at a new tier. In other words, to what extent is the new governance scale distinctive, and does distinctive mean something new, with new powers, responsibilities and freedoms, or the existing approach in a new guise? The latter may be an overtly cynical approach on the part of the government to rescale policy making in particular sectors to a new tier, perhaps because government itself is unable to resolve problems of a political or financial nature, and the new tier is required to attempt to find a solution but under the label of enhancing participation.

The legitimacy of governance structures and questions of state-sponsored governance

Questions concerning the nature and independence of new governance structures from pre-existing government forms raise issues relating to the nature of new scales of policy making within territories when those tiers have been created and organized by the central state. New governance tiers formulated and legislatively created by the central state may be subject to a form of state-sponsored governance, where the responsibilities and freedoms of the new tiers are set within tightly defined parameters and whose operations are determined by the agendas and administrative frameworks of the central state. Proposals to create new non-legislative assemblies or the office of elected mayors may occur within the preferred framework of the central civil service in order to pigeonhole these new tiers within the central state's offices of political accountability and financial management. Such activities may cause some flexibility and discretion within the new tiers once established, but they are nevertheless inflexible in terms of the prospect of the new tiers receiving additional responsibilities, extending power or receiving a transfer of power from pre-existing governing tiers following establishment. State-sponsored governance may even constrain the desires and political objectives of new tiers of governance and further the continued domination of the central state. The restrictions on political and governmental discretion caused by state-sponsored governance may not be a deliberate move to restrict the role and status of the new tiers, but rather a form of convenience administrative management on the part of the central state. A more cynical perspective would suggest a determined move on the part of the central civil service not to relinquish any power or responsibility to alternative governmental tiers.

Attempts to create cross-cutting policy agendas alongside new governance structures

New opportunities to either contribute towards the development of policies or directly formulate policies by new governance tiers will occur within the prescribed boundaries set by the central state, if the central state has sponsored new governance frameworks. This will occur either because the central state has legitimized the new tiers and their responsibilities, or because the new governance modes have to be nevertheless structured within the pre-existing formal legal and policy mechanisms of the government. When new tiers of governance are awarded policy-making functions, or else believe they have the administrative (and possibly political) discretion to set their own agendas, they may devise new structures and methods in order to develop those policies. Devising policies relating to specific sectors and to deal with unique territorial problems may require specific methods of policy-making structures. Those specific policy requirements and specific methodological structures may be incompatible with the form of governance permitted and developed by the formal government scales. The new governance agents may therefore find that they do not possess the mode of working, the organizational structures or the administrative or political means to enact territorially specific policies to suit their own needs. Such situations may only be resolved following protracted negotiations within the governance agencies, and between governance agents and governments.

Engagement with the public and the democratic purpose of governance

The establishment of new governance tiers and structures is intended to foster greater inclusiveness in policy- and decision-making, involving a larger number of participants reaching agreement in a democratic way. Such participatory governance opportunities may take two forms: the governance participation may offer stakeholders the opportunity to share mutual experience in directly formulating policies and in making decisions. Alternatively, the governance participation may only permit the actors to meet together to discuss problems, opportunities and solutions, but may not extend so far as to allow them to frame policies or laws, or to control resources. The latter governance forms are sometimes referred to as a 'talking shop' by cynics of new governance frameworks, although these are, in reality, another aspect of legitimate governance models. Agencies with responsibility for promoting the new governance scales and the administrative and organizational frameworks within which they are contained should state explicitly, which forms of participation the governance model will contain, to avoid raising expectations amongst participants and the creation of later disappointment.

Operational forms

Differences between intergovernmental compatibility

Decentralization and devolution from the central state level to sub-national levels may be part of processes intended to democratize more strategic forms of policy- and decision-making and involve an allocation of more responsibilities or discretion to enable greater aspects of sub-national autonomy over the administrative governance of territories. But the allocation of greater responsibilities to one level may, in turn, cause conflict with the structure, allocation of responsibilities and administration of government at another level, particularly if this latter scale is already subject to formal responsibilities of government. In essence, there may then be tensions and differences between governance structures, operations and purposes at devolved, regional, local or neighbourhood levels. This would reflect the statutory remit of government and newly emerging or even uncertain remits at the devolved level. For example, although the new formal or informal structures at sub-national scale may be intended, directly or indirectly, to transfer responsibilities from the national level, agencies of government at the local level may consider their responsibilities to be under threat or else be subject to control by a newly formed strategic level.

Increasing or decreasing discretion at different governmental tiers

The establishment of new tiers of governance at regional or local level may not be intended to remove responsibilities and discretion from existing tiers of government, but they would by their very nature cause a shift in discretion between the tiers. During the process of new tier of governance establishment, it will take some time for the division of discretion to bed down. This process will be dependent on the formal allocation of responsibilities as set out perhaps in legislation on the form and role of tiers, and on the nature of intergovernmental working between tiers, if one or more is dependent on the other for either formulation or implementation of policies. Traditionally, in the UK, local government has performed an implementation role on aspects of policy sectors for central government, even if local government has been elected separately. These sectors have included education, transport and planning. New forms of governance may occur either because they are permitted under legislation (even if their structure and composition is not prescribed) or because they are ad hoc in nature, responding to local and regional circumstances, needs and political requirements. The prescribed roles and division of responsibilities between formal elected tiers of government will search within the statute for the limits of discretion as part of their working relationships. But the roles and division of responsibilities between formal elected tiers of government and informal or ad hoc tiers of governance will be much more complex, dependent on temporal, sectoral or political circumstances existing within particular relationships. Personnel working within or for these tiers of government and governance may therefore be uncertain about the discretionary limits within which they are operating at any given time. This is likely to cause problems and personnel will have to devote a considerable amount of time to resolve these discretionary uncertainties, since government officials will always search for discretionary safety within their tasks.

Attempts at scalar rationalisation

Those sponsoring new tiers of governance may justify their establishment with reference to the need to simplify structures or rationalize the number of plans and strategies existing across scales. It is likely that new governance agencies alongside existing formal tiers of government will not simplify and rationalize strategies but rather further complicate the institutional structure. The number of strategies needed may indeed be rationalized as governance and government tiers cooperate to produce joint plans. However, such attempts are compounded by the fact that cooperating agencies will possess different objectives and purposes in devising the joint strategies. This conflict will need to be resolved possibly through ad hoc or interim plans and bodies whose principal purpose is to manage and resolve differences in opinion. Where plan rationalization is enacted successfully, and tiers cooperate to produce joint strategies, a key question to pose is whether the plan provides a framework or strategy of consensus and whether it addresses and provides direction on policies and projects, or whether it achieves the lowest common denominator in meeting the agreed points between varied agencies and their objectives and, consequently, lacks strategic direction and bite.

Definitions of institutional structures

Governance modes may allow differing forms of organizational and operational structures within fora to be established in order to meet broader objectives concerning participation, inclusiveness, transparency and policy making. This permits degrees of flexibility within new forums to establish intra-organizational designs best suited to the forums' (and participants') needs. But, equally, there may not be a similar amount of flexibility permitted with regard to the definition and design of institutional structures. So much will depend on the objectives of new governance tiers, which agency has sponsored the new forums, and whether the new tiers have been given specific tasks to perform. This latter issue may either enable or constrain the governance mode in designing structures that meet its objectives. Similarly, the existence of specific objectives may also set the new governance framework within particular forms of working, allied to more formal modes of government that have established predetermined structures. Personnel who work within the new governance forms may also be members of the formal government agencies and may, as a consequence, possess a dual loyalty to both modes of working. Pre-existing institutional structures within government may constrain the ambitions of governance modes, and provide a stark contrast between the more flexible form of working within the governance tier compared to the more rigid and set structures existing within government. This implies that when new institutional structures are established within governance modes, the pre-existing forms of institutional structures evident in government may also require redesigning.

How to consider success in new governance structures and what marks for difference

If there is some uncertainty over the purpose and remit of new governance measures, and a lack of clarity in how outcomes from new governance measures are to feed in to or influence or direct existing government structures and policy making, a further area of concern relates to what outcome exactly from a new governance mode would be considered successful. In establishing new governance processes, there is bound to be some expectation on creating change and differentiation for some clear purpose other than for the fact that it is possible to create change for change's sake. Part of the answer to this problem relates to establishing where the impetus for change in government is emerging from, and whether it is emanating from central government, local government or wider stakeholders. How important is it to identify whether the new governance processes create anything new? What is meant by difference or distinctive in this context? Distinctive could relate to the emerging structures of governance, the degree of inclusiveness and accountability in the new forums alone. Alternatively, distinctive could mean a new opportunity for different outcomes, varied and perhaps broader roles for participants, and possibly changed policy outcomes. Both options are relevant, but it would be important for participants within the new governance networks to recognize under which remit their governance structure is being established. A desire for more inclusiveness and accountability may not actually lead to any desire to change outcomes or to view problems in a different way. This raises the concern that new governance institutions may raise expectations on the part of participants for particular outcomes. If the participants have their origin within particular and defined stances, and these are different to those of other participants, governance may actually accentuate problems and differences within government rather than ameliorate them.

Duplication and fatigue in governance structures

Government departments and participating communities within particular territories may be under extreme pressure to develop new forms of governance across specific territories or policy sectors, many of which may overlap. Local government may not possess sufficient resources or personnel expertise to support a wider a neighbourhood governance network even if desired, not only within its own structure but within the agenda of a governance sponsor such as central government. Governance may develop symptoms of overstretching since there appears to be an emerging desire on the part of government agencies and departments to create new governance structures as a solution to problems per se. Against the old tongue-in-cheek government motto, 'If in doubt, form a committee', governance too is experiencing similar expectations. If the extent of new governance working and novel modus operandi among the agencies of government is increasing at such an alarming rate, confusion may occur among participating groups, communities and the public (and within governance networks themselves) on who exactly is responsible for different strategies, policy development and functions. There may appear to be duplication within certain sectoral areas, across several tiers of government and governance, particularly where the same governance individuals are operating simultaneously across various different networks and interacting with different policy clients. Many individuals within government may also experience partnership fatigue and may lack clarity to enable them to assist governance networks and structures to search for solutions to key problems.

Implementation forms

Expectations and promises of new structures

Governance enables the inclusion of a wider group of participants to become involved in policy- and decision-making processes. A preference for participatory democracy over or alongside representative democracy will enable a larger constituency of individuals to express their opinions and objectives directly within the debating arena. These individuals, specialist interest groups or neighbourhood and territorial interest organizations will have been indirectly excluded from direct policy- and decision-making processes in representative government. Allowing them access and participatory speaking and possibly voting rights within governance will raise their expectations on what the new governance process will deliver for them. Merely giving them a voice within the new governance will not necessarily placate interest groups and they may lobby further for more forms of power once established within the governance process. A greater group of policy- and decision-makers involved in governance may cause expectations that things will be done differently in the future, with a belief that vested interests will be met more explicitly. If participants within governance do not feel that the new processes are making a difference on their terms, or are not enabling them to find a footing within the formal policy-making structure, they will feel disillusioned with the process and may abandon their participation or else resort to alternative methods of influencing. The key issues are whether participants within the new governance processes have been given adequate explanations in advance prior to their participation of what role the new governance modes will perform, what rights participants have, and where the limits of discretion lie.

Relationship between governance processes and policy turbulence with policy making

Policy turbulence occurs when political, financial or personnel circumstances change rapidly within government organizations, causing immediate changes to policy objectives, policy statements and modes of working. These circumstances may, in turn, arise because of internal governmental or external socioeconomic events. Policy turbulence causes difficulty for spatial planning because of the short period of time over which change occurs and the lengthy time it takes for spatial strategies to be prepared. The strategies themselves are the product of a long gestation period, involving several drafts, redrafts and revisions, and involving a broad array of personnel and stakeholders. The shape and contents of a strategy may take several years to resolve and will have been a product of intense argumentation and conflict during preparation stage. Policy turbulence may result in that agreed strategy suddenly becoming defunct, or subject to intense changes which completely reform the ethos, objectives and policy statements of the document. It is quite permissible within the UK for spatial strategies to be ignored in decision-making practice by those authorities responsible for its preparation if it can be justified by the authorities that changed circumstances warrant it irrelevant or out of date. On those occasions when this has occurred, it has usually been as a consequence of changed political priorities on the part of government, or because of changing economic circumstances. If future spatial strategies are the product of not just government agencies and personnel, but also the result of intense inter-collaborative governance, it becomes much more difficult for those strategies to be ignored or amended without broader approval. Spatial strategies are therefore under the ownership of all those agencies that have participated in their drafting, and not only under the ownership of the formal government body with whom the drafting is a legal responsi-bility. Policy turbulence may nevertheless rapidly change the circum-stances surrounding the strategy and will affect the implementation of the strategy. But formal government may, in effect, abuse the governance framework if it attempts to change the strategy without entering into the form of collaborative governance framework that shaped and deter-mined the contents of the strategy in the first place.

Changes within policy-making culture in the move from government to governance

Tensions may emerge in some territories and policy sectors within existing formal institutional government in its path towards governance. Some of these tensions may emanate from central, regional or local government's desire to open up policy making to a larger group of stake-holders and the expectations this then places on the policy-making structure and purpose. In short, there may be a distinction to bear in mind between new wider governance structures, fostered by formally elected government, that are intended to act as an advisory group to formal structures, and the expectations of these new wider governance institutions to formulate policies either in place of existing (or prev-iously operated) government institutions or as a dual role in partnership with existing government institutions. Key questions emerge regarding the extent to which existing government institutions embrace the new wider governance procedures they may have assisted in creating, and how the former has adapted to the latter in its form and operation of working. Such widening-out of government to a larger group of instit-utions, agencies and partnerships should alter the culture of government in its operation and function. Where this has not occurred, this suggests an inability or unwillingness on the part of formal government struc-tures to embrace governance.

Appropriateness of boundaries of governance

A benefit of governance over formal government is that, because of its non-legislative form, the organization and structure of the policy-making do not have to conform to traditional governmental or administrative boundaries. In fact, such formal rigid boundaries may not be appropriate to assist the more open style of debate and governance intended. One reason why a governance mode may be established relates to the very fact that more formal styles of government are inappropriate in some way. In the circumstances, governance may embrace and include disparate organizations, across several scales of government and governance, and extend across territories that do not conform to traditional and standardized government boundaries. Spatial strategies may be devised by a group of actors, each representing very different constituencies, and apply to several local government areas, to sub-regions or cross-regions. A difficulty arises as to how these cross-border strategies are to be legitimized with other sectors and actors that possess boundaries that are more traditional. At some point, given the continued existence of government alongside governance, there will be a requirement for the traditional and fixed form of government to legitimize governance modes and strategy outputs in order either to take into account those strategies within their own objectives or policies, or to implement the strategy's contents into practical reality. This governance–government boundary requirement will not only apply to specific strategies, or specific forms of collaborative effort, but also to particular policy sectors or projects, and will vary across time and space. Such a mixed style of governance and government produces a kaleidoscopic institutional framework whose shape and form continually changes.

Policies may be territorially constrained

When new forms of governance working are established and outputs from collaborative efforts produced, it is inevitable that actors from other territories will look on those modes of working as possible examples to emulate. This activity, which may be described as a form of search for good governance, or a style of policy entrepreneurship, follows similar traits in behaviour in previous years evident in government personnel across territories in their development of specific policies. Government officials, wary of acting inappropriately or *ultra vires* during the formative years of new styles of governance and policy intervention, will watch other territories' behaviour and practices; this is partly as a way to inform themselves of policy and practice development, but also in order not to be caught out in implementing either poor practice or practice that – with hindsight – proves to have negative externalities. Such policy entrepreneurship provides advantages to territorial governance as new policies and practices are established, but it also possesses dangers in seeking predetermined solutions designed for other territories that may not be appropriate to be adopted elsewhere.

Cross-border policy transference may or may not work in all territories, and may precipitate non-distinctive styles of governance, indirectly producing standardized policy solutions that, by their very nature, militate against unique styles of governance.

Conclusions

This chapter has sought to identify, conceptually, the new and emerging relationships between government and governance within the area of spatial planning. Academic interest to date has been focused on what happens at the regional and local territorial scales when either the nation-state permits decentralization and devolution to lower tiers, or when those tiers develop their own capacities – institutionally, territorially and politically – to claim responsibility for policy making. What has been lacking in this debate is an attempt to analyse what happens to traditional or pre-existing styles of government when those new governance processes and tiers are created. This is where existing theory is inadequate. Within the field of spatial planning in particular, questions over the role of the nation-state and its relationship to the decentralized or local tiers remain extremely pertinent, since so much of planning as a governmental activity in history has been directed and steered by central government departments in the national interest. This will create its own legacy for new governing bodies, even if central government gradually withdraws its role. A concern with continued economic growth, the need for further house building, the provision of new or replacement transport infrastructure, the protection of the best landscapes, investment in information technology, provision of infrastructure and food security, are just some of the issues that the UK government regard as priority policy areas. The difficulty the UK government possesses, however, is how to fulfil its election manifesto commitments to establish decentralized governance tiers while at the same time retaining some interest, or even control, over core policy areas that the nation-state needs to concern itself with.

The creation and promotion of governance styles at the regional, sub-regional and local levels since 1997 has led to the welcomed reduction in the role of the nation-state in determining the fortunes of sub-national territories. But such decentralization and devolution processes, structurally and institutionally, have been overlain by simultaneous policy-making transfers from the centre to both the region and the locality. This twin process of institutional decentralization and policy transfer has created a complex and confusing mix of different styles of government and governance across the UK that remain fluid and difficult to comprehend. This confusing array of styles of government and governance is resulting in continued jostling of power between existing forms of government and the newly emerging forms of governance. This power-tension does not necessarily occur between different agencies and different governmental officials; it is often the case that the same governmental personnel have the duty to deliver formal governmental requirements at the same time as mediating or participating as an actor within governance networks and partnerships. The confusion is also occurring within agencies in addition to between them.

As many of the actors within governance arrangements are beginning to discover, the promotion of spatial planning and participatory governance within each scale is a goal with pursuing, but it still requires a form of strategic direction to set some sort of political vision if agreement by lowest common denominator is to be avoided. That mediation and direction role seems to be being referred to traditional forms of government and professionalism, the very institutions that were characteristic of pre-governance styles of working. What governance within spatial planning is creating is greater discretion and autonomy within particular scales and across particular territories. When differences occur in reaching consensus between participants, actors look to more established and more legally certain agents to resolve their difficulties. Those agents are, predominantly and historically, agencies of the nation-state. Central government agencies may resent the desire for their involvement in processes that they have transferred to sub-national tiers. But equally, such involvement may serve a useful purpose in planning in order to provide a perspective representative of the national interest with regard to, for example, the economy, transport and housing. Such practices may become more formalized over time as the nation-state finds it increasingly difficult to let go of policy-making areas on subject areas that it sees it has vested interests in.

What these difficulties suggest is the need to resolve the dilemma of ensuring enhanced self-determination for sub-national territories alongside the need for strategic direction and political vision that extends not only within regions and localities, but also within and from Europe and the UK government. The institutional structures at the regional and local level, for the most part promoted and legitimized by the nation-state, are leading to more bottom-up policy-making and enhanced democratic participation in governance. But they may do so at the possible expense of more sub-national political vision and place-focused strategies, that is, developing unique responses appropriate for particular territories that may require unique institutional design. Within this complex framework of the future government and governance processes within the UK, those officials responsible for its continued operation may attempt to make sense of the upheaval by becoming more concerned within inter- and intra-governmental power jostling, and attempts to stabilize, fix or control fluid governmental processes. If that is allowed to continue, the nation-state will increasingly bear a heavy hand in designing sub-national institutions, legitimizing and formalizing governance practices, and policing and monitoring emerging processes and strategies. The temptation may be too great for central government to withstand: by unleashing the governance beast, government will feel increasingly inclined to attempt to control it. Government does not cease to exist merely because new governance processes are created; government transforms as well, shifts discretion from different parts of the process to others, and repositions itself within the institutional landscape. Such practices may seem inevitable in wider global restructuring and modernization process, but these may invariably produce greater standardization of processes, structures and policies. Ironically, these are the regimes that were the very features of government that governance seemed to be designed to be an antithesis to.

What is of more concern here is with the territory as a geographical and political vessel, rather than with the processes of 'territorialization' and 'de-territorialization'. Having said that, these processes do nevertheless manifest themselves within the processes of devolution, decentralization, spatial planning and the role of the state now unfolding across the UK. And these processes do involve 'spaces of flows' (Castells 1996) through global processes of capital between subnational territories.

Scale may be defined as 'the level of geographical resolution at which a given phenomenon is thought of, acted on or studied' (Agnew 1997: 100). There are various ways of studying scales, including the scaling and rescaling of processes; the relationality of scales between geographical scales upwards and downwards; the amalgam of various scalar organizations creating a vast institutional landscape; scalar fixes, involving the shifting sands of institutions and organizations that are fixed temporarily that create benefits for modern capitalism; and scalar transformations, where one scale transcends into new scales and creates its own legacies and forms (Brenner 2004).

The biggest change currently being enacted in practice is the extension of planning from its narrow regulatory base within various territories and various scales simultaneously, to a broader integrating and spatial governing activity, particularly at sub-national levels (Davoudi and Strange 2009; Haughton et al. 2010; Morphet 2010). This is being rolled out with trepidation, politically, and uncertainty, professionally, but within existing political and socio-geographical territories to ensure legal authority. For many planners, it is a vastly different type of planning from the certain, legal and political activity they have been used to.

Another challenge of spatial planning has been to transcend those existing geographical, territorial and institutional boundaries, if planning is to serve a more forward purpose in the decades ahead. There is general acceptance that historical boundaries, administrative delineations and professional silos will not deliver the type of spatial planning and governance in the future that is, politically, being expected. The more difficult part of change, which could benefit the social and environmental as a counterpoint to the economic and political, is to encourage strategy makers to 'think outside the box' of their own predetermined territory. That is a major barrier to the unfolding of planning into something more meaningful for the future.

Chapter 10

Fluid Spatial Planning as Strategic Intelligence

Let us conclude this examination of planning and governance by trying to make sense of some of the key trends that have occurred in the framing, reconfiguring and re-presenting of the management of territorial change. This was partly achieved by an examination of some planning history, but also by outlining they key drivers of change which have justified the need for planning's intervention to resolve spatial disparities. The story of planning is also about managing the contradictory territorial claims stemming from different types of uses and developments on a finite amount of land. We then went on to examine the changing form and use of planning, across time and space, and how it has become increasingly a hostage of the state and of various, sometimes contradictory, political ideologies that have repositioned its modus operandi at different spatial scales. What becomes immediately apparent is that when viewed holistically across the decades and the different types of planning arrangements that different governments have established and sometimes re-established, the *raison d'être* of planning has shifted dramatically in the wrong direction. This does not only refer to the contentious and turbulent jolts that planning has been subject to as it has been kicked around politically between the central state, the local state, the public sector and private sector, across strategic networks and partnerships, and through the various experiments at the sub-national level. It refers to the fact that the purposes for which planning was created and continues in theory to exist to resolve have been relegated to a subordinate position behind institutionalization and governance for its own sake.

Sure, the conditions of the early twentieth century are somewhat different to those of the twenty-first century, but the drivers of change still impact differentially on people, places and land, and still require managing, and governments still declare them to be in part their responsibility. There remain issues surrounding climate change, managing the consequences of demographic change and migration, of housing accessibility and quality, even in inner-city locations, of transport provision and the availability of infrastructure such as water and energy, of the

228

level of services required in health and education between different places, of the degradation to the environment, of the provision of recreation, leisure, entertainment and shops, and of the provision of employment and economic growth. In theory, professionally and statutorily, planning still exists to deal with these issues. That is one reason why planning has always remained an activity of the central state, even when sub-national or local scales of governance have been prioritized by the central state as the preferential delivery vehicles for policies, and where the private sector undertake the investment and development aspects. But it has also become increasingly difficult in the last 30 years for the central state, and for planning itself, to actually address these issues in a meaningful way. The reason for this is a consequence of the fragmentation of the state into a range of governmental, quasi-governmental, private and partnership bodies, each with its own remit, strategies, policies and decision and delivery frameworks, even sector by sector. That does not, however, stop governments and ministers proclaiming a desire to 'do something' about housing, or transport, or high-street shopping, even if the powers available to do them to resolve these issues are actually quite limited in this complex, fragmented and frankly overpopulated institutional structure. Such are the hallmarks of a governance model.

The role the planning process plays in this reconfigured landscape is not one of direct service provision to perform the 'do something' job, as it had been in the first three-quarters of the twentieth century. Rather, the role of planning in the twenty-first century is to mediate between the various actors required to be brought together to enable decisions or development to occur in a way the visionaries imagine. Planning has become much more of an integration service, a function of the governmental process and of the central state to manage others, as it is about resolving land-use disputes directly. And that role also extends into managing democratic issues – the people question – including encouraging new voices and involvement by citizens and businesses in the decision and development dealings. These twenty-first-century roles of planning, I contend, are not sufficiently recognized by either politicians or the public who, for the most part, see planning in its historical light with occasional rants about what 'the planners' are doing here or there, or the decisions they are making. It is the integration and democratic roles of planning that ensure planning's survival in the twenty-first century; they have given planning an implicit legitimacy. Ironically enough, the more governments fragment the state into smaller forms and encourage more pluralistic forms of decision making, the more planning and planning skills are called upon – often behind the scenes in a strategic enabling activity way – to integrate those smaller forms and ensure transparency and democratic accountability.

Planning as a transitional force

Developments and changes in, on and to the land have often occurred beyond expectations of the experts or the trends and projections of the planners, from the postwar period to the beginning of a new century. There is nothing surprising about this – looking strategically at future land-use trends is not a hard or exact science. Trends can tell us a little about the sort of issues we need to keep an eye on, the patterns of development and market behaviour, and where investment and resources need to be allocated. But the world will always develop in a different way to that predicted: new technology, external forces, the political process and, above all, people's behaviour will all create different patterns and trends that will need to be taken into account in planning for the present and the future. Planners are trained to plan, to assess the evidence of where we have come from and predict where we may be heading, to evaluate outcomes, but also have to accept that the future is uncertain, prone to different forms of political intervention and redesign, and will no doubt turn out differently to how they imagine. It does not mean we should not plan in the first place. Planning still performs a useful role in thinking about the spatial variations of change, different service requirements and infrastructure needs over long time periods. But planners have to accept early in their careers that there will be successes from planning intervention and there will be failures. And there will be unforeseen implications from the interventions that occur that will also need to be addressed at some unknown point in the future. Think of it as a domino effect.

These realistic implications of planning do not sit comfortably in a modern democracy and polity which is highly politicized and sensitive to the need to be seen to make rapid responses. Twenty-four-hour news coverage, the role of special advisers alongside the bureaucratic machinery of government, and politicians wanting to be seen to address straightforward matters with easy-to-disseminate-and-digest solutions within a five-year term of office are not, by their very nature, strategic, long-term and uncertain. There have been four distinct phases and changes to planning in England since 1997 alone representing different central government priorities. Planning policies can take a considerable amount of time to take effect, considering how the political system translates ideas, formulates them into policy and goes on to implement them on the ground. Planning outcomes usually require partnership between different arms of the state and the public sector, and cooperation, financing and delivery from the private sector. These liaisons can take years in themselves to come about, even for individual projects. It takes even longer to witness the consequences of those ideas, policies and implementations in different locations. Those politicians eager to claim success for initiating projects will probably have already moved on by the time their dreams are realized. That is not necessarily because planning is slow (although it is true that some planning authorities are more efficient than others), it is rather because of the time it takes to enter into partnerships, to negotiate and bargain over proposals, to mediate between groups in order to reach compromise, to be transparent and consultative, to align proposals with finance and resourcing, and above all to navigate projects through the crowded governance structure where so many different essential actors and organizations are required to see a project realized on the ground. If you consider the time it takes for a political manifesto commitment to be drafted into a legislative bill, to be steered through Parliament and to receive royal assent and eventually be instigated practically, perhaps planning goes through a similar long-winded gestation of change to achieve results – it is also perhaps a little too much like the political system for comfort for most politicians.

Planning is often criticized for its over-optimism, its inability to update plans quickly and because economic, social and environmental change occurs despite, frequently not because of, planning. It is true that change has occurred on the ground in ways that have been different to the policy commitment. Under the postwar planning regime, despite the existence of green-belt policies and a political commitment to urban containment, development still occurred outside towns and cities in the countryside. Since the 1940s and continuously in the decades since, growth around existing urban areas has been accommodated beyond the green belt by the creation of central government-designated new development areas – first, a series of 'new towns', then through 'sustainable community growth areas', and more recently by 'eco-towns', often on land which had previously been agricultural, in rural locations around Britain and unrelated initially to local planning policies. Policies have not been abandoned, but rather have been compromised by other policies, possibly of other authorities. In this case, the new development sites may not have been the choice of local planners or local people, but were deemed necessary by national government – perhaps because their assessment and strategic needs evidence was different to that at the local level, or because the land was in public ownership and more readily available. And so long as there is a legal and a political necessity to 'take account of' national policies at the local level (as the phraseology states), then central government will always be able to tweak local planning systems to suit its own agenda.

That is one benefit, or disadvantage – depending on your point of view – of a sovereign state possessing a discretionary planning process. It is highly political, centralist, changeable and not enshrined in constitutional rights and responsibilities other than through statute, policy statements and judicial interpretation. In other words, the architecture of the planning policy framework is so flexible that no one policy commitment is enduring, sacrosanct or even binding on the very planning agencies that are charged politically with its design and operation. We do not possess a pragmatic planning system – make it up and justify it as we go along – since we have legislative commitments to make plans and develop policies for implementation. But we do have an element of discretionary judgement to enable us to change our minds or depart from an agreed position, providing we justify it. For politicians, that is a godsend. It also means that the system is sufficiently flexible to be able to take account of short-term changes, such as economic recession or recovery. There is no need to pass a new Act every time we want to amend the planning system or policy commitment, we merely change the policy to reflect different times and circumstances. That is because of the increased number of agendas that planning has some responsibility for today. The UK possesses one of the most flexible planning systems in the world compared to many other countries which have a much more rigid, regulatory or zoning planning system with plans acting as blueprints for future action. The UK's development plans, by contrast, are mere sentiments to take into account. The story of the UK's land-use and spatial planning processes is one of constant political compromises between the certain and the discretionary. This book has been devoted to that story.

Pinning down spatial planning

Spatial planning arrived on the institutional scene because there was a strategic need for it: it provided a territorial synoptic perspective of change coupled with an integration imperative. But the way it unfolded in the UK was quite unique. It was never a singular activity, but a plural one, broad-ranging and varied. We can now say that spatial planning in the UK as an intention has been viewed over the last 20 years as five different possibilities, as outlined in Table 10.1.

These components can be explained further.

(1) *Integration* – the need and opportunity to integrate spatial development through new strategies or partnerships including activities such as economic development, transport, planning, sustainable development, energy, water and biodiversity (Bianconi, Gallent and Greatbach 2006).
(2) *Consensus building* – the scope for and implications of policy divergence and intra- and inter-regional/local rivalry and competition between various actors and institutions (Raco, Parker and Doak 2006; Tewdwr-Jones, Morphet and Allmendinger 2006).

Table 10.1 *Diverse components of the UK's spatial planning anatomy*

Component	Origin
Integration	Local government/planning legislation, academic/professional
Consensus building	Democratic deficit, collaborative governance
Differentiation	Place-shaping agenda of government
Strategic governance	Joined-up governance, addressing the fragmented state
Identity building	Economic competitiveness, pro-growth agenda of government

Source: Tewdwr-Jones, Gallent and Morphet (2010).

(3) *Differentiation* – the tension between regional autonomy, a reawakening of identity, and the national interest, including wider questions concerning the balance between the two and ongoing debate about the role of the centre (Dietrichs 1989).

(4) *Strategic governance* – the relationship between evolving sub-national, city-regional, local and neighbourhood agendas and existing institutions, processes and stakeholders, and whether this supports or inhibits new distinctive forms of strategy making, and on whose terms (Pearce and Ayres 2006).

(5) *Identity building* – the role and extent of 'place building' and the ways in which the territory is discursively constructed by differing actors, being politically, socially and symbolically shaped and contested in various ways (Counsell and Haughton 2003; Albrechts 2006).

As far as the relationship between spatial planning and traditional forms of land-use planning is concerned, this remains an uncertain question in the current fluid form of planning in the UK. The focus on vision setting, the alignment of planning strategies with those public bodies that possess resource allocations, and the closer relationship between policy formulation and implementation and delivery, could – in the future – deliver a very different planning process, where the regulatory arm of planning becomes more akin to a zoning process, if this concept is taken to its logical conclusions. Such a move does not seem light-years away in some parts of England, partly because the politicized reforms after 2011 have enabled stronger local planning regulatory and neighbourhood practices.

Spatial planning in the UK can therefore be characterized by both the familiar and different. It is a child that has matured and broken free from its European parent, and it has taken on a governmental and coordinating responsibility at all levels of government that places it potentially as a delivery mechanism with some political clout. In the 2000s it returned a corporate and strategic role for planning after 25 years of absence and it occurred in diverse and subtly different ways in different parts of the UK that bear the hallmarks of the re-territorialization and rescaling of policy making. Some of these roles were, however, short-lived: a new government after 2010 misunderstood the reality of planning in the twenty-first century and dismantled elements of the very fabric of the governance process needed to resolve land-use tensions within a highly contested, democratic and institutionally fragmented state. These may well be the features of the spatial planning label that form the intentions for future UK governments, but whether they will be adopted or bought in practically by a future administration is another question. What is more certain, however, is that the spatial planning debate in the UK is occurring through political, scientific and professional lenses, even if it is not a current agenda of government. In the academic field, in particular, it has generated important and potentially stimulating ideas that extend way beyond the planning discipline. These debates embrace ideas about space, place and territory, about land-use pressures and tipping points, and medium- to long-term perspectives that are prevalent within geography at the present time.

Strategic intelligence and sustainable land use

Whether one 'believes' in spatial planning or not, or possesses a particular perspective of what spatial planning is, the preceding section – indeed most of this book – should have demonstrated an undeniable fact: the processes we possess to resolve land-use change have become too associated with the institutional trappings of the state and too far caught between malleable party political ideologies. A new approach to how we manage land use and spatial change within government and across different territories is vital if we are going to address climate change and sustainability and help realize greater societal benefits. At present, the management of land-use change:

- is fragmented, with different governance arrangements for different sectors;
- involves decisions taken at different levels which together do not reflect a coherent strategic approach based on clear national objectives;

- combines market mechanisms and regulation in ways which are often in conflict, generating severe pressures in some sectors;
- is delivering outcomes which are sometimes hard to reconcile with evidence on the full range of values of the land in different uses;
- faces considerable pressures in the future, as population grows and key policy priorities such as climate change pose significant challenges.

Current institutional arrangements and planning procedures sit somewhat uncomfortably alongside private ownership of land and the property markets. Some decisions about land use at local level are heavily constrained by the lack of intelligence, or because some of the responsibilities to take into account wider issues are the preserve of other agencies and bodies. It is also the case that planning has not been required to take account of the full range of factors affecting the true social value of land. At a time when fiscal issues are starting to play a more prominent role in incentivizing development and shaping projects, it seems likely that financial incentives, in the context of local land markets and local planning institutions, may need to become aligned with the declared objectives of land-use policy.

The structures in place to deliver infrastructure development and land-use changes within or adjacent to urban areas are at least equally problematic. Urban land has been increasingly managed by a range of public and quasi-public authorities, through ad hoc delivery vehicles standing outside elected local government and at arm's length from central government. In these cases it can be hard to balance strategic, national or regional considerations against strong opposition from local residents. Here the issue is the scale at which decisions are best made and the framework in place for taking them in a democratically acceptable way. New arrangements have recently been put in place to address some of these problems, but only in relation to major infrastructure. The limited scope of the planning process at present militates against a wider strategic approach to local or even neighbourhood decisions. The challenge is to devise reforms that would deliver land-use decisions in a more robust and efficient way, based on the uniqueness of land in different locations, in order to produce better overall value for the country while reflecting the inevitable trade-offs involved. The existing planning process is the wrong starting point. This will require a more holistic approach to managing the land that should take account of the many factors, external considerations, policy priorities and individual preferences that influence outcomes. As such, it is primarily a governance challenge and a new understanding is needed in order to improve the basis on which planning policies are devised and decisions are taken that, in turn, will generate better outcomes from land. There are a number of key governance challenges associated with this:

- The need for mechanisms and governance structures which require land-use decisions at all levels to be taken with regard to the full range of services and values of land in different possible uses, given both individual preferences and strategic policy objectives.
- The need for better data and intelligence, information flows and agreed methodologies to inform these decisions.
- The need to ensure that decisions taken in different sectors are consistent in reflecting this overall approach.
- The need to ensure appropriate incentives for land-use change and duties on landowners which encourage desired behaviours consistent with this approach and minimize tensions occurring within the system.
- The need to change policy to better link land-use and management policy to climate change mitigation and adaptation efforts.
- The need to ensure that governance of land reflects future needs as well as present ones.
- The need to embed a better understanding the value and function of biodiversity and ecosystem services in the formulation and adoption of local and strategic land-use policies.
- The need to reflect spatial considerations and geography most effectively in land-use policy.
- The need to truly understand place identity and place uniqueness.

This suggests that there is a fundamental need to go back to first principles before even considering the design and delivery of spatial policies that ensure the effectiveness of the land-use system: first, generating agreement about the objectives of the land and the services required – economic, environmental and social; secondly, quantifying and prioritizing the desired services; and thirdly, aligning individual and institutional preferences with these objectives. As land delivers a variety of services which at present are the focus of individual ministries or processes, consistency will require coordination and integration across a currently disparate set of agencies and activities.

As there is no single government department or agency with a policy or legislative remit that sets priorities for land use, this integration is difficult to achieve. Rather, there are many government bodies, operating at various levels of policy and decision-making and within different legal frameworks, that seek to achieve very different outcomes. The adoption of a coherent set of clearly articulated strategic national objectives for how land is used and managed could create a greater impetus to recognize land as a national asset and allow land-allocation mechanisms to be adapted to better deliver these objectives over time. Plans, strategies and guides at national, regional and local scales created under clearly articulated national objectives would create greater certainty for landowners and managers. A commitment to more coordinated action, based on a more integrated understanding of the land's potential uses and how change creates impacts spatially over time, would create the basis for realizing greater value, both financial and non-financial.

A spatial framework or robust strategic intelligence is essential to achieve an integrated approach to the future use of the land. Such intelligence is needed to provide certainty and direction for all the governance processes, whatever the balance between regulation and market mechanisms and different levels of decision making. At minimum, it could simply lay down a common approach to decision making and the methodology to be used. At present this varies greatly across sectors and decision levels. It could also articulate the preferred level of decision-making for certain types of land use and climate change. The nation's infrastructure needs, such as airports, ports, major road and rail projects, energy and water, cut across the boundaries of established administrative regions and localities. Such projects are difficult to plan and assess on a local, or even regional, basis. Similarly, it could be difficult to form a national picture of the benefits and flow of ecosystems services spatially and over time at the local level. Other decisions are more suited to local-level decisions because the impacts, whether positive or negative, are experienced locally. There is a risk that incremental decision-making on individual projects and land choices without strategic direction will continue to create unintended consequences and unsustainable outcomes. A common and holistic approach to decisions across all sectors and levels of government, based on the best possible data and agreed approaches to establishing values, would help to minimize this risk.

The need to define clear national objectives for land use also depends to a great degree on sensitivity to the enormous variation in the needs and opportunities across the UK, and this variation challenges the relevance of standardized approaches or policies for particular types of land. All land is different, it possesses multiple values, both ecologically and economically, and helps create a sense of place and identity. Defining national land objectives for a country as a whole does not mean the imposition of standardized or uniform solutions. Rather, it should allow the different assets of land in different locations to inform decisions on how best to make the most of their comparative advantage and generate robust policies and choices about how different types and locations of land can be used to best advantage. This would require a stronger evidence base to underpin choices; currently evidence is either absent or patchy across the country, and even where it is available there may be uncertainty as to how it should be taken into account by decision makers.

A better understanding of the locational aspect of place assets is needed. The geographical pattern of landscapes, resources, capability, ecosystems and the arrangement of human activities constitute unique places that are the outcomes of both unintentional and purposeful action. This sense of place helps create communities and social cohesion, but also influences perceptions and attitudinal responses, manifested through markets and other mechanisms, which condition further spatial changes to the land. Incremental local land-use changes can cumulatively become a matter of national importance. Interests of the wider community or segments of the nation may be underrepresented in local decisions, and consequently be given insufficient weight. There is an opportunity to devise a system that embeds a better understanding of what each different piece of land offers to us, not just locally for individual choices but also nationally, and how that understanding can best shape land use in the national interest (see Figure 10.1).

A central challenge to embedding a deeper understanding of land and place assets and the wider long-term impact of land use change lies in governmental mechanisms and the various spatial scales to which policy- and decision-making relates. As we have seen throughout this book, the UK has tended to use administrative areas as the spatial frameworks to formulate and deliver land-use policies and initiatives. But the boundaries of administrative areas such as regions and local

Figure 10.1 *The value of urban green spaces:*
Walthamstow Marshes, London

Located just on the edge of the Olympic Park and adjacent to Hackney in the Lea Valley, this natural area is rich in biodiversity and serves as a recreational area for the urban population, but crucially acts as a flood inundation area in periods of extreme rainfall.

authorities do not necessarily relate to the functional and economic flows across the land (see Figure 10.2). Some specific policies focus on networks, such as the transport system, that stretch across various governmental and geographical boundaries. These may not sit well with strategies and plans for the growth of towns and cities that are clustered in specific places. Changes in demand for the use of land, deriving from socioeconomic and environmental factors, do not start and stop at administrative boundaries. Movement of people and goods and flows of services – the way we conduct our daily lives – are increasingly difficult to handle through investment decisions and strategies that are often bounded within a local or regional planning framework. These also tend to focus on what we can see on the surface of the land and how various land uses interact; they do not look at what each parcel of land can offer us ecologically or otherwise. The flows in activities and services over and on the land, over time, create the need for a different perspective of land-use linkages and opportunities. The forces that drive change in and over the land interact in complex ways, and sector-specific policy responses (in housing, transport or agriculture, for example) may not be sufficiently effective in addressing the range of different considerations relevant to land-use decisions in particular places.

The spatial scale at which land-use decisions are made, and the ways in which present institutional arrangements interact, are issues which need to be addressed in considering potential reforms to the both planning and the governance system. But irrespective of how far institutional change is desirable or practical, an overarching perspective is still needed to delineate how particular types of land-use decisions are made, on what basis and by whom. The purpose of such an exercise is not to identify a particular set of functional solutions to how to manage land-use change better, but to indicate possible changes of approach which should be embodied in a better system, and what issues therefore need to be addressed. More detailed work could well result in a very diverse, mixed patchwork of administrative arrangements and policy instruments to provide a more realistic and appropriate planning framework. This would then help to deliver better results from consideration of all our land expectations based on the assets of unique places, while meeting future long-term changes. The basis for revising our planning and governance arrangements is the idea that by combining a more sophisticated understanding of how land creates assets for society with a governance framework which more proactively identifies a wider range of place benefits, the performance of both the land and planning could be greatly improved.

Achieving better places will continue to require a range of policy instruments, including regulatory and economic instruments related directly to the problems of places as they have been assessed and analysed. It may involve changes such as proactive fostering and of partnerships

Figure 10.2 *Spaces of flows: Train travel and commuting patterns*

A Pendolino train at Liverpool Lime Street Station awaiting its next diagrammed working to London. Journey times are currently approximately 2 hours 10 minutes. The introduction of high-speed rail services after 2030 would reduce the time taken to just one and a half hours. Will high-speed rail benefit northern cities' economies, or merely extend London's commuter belt over a much greater distance?

between businesses and communities, encouraging land-management regimes to deliver multiple benefits, and allocating land parcels among different uses more strategically, but at the same time keeping a perspective on how people and community (rather than planners and developers) view places. An underlying theme is the need to 'mainstream' choices and decisions which can be expected to deliver better outcomes, while retaining sufficient overall control to ensure that key objectives (such as avoidance of urban sprawl) are met. A better and deeper understanding of place uniqueness and place assets, how benefits flow, and recognition that existing governance structures may be inadequate to address this deeper meaning of places, would make it possible to create an intelligence which is more likely to create benefits for society in a sustainable way. The benefits of utilizing this deeper spatial intelligence include identifying:

- Problems of land in urban and rural areas which are addressed inadequately and, if left unresolved, are likely to get worse or dramatically reduce well-being.

- Vulnerabilities or systemic weaknesses on which external influences and forces could cause a spiralling of unintended and adverse consequences.
- Geographical pressure points where a combination of influences are creating particular pressures.
- Policy dilemmas where targets and commitments could lead to unintended consequences or produce conflicting outcomes.
- Drivers which produce uncertain outcomes over which we have little control.

A satisfactory strategic intelligence base on land and spatial change would need to enable the land to meet the challenges identified in Chapter 2, in ways which combine best use of evidence taking full account of the range of views and interests involved. As well as promoting more informed decisions, based on a more holistic understanding of land-use impacts, and aligning incentives with objectives to create greater harmony in the system, it would need to improve coordination across sectoral boundaries and spatially. In order to produce outcomes which are socially and politically acceptable it should also improve the two-way flows of knowledge from local to national level and empower communities, whilst delivering wider social, economic and environmental benefits.

In order to start thinking of devising a spatial planning approach with a stronger strategic intelligence capability based on place and land uniqueness while also potentially delivering real sustainable benefits, a number of key issues need to be addressed. The most prominent issue is how to deal with more strategic issues in an era of small government and an increasingly devolved governmental structure where decisions are delegated to neighbourhoods and citizens. This is a significant problem, for any more holistic evidence-based role requires, in theory, either higher tiers of the state or the research and scientific communities to monitor and assess incremental change. That does not mean a need to re-create a central state or top-down forms of decision making. Rather, it is about recognizing the overriding duty of national government in its strategic and intelligence duties relating to territorial change, something the Coalition government seems to have abdicated responsibility for. As a consequence, there is a need to establish clear land use and management objectives and priorities, and the development of institutional structures that can properly take account of the full range of services that land can supply. There is, critically, a desire to set out an holistic, evidence-based approach to decision making. Key to ensure recognition of place uniqueness is the need to generate the evidence and intelligence base about land and place to identify the multiple uses of land, which might include the development of new forms of modelling and scenario work, and a deeper understanding of land capacity to deliver results. Strategic intelligence and planning should not be isolated from finance and resources, and so there is also a need to devise an appropriate range of incentives, compensation and mitigation measures and relate these to particular problems and opportunities in various settings. Part of planning's historic role is to handle the range of economic and environmental pressures over time while coping with uncertainties and ensuring resilience in the land system. Those strategic attributes are essential. This would include taking future-proof decisions or devising policies that are robust in the face of changing circumstances.

Figure 10.3 illustrates a strategic spatial intelligence process, with a clear identification of first principles and what is expected from land and territory, before going on to think of the implications holistically of each possible outcome from land and planning decisions prior to developing a strategy, and relating these to the uniqueness of land, territory and place. Only by undertaking this more informed strategic analysis of territorial assessment could a truly place-based decision process be realized.

The task of undertaking an assessment of the deeper meanings of the land, based on place, the medium- to long-term drivers of change, and

Figure 10.3   *Place-based spatial strategic intelligence*

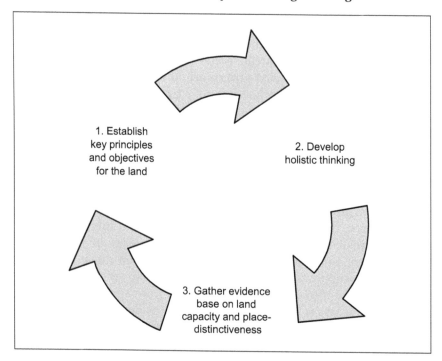

the range of different outcomes that could benefit society and generate well-being, is not an easy one to insert within an existing planning process. Historically, in many countries, planning has often only been concerned with aesthetic impacts, making short-term or incremental economic gains, and has been dissected governmentally and institutionally between too many vested and self-serving interests. This creates its own legacies. But we have reached a stage of the planet's life when wider and more important issues relating to climate change, population needs and global demographic trends, people's health and economic vulnerability need to feature much more prominently within a nation's planning decisions but are linked, and this is absolutely critical, to land and its uniqueness as found in different territories. These global and national trends cannot become bogged down to an even greater extent within the political machinations and contested responsibilities between scales of governance and the various agencies of an individual state.

There is now a greater need for a new form of planning, and for spatial planning, to address these larger strategic concerns, linking global trends and uncertainties of the present and future, with possible impacts and solutions within unique places and on unique land parcels. A more critical role for planning is essential in assessing spatial change and land use trends *sans frontières*. Planning and sustainability in their wider global guise need to be at the heart of political intervention, where sustainability is not defined as some narrow economic growth agenda or subsumed within a political neo-liberal paradigm. Questions concerning our land, its assets, the future of places and their resilience, within an intelligence and modelling process that looks at the bigger picture and long term, and assessing their possible implications, would serve to give spatial planning a strategic spirit and purpose after a period of time where planning has tended to lose its way.

One way this could be achieved through the planning system is by striving to achieve territorial and spatial resilience, where the assets and potential of the land are gathered, their vulnerability modelled, their multiple benefits assessed and their position within individual places recorded, prior to thinking about the future uses of land and formulating policies for change and development (see Figure 10.4).

Conclusions

Overall, perhaps one of the fundamental features of recent forms of spatial planning compared to historical forms of planning is that it has extended planning into a positive tool for participants. It is proactive, not reactive. Spatial strategy-making extends beyond the legal confines of statutory town and country planning in order to inspire, give confi-

Figure 10.4 *Test of territorial and spatial resilience*

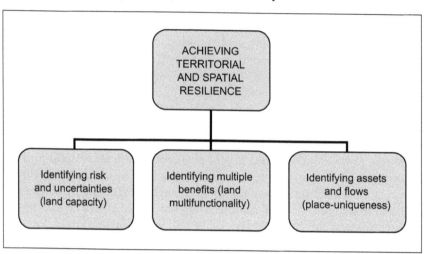

dence and provide understanding. It is an enabling mechanism. Development decisions will remain within the parameters of the statutory framework provided by the planning Acts; but the policy-making side of planning is opened up in the interests of transparency, fairness and mutual learning. The core principles of spatial planning relate not only to policy development, but also coordination, implementation, financing and resourcing. But it also has to ensure that it informs politics and governance, rather than sits as a tool within the political structure.

The key challenges relate to the requirements of finding visionary aspects of planning and of making connections within increased complexity. Spatial planning should promote innovation and experimentation, the development of creativity, a sense of confidence and new capacities on the part of planners. More people should become involved within planning through consideration of places and how they might change in the future; participants need to be nurtured, provided with knowledge, and helped to develop critical understanding of events and situations. Planners will need to be realistic: no one suggests that these new processes of spatial planning will be an easy activity from the outset, and there will be those who wish to judge spatial planning too quickly and talk of its failure; but it is vital for people to be brought along in debates about these trends rather than treated with arrogance.

Planning can no longer be a tool of the central state: it will increasingly become an activity of the many, rather than of the few. Perhaps a true sign of spatial planning's success will be when it is no longer 'owned' by planners but by those agencies and individuals who see a value for it. Partnership processes seem likely to increase the ownership of strategies and plans, as part of new governance networks and pluralism, but there will have to be clear lines of delineation between the role of government and the role of individuals in dealing with some bigger land-use and climate-change issues. This would not be removing democracy, merely shifting different types of democracy to different agencies with defined responsibilities. Plans and planning can assist in fostering unique places that people feel proud of based on a real assessment of evidence and difference. Planners, either in the public or private sectors, will still be called upon to search for spatial expressions of a range of sectoral issues and support communities and others in making sense of change, thereby contributing towards expressing a voice within the management of sustainable development. After all, as Haughton et al. (2010: 1) state, 'spatial planning is about better place-making'. None of this is particularly new, even if some of the labels have changed; they are some of the reasons why planning was enacted in the first place over a hundred years ago. In the twenty-first century, we do have more expectations as a society, we make more demands on the land, we are prepared to contest change more prominently, and we are impatient. As complexity increases, so does the work of planning in drawing together these dilemmas and making sense of them. That means planning needs to change periodically as a function of government in order to respond to the challenges we face. The problem occurs when the architecture of planning changes, not because of societal or environmental need, but because of political ideological reasons or as a function of institutional restructuring. And when that happens there is a time for a much more fundamental debate about planning's value and purpose. Science, research, strategic thinking and place identity need to become central to planning's heart as part of a spatial renaissance but also to help create societal well-being. To those individual ministers, officials and special advisers who possess a partial or even warped view of planning's role, historically and contemporarily, it is worth reminding them that *place matters*. Ultimately, this is not the story of planning; it is the story of the way we live.

References

6, P., Leat, D., Seltzer, K. and Stoker, G. (2002) *Towards Holistic Governance: The New Reform Agenda*, Palgrave Macmillan, Basingstoke.

Adams, D., Russell, L. and Taylor-Russell, C. (1994) *Land for Industrial Development*. Spon, London.

Adams, D., Disbury, A., Hutchison, N. and Munjoma, T. (2002) Vacant urban land: exploring ownership strategies and actions, *Town Planning Review*, **73**, 395–418.

Adams, D. and Watkins, C. (2002) *Greenfields, Brownfields and Housing Development*, Blackwell, London.

Adcock, R. and D. Collier (2001) Connecting ideas with facts: The validity of measurement, *American Political Science Review*, **95**(3), 529–46.

Agnew, J. (1997) The dramaturgy of horizons: Geographical scale in the 'reconstruction of Italy' by the new Italian political parties, 1992–1995, *Political Geography*, **16**(2), 99–121.

Agnew, J. (1999) Mapping political power beyond state boundaries: territory, identity, and movement in world politics, *Millennium*, **28**, 499–521.

Albrechts, L. (2006) Shifts in strategic spatial planning? Some evidence from Europe and Australia, *Environment and Planning A*, **38**(6), 1149–70.

Alden, J. (2001) Devolution since Kilbrandon and scenarios for the future of spatial planning in the United Kingdom and European Union, *International Planning Studies*, **6**(2), 117–32.

Alden, J. and Offord, C. (1996) Regional planning guidance, in Tewdwr-Jones, M. (ed.) *British Planning Policy in Transition*, UCL Press, London.

Alesina A. and E. Spolaore (2003) *The Size of Nations*, MIT Press, London.

Alexander, E. (1997), A mile or a millimetre? Measuring the 'planning theory-practice gap', *Environment and Planning B: Planning and Design*, 24(1), 3–6.

Allen, C. (2008) *Housing Market Renewal and Social Class*, Routledge, London.

Allmendinger, P. (2001) *Planning in Postmodern Times*, Routledge, London.

Allmendinger, P. (2002) Planning under a Scottish Parliament: A missed opportunity?, *European Planning Studies*, **10**(6), 793–98.

Allmendinger, P. (2003) From New Right to New Left in UK planning, *Urban Policy and Research*, **21**(1), 57–79.

Allmendinger, P. (2006) Zoning by stealth? The diminution of discretionary planning, *International Planning Studies*, **11**(2), 137–43.

Allmendinger, P. (2011) *New Labour and Planning: From New Right to New Left*, Routledge, London.

Allmendinger, P. and Haughton, G. (2007) The fluid scales and scope of UK spatial planning, *Environment and Planning A*, **39**(6), 1478–96.

Allmendinger, P. and Haughton, G. (2009) Soft spaces, fuzzy boundaries and metagovernance: The new spatial planning in the Thames Gateway, *Environment and Planning A*, **41**, 617–33.

Allmendinger, P. and Haughton, G. (2010) Critical reflections on spatial planning, *Environment and Planning A*, **41**, 2544–9.

Allmendinger, P. and Haughton, G. (2011) Moving on – from spatial planning to localism and beyond, *Town and Country Planning*, April, 184–7.

Allmendinger P., Morphet, J. and Tewdwr-Jones, M. (2005) Devolution and the modernisation of local government: Prospects for planning, *European Planning Studies*, **13**(3), 349–70.

Allmendinger, P. and Tewdwr-Jones, M. (1997) Post-Thatcherite urban planning and politics: a Major change?, *International Journal of Urban and Regional Research*, **21**(1), 100–16.

Allmendinger, P. and Tewdwr-Jones, M. (2000a) New Labour, new planning? The trajectory of planning in Blair's Britain, *Urban Studies*, **37**(8), 1379–1402.

Allmendinger, P. and Tewdwr-Jones, M. (2000b) Spatial dimensions and institutional uncertainties of planning and the 'new regionalism', *Environment and Planning C: Government and Policy*, **18**(6), 711–26.

Allmendinger, P. and Tewdwr-Jones, M. (eds) (2002a) *Planning Futures: New Directions for Planning Theory*, Routledge, London.

Allmendinger, P. and Tewdwr-Jones, M. (2002b) The communicative turn in urban planning: unravelling paradigmatic, imperialistic and moralistic dimensions, *Space and Polity*, **6**(1), 5–24.

Allmendinger, P. and Thomas, H. (eds.) (1998) *Urban Planning and the British New Right*, Routledge, London.

Amin, A. (1996) Beyond associative governance, *New Political Economy*, **1**(3), 309–33.

Amin, A. and Hausner, J., (1997) Interactive governance and social complexity, in *Beyond Market and Hierarchy: Interactive Governance and Social Complexity*, Edward Elgar, Cheltenham, pp. 1–31.

Amin, A., Massey, D. and Thrift, N. (2003) *Decentering the Nation: A Radical Approach to Regional Inequality, Catalyst Paper 8*, Catalyst, London.

Amin A. and Thrift, N. (1992) Neo-Marshallian nodes in global networks, *International Journal of Urban and Regional Research*, **16**, 571–87.

Amin A. and Thrift, N. (1995) Globalisation, institutional 'thickness' and the local economy, in Healey, P., Cameron, S., Davoudi, S., Graham, S. and Mandani-Pour, A., *Managing Cities: The New Urban Context*, John Wiley, Chichester, pp. 91–108.

Armstrong, H. (2001) Regional Selective Assistance: Is the spending enough and is it targeting the right places?, *Regional Studies*, **35**, 247–58.

Arnstein, S. (1969) The ladder of citizen participation, *Journal of the Institute of American Planners*, **35**(4), 216–24.

Arup Planning (2004) *Standard Application Forms and a Review of the Acknowledgement, Registration and Validation Process for Planning Applications and Other Consent Regimes*, CLG, London.

Ashworth, W. (1954) *The Genesis of Modern British Town Planning*, Routledge & Kegan Paul, London.

Audsley, E., Brander, M., Chatterton, J., Murphy-Bokern, D., Webster, C. and Williams, A. (2009) *How Low Can We Go? An Assessment of Greenhouse Gas Emissions from the UK Food System and the Scope for Reduction by*

2050. Report to WWF and Food Climate Research Network, Cranfield University, Bedford.

Bache, I. and Nugent, N. (2007) Europe, in Seldon, A. (ed.) *Blair's Britain*, Cambridge University Press, Cambridge.

Bailey, N. (2009) Managing the metropolis: Economic change, institutional reform and spatial planning in London, in Davoudi, S. and Strange, I. (eds) *Conceptions of Space and Place in Strategic Spatial Planning*, Routledge, London, pp. 181–205.

Baker, M. (1998) Planning for the English regions: A review of the Secretary of State's regional planning guidance, *Planning Practice and Research*, 13(2), 153–69.

Baker, M., Deas, I. and Wong, C. (1999) Obscure ritual or administrative luxury? Integrating strategic planning and regional development, *Environment and Planning B: Planning and Design*, 26(5), 763–82.

Barker, K. (2004) *Delivering Stability: Securing Future Housing Needs*, HM Treasury, London.

Barker, K. (2006) *Barker Review of Land-use Planning Interim Report*. HM Treasury, London.

Batchler, J. and Turok, I. (eds) (1997) *The Coherence of EU Regional Policy*, Jessica Kingsley, London.

Bateman, I. (2009) Bringing the real world into economic analyses of land use value: Incorporating spatial complexity, *Land Use Policy*, 26(1), S30–42.

Beaverstock, J.V., Smith, R.G. and Taylor, P.J. (1999) A roster of world cities, *Cities*, 16, 445–58.

Beddington, J. (2009) Food, energy, water and the climate: A perfect storm of global events?,' speech to the National University of Science, Vietnam, September.

Bennett, R.J. (1997) Administrative systems and economic spaces, *Regional Studies*, 31, 323–36.

Berry, J., Brown, L. and McGreal, S. (2001) The planning system in Northern Ireland post-devolution, *European Planning Studies*, 9(6), 781–91.

Berry, J. and McGreal, S. (1995) European cities: The interaction of planning systems, property markets and real estate investment, in Berry, J. and McGreal, S. (eds) *European Cities, Planning Systems and Property Markets*, Spon, London, pp. 1–16.

Best, R.H. (1981) *Land Use and Living Space*, Methuen, London.

Bevan, A. and Estrin, S. (2004) The determinants of foreign direct investment into European transition economies, *Journal of Comparative Economics*, 32(4), 775–87.

Bianconi, M., Gallent, N. and Greatbatch, I. (2006) The changing geography of subregional planning in England, *Environment and Planning C: Government and Policy*, 24(3), 317–30.

Blackman, T. (1997) Urban planning in the United Kingdom, in Pacione, M. (ed.) *Britain's Cities: Geographies of Division in Urban Britain*, Routledge, London, pp. 128–49.

Boddy, M. et al. (1997) *City for the 21st Century? Globalisation, Planning and Urban Change in Contemporary Britain*, Policy Press, Bristol.

Börzel, T.A. (2002) Pace-setting, foot-dragging, and fence-sitting: Member state responses to Europeanization, *Journal of Common Market Studies*, **40**(2): 193–214.

Börzel, T. (2002a) *States and Regions in the European Union*, Cambridge University Press, Cambridge.

Börzel, T. and Risse, T. (2003) Conceptualising the domestic impact of Europe, in Featherstone, K. and Radaelli, C.M. (eds.) *The Politics of Europeanization*, Oxford University Press, Oxford, pp. 57–80.

Börzel, T.A. (2004) How the European Union interacts with its member states, in Lequesne, C. and Bulmer, S. (eds) *Member States and the European Union*, Oxford University Press, Oxford.

Boyer, R. and Hollingsworth, J.R. (1997) *Contemporary Capitalism: The Embeddedness of Institutions*, Cambridge University Press, Cambridge.

Breheny, M. (1991) The renaissance of strategic planning?, *Environment and Planning B: Planning and Design*, **18**(3), 233–49.

Brenner, N. (1999) Globalisation as reterritorialisation: The re-scaling of urban governance in the European Union, *Urban Studies*, 36, 431–52.

Brenner, N. (2003) Metropolitan institutional reform and the rescaling of state space in contemporary western Europe, *European Urban and Regional Studies*, **10**, 297–324.

Brenner, N. (2004) *New State Spaces: Urban Governance and the Rescaling of Statehood*, Oxford University Press, Oxford.

British Chambers of Commerce (1997) *Regional Policy*, BCC, London.

Bruton, M. (ed.) (1974) *The Spirit and Purpose of Planning*, Hutchinson, London.

Bruton, M. and Nicholson, D. (1985) Strategic land use planning and the British development plan system, *Town Planning Review*, **56**, 21–41.

Byrne, T. (2001) *Local Government in Britain*, Penguin, Harmondsworth.

Cabinet Office (1999) *Modernising Government*, Cabinet Office, London.

Cabinet Office (2008) *Food Matters: Towards a Strategy for the 21st Century*, Cabinet Office Strategy Unit, London.

Cameron, D. (2011) speech on the 'Big Society', London, 14 February.

Caporaso, J. and Stone Sweet, A. (2001) Institutional Logics of European Integration, in Stone Sweet, A., Sandholtz, W. and Fligstein, N. (eds.) *The Institutionalization of Europe*, Oxford University Press, Oxford.

Caprik, P. (2010), Regional promotion and competition: An examination of approaches to FDI attraction in the Czech Republic, in Adams, N., Cotella, G. and Nunes, R. (eds), *Territorial Development, Cohesion and Spatial Planning: Building on EU Enlargement*, Routledge, London.

Carbonell, A. and Yaro, R. (2005) American spatial development and the new megalopolis, *Land Lines*, **17**(2), available at http://www.lincolninst.edu/pubs/PubDetail.aspx?pubid=1009, accessed 19 February 2008.

Carstensen, K. and Toubal, F. (2004) Foreign direct investment in Central and Eastern European countries: A dynamic panel analysis, *Journal of Comparative Economics*, **32**(1), 3–22.

Castells, M. (1996) *The Rise of the Network Society*, Blackwell, Oxford.

CBI (1997) *Regions for Business: Improving Policy Design and Delivery*, CBI, London.

CEC (1984) *Recommendation R84/2 Du Comité des Minstres aux états members relative a la Charte Européenne de l'Amènagement du Territoire,* Strasbourg.

CEC (1991) *Europe 2000,* Office for Official Publications of the European Communities, Luxembourg.

CEC (1994) *Europe 2000+,* Office for Official Publications of the European Communities, Luxembourg.

CEC (1997) *The EU Compendium of Spatial Planning Systems and Policies,* CEC, Luxembourg.

CEC (1999) *European Spatial Development Perspective: Towards Balanced and Sustainable Development of the Territory of the EU,* Office of the Official Publications of the European Communities, Luxembourg.

CEC (2004) *A New Partnership for Cohesion: Convergence, Competitiveness, Cooperation, Third Report on Economic and Social Cohesion,* CEC, Luxembourg.

CEC (2008) *Green Book on Territorial Cohesion,* CEC, Luxembourg.

Chapman, W. (2005) Planning policy guidance, speech to the RTPI Planning and Environment Training Conference, London, May.

Chatterton, J., Viavattene, C., Morris, J., Penning-Rowsell, E. and Tapsell S. (2009) *The Costs of the Summer 2007 Floods in England, Report to the Environment Agency Science Project SC070039,* Cranfield University, Bedford.

Cherry, G.E. (1974) The development of planning thought, in Bruton, M. (ed.) *The Spirit and Purpose of Planning,* Hutchinson, London, pp. 66–84.

Cheshire, P. (2008) Reflections on the nature and policy implications of planning restrictions on housing supply: Discussion of 'Planning policy, planning practice, and housing supply' by Kate Barker, *Oxford Review of Economic Policy,* 24(1), 50–8.

Cheshire, P. and Hay, D.G. (1989) *Urban Problems in Western Europe,* Unwin, London.

Cheshire, P. and Sheppard, S. (2003) *The Introduction of Price Signals into Land Use Planning Decision Making: A Proposal,* Department of Geography and Environment, London School of Economics and Political Science, London.

Chilton, P.J., Guha, P., Peach, D.W., Stuart, M.E. and Whitehead, E.J. (2004) *Implications of Changing Groundwater Quality for Water Resources and the UK Water Industry. Phase 3: Financial and Water Resources Impact, Final Report,* UKWIR Report 04/WR/09/8.

CLG (Department for Communities and Local Government) (2006) *Strong and Prosperous Community.* White Paper, Stationery Office, London.

CLG (2007a) *Creating Strong, Safe and Prosperous Communities.* Statutory Guidance Consultation Draft, CLG, London.

CLG (2007b) *Generalised Land Use Database Statistics for England 2005.* Department of Communities and Local Government, London.

CLG (2007c), *National Evaluation of Local Strategic Partnerships.* CLG, London.

CLG (2010) Localism Bill starts a new era of people power. Press release, CLG, 13 December.

CLG/BERR (2007) *Taking Forward the Review of Sub-national Economic Development and Regeneration*, CLG, London.

Clotworthy, J. and Harris, N. (1996) Planning policy implications of local government reorganisation, in Tewdwr-Jones, M. (ed.) *British Planning Policy in Transition: Planning in the 1990s*, UCL Press, London.

Cochrane, A., Peck, J. and Tickell, A. (1996) Manchester plays games: Exploring the local politics of globalisation, *Urban Studies* 33(8), 1319–36.

Cole, A. and Drake, H. (2000) The Europeanization of the French polity: Continuity, change and adaptation, *Journal of European Public Policy*, 7(1), 26–43.

Comber, A.J. (2008) Land use or land cover?, *Journal of Land Use Science*, 3(4), 199–202.

Commission for Integrated Transport (l2009) *Planning for Sustainable Travel*, available at http://www.plan4sustainabletravel.org/downloads/cfit_background_report.pdf

Conservative Party (2010) *Open Source*, Green Paper, Central Office, London.

Cooke, P. (1983) *Theories of Planning and Spatial Development*, Hutchinson, London.

Cooke P. (ed.) (1989) *Localities*, Unwin Hyman, London.

Cooke P. and Morgan, K. (1993) The network paradigm: New departures in corporate and regional development, *Environment and Planning D, Society and Space*, 11, 543–64.

Cooke P. and Morgan, K. (1998) *The Associational Economy: Firms, Regions and Innovation*, Oxford University Press, Oxford.

Cope, S. (2001) The Europeanisation of British policy-making, in Savage, S.P. and Atkinson, R. (eds) *Public Policy Under Blair*, Palgrave, Basingstoke.

Corry D. and Stoker, G. (2002) *The New Localism*, NLGN, London.

Corry D., Hatter, W., Parker, I., Randle, A. and Stoker, G. (2004) *Joining-up Local Democracy: Governance Systems for New Localism*, NLGN, London.

Couclelis H. (2005) 'Where has the future gone?' Rethinking the role of integrated land-use models in spatial planning, *Environment and Planning A*, 37(8), 1353–71.

Counsell, D. and Haughton, G. (2003) Regional planning tensions: Planning for economic growth and sustainable development in two contrasting English regions, *Environment and Planning C: Government and Policy*, 21(2), 225–39.

Counsell, D., Haughton, G., Allmendinger, P. and Vigar, G. (2003) From land use plans to spatial development strategies: New directions in planning in the UK, *Town and Country Planning*, January, 15–19.

Cowell, R. and Martin, S. (2003) The joy of joining up: Modes of integrating the local government modernisation agenda, *Environment and Planning C: Government and Policy*, 21(2), 159–79.

Cowell R. and Owens, S. (2006) Governing space: Planning reform and the politics of sustainability, *Environment and Planning C: Government and Policy*, 24(3), 403–21.

Cowles, M., Caporaso, J. and Risse, T. (2001) (eds.) *Transforming Europe: Europeanization and Domestic Change*, Cornell University Press, Ithaca, NY.

CPRE (1994) *Greening the Regions: Regional Planning Guidance – A Review and Assessment of Current Practice*, CPRE, London.

Cullingworth, J.B. (ed.) (1999) *British Planning: 50 Years of Urban and Regional Policy*, Athlone, London.

Cullingworth, B. and Nadin, V. (2006) *Town and Country Planning in the UK*, 14th edn, Routledge, London.

Dabrowski, M. (2010) Institutional change, partnership and regional networks: Civic engagement and the implementation of structural funds in Poland, in Adams, N., Cotella, G. and Nunes, R. (eds) *Territorial Development, Cohesion and Spatial Planning: Building on EU Enlargement*, Routledge, London.

Davies, H.W.E. (1994) Towards a European planning system?, *Planning Practice and Research*, 9(1), 63–9.

Davoudi, S, (2003) Polycentricity in European spatial planning: From an analytical tool to a normative agenda, *European Planning Studies*, 11(8), 979–99.

Davoudi, S. and Strange, I. (eds) (2009) *Conceptions of Space and Place in Strategic Spatial Planning*, Routledge, London.

Deas, I. (2006) The contested creation of new state spaces: Contrasting conceptions of regional strategy building in North West England, in Tewdwr-Jones, M. and Allmendinger, P. (eds) *Territory, Identity and Spatial Planning: Spatial Governance in a Fragmented Nation*, Routledge, London, pp. 83–105.

DEFRA (2008) *Future Water: The Government's Water Strategy for England*, Department for Environment, Food and Rural Affairs, London.

Deloitte MCS (2008) *The Economic Case for the Visitor Economy: Final Report for Visit Britain*. Deloitte MCS, London.

DETR (1998a) *Local Democracy and Community Leadership, Consultation Paper*, Department for Transport, Local Government and the Regions, London.

DETR (1998b) *Modernising Planning: A Statement by the Minister for the Regions, Regeneration and Planning*, Department for Transport, Local Government and the Regions, London.

DETR (1998c) *New Leadership for London: The Government's Proposals for a Greater London Authority, Consultation Paper*, Department for Transport, Local Government and the Regions, London.

DETR (1998d) *The Future of Regional Planning Guidance, Consultation Paper*, Department for Transport, Local Government and the Regions, London.

DETR (1998e) *The Impact of the EU on UK Planning*, Department for Transport, Local Government and the Regions, London.

DETR (2000a) *New Council Constitutions Guidance Pack*, Department for Transport, Local Government and the Regions, London.

DETR (2000b) *Preparing Community Strategies: Government Guidance to Local Authorities*, Department for Transport, Local Government and the Regions, London.

DfT (2003) *Transport Statistics Great Britain*, TSO, Norwich.

Diamond, D. (1979) The uses of strategic planning: The example of national planning guidelines in Scotland, *Town Planning Review*, 50(1), 18–25.

Dicken, P. and Tickell, A. (1992) Competitors or collaborators? The structure and relationships of inward investment in Northern England, *Regional Studies*, 26, 99–106.

Dickinson, R.E. (1967) *The City Region in Western Europe*, Routledge, London.

Dietrichs, B. (1989) Regional planning, *Environment and Planning C: Government and Policy*, 7(4), 395–402.

Di Maggio, P. (1993) On metropolitan dominance: New York in the urban network, in Shelter, M. (ed.) *Capital of the American Century: The National and International Influence of New York*, Russell Sage, New York.

DoE (1989) *The Future of Development Plans White Paper*, HMSO, London.

DoE/WO (1988) Circular 1/88: Planning Policy Guidance Notes and Minerals Planning Guidance Notes, HMSO, London.

DoE/WO (1992) PPG1: General Policy and Principles, HMSO, London.

Doucet, P. (2006) Territorial cohesion of tomorrow: A path to co-operation or competition?, *European Planning Studies*, 14(10), 1473–85.

DRDNI (2001) *Regional Development Strategy for Northern Ireland*, Department for Regional Developmehnt Northern Ireland, Belfast.

DTI (2006) *UK Energy and CO_2 Emissions Projections*, Department of Trade and Industry, London.

DTLR (2001) *Planning: Delivering a Fundamental Change*, HMSO, London.

DTLR (2001) *Strong Local Leadership: Quality Public Services*, Department of Environment, Transport and the Regions, London.

Dühr, S. (2007) *The Visual Language of Spatial Planning: Exploring Cartographic Representations for Spatial Planning in Europe*, Routledge, London.

Dühr, S., Colomb, C. and Nadin, V. (2010) *European Spatial Planning and Territorial Cooperation*, Routledge, London.

Duncan, S. and Goodwin, M. (1988) *The Local State and Uneven Development*, Polity Press, Cambridge.

Dyson, K. (2000) Europeanization, Whitehall culture and the Treasury as institutional veto player: A constructivist approach to economic and monetary union, *Public Administration*, 78(4): 897–914.

Eddington, R. (2006) *Transport's Role in Sustaining the UK's Productivity and Competitiveness*, Stationery Office, London.

Elson, M. (1986) *Green Belts: Conflict Mediation in the Urban Fringe*, Heinemann, London.

Environment Agency (2008) *Climate Change and River Flows in the 2050s: Science summary SC070079/SSI*, Environment Agency, Bristol.

Environment Agency (2009) *Flooding in England: A National Assessment of Flood Risk*, Environment Agency, Bristol.

Enviros (2005) *The Costs of Supplying Renewable Energy*, report prepared for the DTI, available at http://www.berr.gov.uk/files/file21118.pdf

ERM (Environmental Resources Management) (2005) *Draft Sustainability Appraisal Report on the Consultation Draft of the South East Plan*, ERM, London.

ESPON (2005) *Project 2.3.1 Application and Effects of the ESDP in the Member States – First Interim Report*, Luxembourg.

ESPON (2006) *Project 2.3.1 Application and Effects of the ESDP in the Member States – Second Interim Report*, Luxembourg.

Evans, A.W. (1991) Rabbit hutches on postage stamps: Planning, development and political economy, *Urban Studies*, 28, 853–70.

Evans, A.E. (2003) Shouting very loudly: Economists, planning and politics, *Town Planning Review*, 74, 195–212.

Evans, R. and Harding, A. (1997) Regionalisation, regional institutions and economic development, *Policy and Politics*, **25**, 19–30.

Evers, D. (2008) Reflections on territorial cohesion and European spatial planning, *Tijdschrift voor Economische en sociale geografie*, **99**(3), 303–15.

Ezcurra, R., Pascual, P., Rapún, M. (2007) Regional disparities in the EU: An analysis of regional polarization, *Annals of Regional Science*, **41**(2), 401–29.

Faludi, A. (2001) The application of the European Spatial Development Perspective: Evidence from the northwest metropolitan area, *European Planning Studies*, **9**(5), 663–75.

Faludi, A. (2002) Positioning European spatial planning, *European Planning Studies*, **10**(7), 897–909.

Faludi, A. (ed.) (2003) The application of the European Spatial Development Perspective, special issue, *Town Planning Review*, **74**(1), 1–140.

Faludi, A. (2004) Spatial planning traditions in Europe: Their role in the ESDP process, *International Planning Studies*, **9**(2–3), 155–72.

Faludi, A. (2005) Territorial cohesion: An unidentified political objective, *Town Planning Review*, **76**(1), 1–13.

Faludi, A. (2006) From European spatial development to territorial cohesion policy, *Regional Studies*, **40**(6), 667–78.

Faludi, A. (ed.) (2007) *Territorial Cohesion and the European Model of Society*, Lincoln Institute of Land Policy, Cambridge, MA.

Faludi, A. (2009) A turning point in the development of European Spatial Planning? The territorial agenda of the EU and the first action programme, *Progress in Planning*, **71**(1), 1–42.

Faludi, A. and Waterhout, B. (2002) *The Making of the European Spatial Development Perspective*, Routledge, London.

FAO (Food and Agriculture Organization) (2005) *The State of Food Insecurity in the World 2005*, Food and Agriculture Organization of the United Nations, Rome, Italy.

Featherstone, K. (1998) Europeanization and the centre periphery: The case of Greece in the 1990s, *South European Society and Politics*, **3**(1): 23–39.

Featherstone, K. (2003) In the name of Europe, in K. Featherstone and C.M. Radaelli (eds.) *The Politics of Europeanization*, Oxford University Press, Oxford, pp. 3–26.

Featherstone, K. and Kazamias, G.A. (2001) *Europeanization and the Southern Periphery*, Frank Cass, London.

Featherstone, K. and Radaelli, C. (eds) (2003) *The Politics of Europeanization*, Oxford University Press, Oxford.

Fischer, F. and Forester, J. (eds) (1993) *The Argumentative Turn in Policy Analysis and Planning*, UCL Press, London.

Flyvbjerg B. (1998) *Rationality and Power: Democracy in Practice*, University of Chicago Press, Chicago.

Forester, J. (1989) *Planning in the Face of Power*, University of California Press, Berkeley.

Forester, J. (1993) *Critical Theory, Public Policy and Planning Practice*, State University of New York Press, Albany.

Forester, J. (1999) *The Deliberative Practitioner*, MIT Press, Cambridge, MA.

Freire, P. (1998) *Pedagogy of Hope*, Continuum, New York.

Friedmann, J. (1995) Where we stand: A decade of world city research, in Knox, P.L. and Taylor, P.J. (eds) *World Cities in a World System*, Cambridge University Press, Cambridge.

Friedmann, J. (2004) Strategic spatial planning and the longer range, *Planning Theory and Practice*, 5(1), 49–56.

Gallent, N. (2007) Household projects and strategic housing allocations, in Dimitriou, H.T. and Thompson, R. (eds) *Strategic and Regional Planning in the UK*, Routledge, London.

Gallent, N. (2009) The future of housing and homes, *Land Use Policy*, 26(1), S93–102.

Gallent, N. and Tewdwr-Jones, M. (2007) *Decent Homes for All: Reviewing Planning's Role in Housing Provision*, Routledge, London.

Getimis, P. (2003) Improving European union regional policy by learning from the past in view of Enlargement, *European Planning Studies*, 11(1), 77–87.

Giannakourou, G. (1996) Towards a European spatial planning policy: Theoretical dilemmas and institutional implications, *European Planning Studies*, 4(5), 595–613.

Giannakourou, G. (1998) The Europeanisation of national spatial planning policies, in Bengs, C. and Böhme, K. (eds) *The Progress of European Spatial Planning, Nordregio report 1998:1*, Nordregio, Stockholm, pp. 25–34.

Giannakourou, G. (2005) Transforming spatial planning policy in Mediterranean countries: Europeanisation and domestic change, *European Planning Studies*, 13(2), 319–31.

Giddens A. (2000) *The Third Way and its Critics*, Polity Press, Cambridge.

Glasson, J. and Marshall, T. (2007) *Regional Planning*, Routledge, London.

Goetz, K. (2002) Four worlds of Europeanization, paper prepared for the ECPR Joint Sessions of Workshops, Turin, Italy, 22–27 March.

Goetz, K.H. and Hix, S. (2000) Europeanised politics? European integration and national political systems, *West European Politics*, 23(4) (special issue).

Goldsmith, P. (1993) The Europeanisation of local government, *Urban Studies*, 30(4/5), 683–99.

Goodstadt, V. and U'ren, G. (1999) Which way now for Scottish planning?, *Planning*, 22 January, 11.

Goodwin, M. and Duncan, S. (1986) The local state and local economic policy: Political mobilisation or economic regeneration, *Capital and Class*, 27, 14–36.

GOS (Government Office for Science) (2010) *Foresight: Land Use Futures*, GOS, London.

GOS (Government Office for Science) (2011) *Foresight: Food Security*, GOS, London.

Graham, S. and Marvin, S. (2001) *Splintering Urbanism: Networked Infrastructures, Technological Mobilities and the Urban Condition*, Routledge, London.

Gualini, E. (2004) *Multi-Level Governance and Institutional Change: The Europeanisation of Regional Policy in Italy*, Ashgate, London.

Gualini, E. (2005) Europeanization and governance rescaling: 'territorial cohesion' as opportunity for 're-politicizing' European spatial policy and planning? Paper presented at the AESOP conference, Vienna.

Habermas, J. (1984) *The Theory of Communicative Action; Volume 1: Reason and the Rationalization of Society*, trans. McCarthy, T., Polity Press, Cambridge.

Hague, C. (1990) Scotland: Back to the future for planning, in Montgomery, J. and Thornley, A. (eds) *Radical Planning Initiatives: New Directions for Urban Planning in the 1990s*, Gower, Aldershot.

Hall, P. (1993) Forces shaping urban Europe, *Urban Studies*, 30(6), 631–58.

Hall, P. (2007) The United Kingdom's experience in revitalising inner cities, in Ingram, G. and Hong, Y. (eds) *Land Policies and their Outcomes*, Lincoln Institute of Land Policy, Cambridge, MA.

Hall, P., Gracey, H., Drewett, R. and Thomas, R. (1973) *The Containment of Urban England*, Allen & Unwin, London.

Hall, P. and Pain, K. (2006) *The Polycentric City*, Earthscan, London.

Hall, P. and Tewdwr-Jones, M. (2011) *Urban and Regional Planning*, 5th edn, Routledge, London.

Hall, P.A. and Soskice, D. (2001) *Varieties of Capitalism: The Institutional Foundations of Comparative Advantage*, Oxford University Press, Oxford.

Harding, A. (1996) *Coalition Formation and Urban Redevelopment: A Cross-National Study*, ESRC, Swindon.

Harper, T.J. and Stein S.M. (1995) Out of the postmodern abyss: Preserving the rationale for liberal planning, *Journal of Planning Education and Research*, 14, 233–44.

Harris, J. and Tewdwr-Jones, M. (2010) Ecosystem services and planning, *Town and Country Planning*, May.

Harris, N. (2001) Spatial development policies and territorial governance in an era of globalisation and localisation, in *Towards a New Role for Spatial Planning*, OECD, Paris, pp. 33–54.

Harris, N. and Hooper, A. (2006) Redefining 'the space that is Wales': Place, planning and the Wales Spatial Plan, in Allmendinger, P. and Tewdwr-Jones, M. (eds) *Territory, Identity and Spatial Planning*, Routledge, London.

Harris, N., Hooper, A. and Bishop, K. (2002) Constructing the practice of 'spatial planning': A national spatial planning framework for Wales, *Environment and Planning C: Government and Policy*, 20(4), 555–72.

Harris, N. and Tewdwr-Jones, M. (1995), The implications for planning of local government reorganisation in Wales: Purpose, process and practice, *Environment and Planning C: Government and Policy*, 13(1), 47–66.

Harrison, J. (2007) From competitive regions to competitive city-regions: A new orthodoxy, but some old mistakes, *Journal of Economic Geography*, 7(3), 311–32.

Harrison, J. (2010) Networks of connectivity, territorial fragmentation, uneven development: The new politics of city-regionalism, *Political Geography* 29(1), 17–27.

Harvey, D. (1989) From managerialism to entrepreneurialism: The transformation in urban governance in late capitalism, *Geografiska Annaler*, 71B(1), 3–17.

Harvie, C. (1991) English regionalism: The dog that never barked, in Crick, B. (ed.) *National Identities*, Blackwell, London.

Haughton, G. et al. (1997) Turf wars: The battle for control over English local economic development, *Local Government Studies*, 23(1), 88–106.

Haughton, G. and Counsell, D. (2004) *Regions, Spatial Strategies and Sustainable Development*, Routledge, London.

Haughton, G., Allmendinger, P., Counsell, D. and Vigar, G. (2010) *The New Spatial Planning*, Routledge, London.

Hayton, K. (1996) Planning policy in Scotland, in Tewdwr-Jones, M. (ed.) *British Planning Policy in Transition*, UCL Press, London.

Hayton, K. (1997) Planning in a Scottish Parliament, *Town and Country Planning*, July/August, **64**, 45–7.

Healey, P. (1992a) Planning through debate, *Town Planning Review*, 63, 143–62.

Healey, P. (1992b) The reorganisation of the state and market in planning, *Urban Studies*, **29**(3), 411–34.

Healey, P. (1993) The communicative work of development plans, *Environment and Planning B: Planning and Design*, 20(10), 83–104.

Healey, P. (1997) *Collaborative Planning: Shaping Places in Fragmented Societies*, Macmillan, Basingstoke.

Healey P. (1998) Building institutional capacity through collaborative approaches to urban planning, *Environment and Planning A*, 30(9), 1531–46.

Healey, P. (1999) Deconstructing communicative planning theory: A reply to Tewdwr-Jones and Allmendinger, *Environment and Planning A*, **31**(6), 1129–35.

Healey, P. (2001) New approaches to the content and process of spatial development frameworks, in *Towards a New Role for Spatial Planning*, OECD, Paris, pp. 143–63.

Healey, P. (2006) Territory, integration and spatial planning, in Tewdwr-Jones, M. and Allmendinger, P. (eds) *Territory, Identity and Spatial Planning: Spatial Governance in a Fragmented Nation*, Routledge, London.

Healey, P. (2007) *Urban Complexity and Spatial Strategies: Towards a Relational Planning for Our Times*, Routledge, London.

Healey, P., Cameron, S., Davoudi, S., Graham, S. and Mandani-Pour, A. (eds.) (1995) *Managing Cities: The New Urban Context*, John Wiley, Chichester.

Healey, P. and Williams, R. (1993) European urban planning systems: Diversity and convergence, *Urban Studies*, 30, 701–20.

Hedetoft, U. (1995) National identities and European integration 'from below': Bringing people back in, *Journal of European Integration*, 26(1), 1–28.

Herrschel, T. and Newman, P. (2002) *Governance of Europe's City Regions*, Routledge, London.

Hirst, P. (1994) *Associative Democracy*, Polity Press, Cambridge.

Hirst, P. and Thompson, G. (1999) *Globalisation in Question*, Polity Press, Cambridge.

Hix, S. and Goetz, K. (eds.) (2000) *Europeanised Politics? European Integration and National Political Systems*, Frank Cass, London.

HM Government (1997) Building Partnerships for Prosperity: Sustainable Growth, Competitiveness and Employment in the English Regions, Cm 3814. Stationery Office, London.

HM Government (2002) *Your Region, Your Choice: Revitalising the English Regions*, Cm5511, Stationery Office, London.

HM Government (2007a) *Planning for a Sustainable Future*, Stationery Office, London.

HM Government (2007b) *Review of sub-national economic development and regeneration*, Stationery Office, London.

HM Government (2009) *The UK Low Carbon Transition Plan: National Strategy for Climate and Energy Flooding*, Stationery Office, London.

HM Government (2011) *Natural Environment White Paper*, Stationery Office, London.

Hoch, C. (1994) *What Planners Do: Power, Politics and Persuasion*, Planners Press, Chicago.

Home, R. (2009) Land ownership in the United Kingdom: Trends, preferences and future challenges, *Land Use Policy*, **26**(1), S103–108.

Hudson, R. (2003) Fuzzy concepts and sloppy thinking: Reflections on recent developments in critical regional studies, *Regional Studies*, **37**(6/7), 741–6.

Hudson, R., Dunford, M., Hamilton, D. and Kotter, R. (1997) Developing regional strategies for economy success, *European Urban and Regional Studies*, **4**(4), 365–73.

IDeA (2001) *Political Executives and the New Ethical Framework*, IdeA, London.

Imrie, R. and Raco, M. (1999) How new is the new local governance? Lessons from the United Kingdom, *Transactions of the Institute of British Geographers*, n.s., **24**(1), 45–63.

Imrie, R. and Raco, M. (eds) (2003) *Urban Renaissance: New Labour, Community and Urban Policy*, Policy Press, Bristol.

Imrie, R. and Thomas, H. (eds) (1993) *British Urban Policy and the Urban Development Corporations*, Paul Chapman, London.

Innes, J. (**1995**) Planning theory's emerging paradigm: Communicative action and interactive practice, *Journal of Planning Education and Research*, **14**(3), 183–90.

Innes, J. and Booher, D. (2003) Collaborative policymaking: Governance through dialogue, in Hajer, M.A. and Wagenaar, H. (eds) *Deliberative Policy Analysis: Understanding Governance in the Network Society*, Cambridge University Press, Cambridge, pp 33–59.

Insight Social Research (1989) *Local Attitudes to Central Advice*, J. Sainsbury, London.

Ioakimidis, P.C. (1996) Contradictions between policy and performance, in Featherstone, K. and Ifantis, K. (eds) *Greece in a Changing Europe*, Manchester: Manchester University Press.

Jacquot, S. and Woll, C. (2003) Usage of European integration: Europeanization from a sociological perspective, *European Integration Online Papers*, **7**(12), available at http://eiop.or.at/ eiop/texte/2003–012a.htm

Janin Rivolin, U. (2003) Shaping European spatial planning: How Italy's experience can contribute, in Faludi, A. (ed.) The application of the European Spatial Development Perspective, Special Issue, *Town Planning Review*, **74**(1), 51–76.

Janin Rivolin, U. and Faludi, A. (2005) The Hidden Face of European Spatial Planning: innovations in governance, *European Planning Studies*, **13**(2), 195–215.

Jarvis, R. (1996) Structure planning and strategic planning guidance in Wales, in Tewdwr-Jones, M. (ed.) *British Planning Policy in Transition*, UCL Press, London.

Jenkins, S. (2011a) Call this planning reform? It's a recipe for civil war, *Guardian*, 13 September, accessed online 14 October 2011.

Jenkins, S. (2011b) This localism bill will sacrifice our countryside to market forces, *Guardian*, 28 July, accessed 14 October 2011.

Jensen, O.B. and Richardson, T. (2004) *Making European Space: Mobility, Power and Territorial Identity*, London, Routledge.

Jessop, B. (1994) Post-Fordism and the state, in Amin, A. (ed.) *Post-Fordism: A Reader*, Blackwell, Oxford.

Jessop, B. (1995) The future of the nation state in Europe: Erosion or reorganization?, *WP50, Political Economy of Local Governance Series*, Department of Sociology, University of Lancaster, Lancaster.

Jessop, B. (1996) Interpretive sociology and the dialectic of structure and agency, *Theory, Culture and Society*, **13**(1), 119–28.

Jessop, B. (1997a) The entrepeneurial city: Re-imaging localities, re-designing economic governance, or restructuring capital?, in Jewson, N. and MacGregor, S. (eds.) *Transforming Cities: Contested Governance and New Spatial Divisions*, Routledge, London, pp. 28–41.

Jessop, B. (1997b) The future of the national state: Erosion or organisation? General reflections on the West European Case, mimeo, Department of Sociology, University of Lancaster, Lancaster.

Jessop, B. (1999) Reflections on globalization and its (il)logics, in Dicken, P., Olds, K., Kelly, P. and Yeung, H. (eds) *Globalisation and the Asia-Pacific*, Routledge, London.

Jessop, B. (2000) The crisis of the national spatio-temporal fix and the tendential ecological dominance of globalizing capitalism, *International Journal of Urban and Regional Research*, **24**(2), 323–59.

Jessop, B. (2004) Critical semiotic analysis and cultural political economy, *Critical Discourse Studies*, **1**(2), 159–74.

John, P. (1997) Sub-national partnerships and European integration: The difficult case of London and the South East, in Bradbury, J. and Mawson, J. (eds) *British Regionalism and Devolution: The Challenges of State Reform and European Integration*, Jessica Kingsley, London, pp. 235–53.

Jonas, A. and Ward, K.G. (1999) Toward new urban and regional policy frameworks for Europe: Competitive regionalism 'bottom up' and 'top down', paper presented to the Regional Association Studies Sixth International Conference, 'Regional Potentials in an Integrating Europe', University of the Basque Country, Bilbao, Spain, September.

Jonas, A. and Ward, K.G. (2007) Introduction to a debate on city-regions: New geographies of governance, democracy and social reproduction, *International Journal of Urban and Regional Research*, **31**, 169–78.

Jones, M. (1998) Restructuring the local state: Economic governance or social regulation?, *Political Geography* **17**(8), 959–88.

Jones, M. (1999) The regional state and economic regulation: Regional regeneration or political mobilisation?, paper presented at the Sixth International Conference of the Regional Studies Association 'Regional Potentials in an Integrating Europe', University of the Basque Country, Bilbao, September.

Jones, M. (2001) The rise of the regional state in economic governance: 'partnerships for prosperity' or new scales of state power?, *Environment and Planning A*, **33**: 1185–1211.

Jones, M. and MacLeod, G. (1999) Towards a regional renaissance? Reconfiguring and rescaling England's economic governance, *Transactions of the Institute of British Geographers*, n.s. **24**(3), 295–314.

Keating, M. (1997) The invention of regions: Political restructuring and territorial government in western Europe, *Environment and Planning C, Government and Policy*, **15**: 383–98.

Keeble, L. (1961) *Town Planning at the Crossroads*, Estates Gazette, London.

Kendle, J. (1997) *Federal Britain: A History*, Routledge, London.

Kitchen, T. (1997) *Plans, Policies, Politics, People*, Paul Chapman, London.

Knill, C. and Lehmkuhl, D. (1999) How European matters: Different mechanisms of Europeanization, *European Integration Online Papers*, **3**(7), available at http://eiop.or.at/eiop/texte/1999–007.htm

Kohler-Koch, B. and Eising, R. (1999) (eds) *The Transformation of Governance in Europe*, Routledge, London.

Kunzmann, K. (2006) The Europeanization of spatial planning, in Adams, N., Alden, J. and Harris, N. (eds) *Regional Development and Spatial Planning in an Enlarged Europe*, Ashgate, Aldershot, pp. 43–64.

Kunzmann, K., Jenssen, B., Lemke, M. and Rojahn, G. (1977) *A Concept for a European Regional Policy Council of Europe, European Regional Study Series 3*, Strasbourg.

Labour Party (1995) *A Choice for England: A Consultation Paper on Labour's Plans for English Regional Government*, Labour Party, London

Lagendijk, A. (1997) Towards an integrated automotive industry in Europe: A 'merging filière' perspective, *European Urban and Regional Studies*, **4**(1), 5–18.

Lagendijk, A. (2003) Towards conceptual quality in regional studies: The need for subtle critique – a response to Markusen, *Regional Studies*, **37**(6/7), 719–28.

Ladrech, R. (1994) Europeanisation and domestic Politics and institutions: The case of France, *Journal of Common Market Studies*, **32**(1), 69–88.

Land Use Consultants (1995) *The Effectiveness of PPGs*, LUC, London.

Lawton, T.C. (1999) Governing the skies: Conditions for the Europeanisation of airline policy, *Journal of Public Policy*, **19**(1), 91–112.

Lawton-Smith, H., Tracey, P. and Clark, G.L. (2003) European policy and the regions: A review and analysis of tensions, *European Planning Studies*, **11**(7), 859–73.

Le Grand, J. and Bartlett, W. (1993) *Quasi-Markets and Public Policy*, Macmillan, Basingstoke.

Leitch Review (2006) *Leitch Review of Skills: Prosperity for All in the Global Economy Final Report*, HM Treasury, London.

LGA (Local Government Association) (2000) *Reforming Local Planning: Planning for Communities*. IDeA, London.

Lincoln Institute of Land Policy and Regional Plan Association (2004) *Toward an American spatial development perspective, Policy Roundtable Report*, September, available from the Lincoln Institute.

Lindblom, C. (1959) The science of 'muddling through', *Public Administration Review*, **19**, 79–88.

Lloyd, G. and Illsley, B. (1999) Planning and devolved government in the United Kingdom, *Town Planning Review*, 70(4), 409–32.

Lloyd, G. and Peel, D. (2006) City-regionalism: The social reconstruction of an idea in practice, in Tewdwr-Jones, M. and Allmendinger, P. (eds) *Territory, Identity and Spatial Planning: Spatial Governance in a Fragmented Nation*, Routledge, London, pp. 285–304.

Lloyd, P. and Meegan, R. (1996) Contested governance: European exposure in the English regions, in Alden, J. and Boland, P. (eds) *Regional Development Strategies: a European Perspective*, Jessica Kingsley, London, pp. 55–85.

Lovering J. (1997) *Misleading and Misreading Wales: The New regionalism, Papers in Planning Research 166*, Department of City and Regional Planning, Cardiff University, Cardiff.

Lovering, J. (1999 Theory led by policy: The inadequacies of the 'new regionalism' (illustrated from the case of Wales), *International Journal of Urban and Regional Research*, **23**, 379–95.

Lung, Y. (2004) The changing geography of the European automobile system, *International Journal of Automotive Technology and Management*, 4(2/3), 137–65.

Lynch, P. (1999) New Labour and the English Regional Development Agencies: Devolution as evolution, *Regional Studies*, 31(1), 73–89.

Lyons, Sir M. (2006) *Well Placed to Deliver? Shaping the Pattern of Government Service, Final Report of the Independent Review of Public Sector Relocation*, HM Treasury, London.

MacGinty, R. (2006) 'We'll have more please, but not now and not like that': Public attitudes to the Assembly in Northern Ireland, in Tewdwr-Jones, M. and Allmendinger, P. (eds) *Territory, Identity and Spatial Planning: Spatial Governance in a Fragmented Nation*, Routledge, London, pp. 255–68.

MacKinnon, D. (2011) Reconstructing scale: Towards a new scalar politics, *Progress in Human Geography*, **35**(1), 21–36.

MacLennan, D. (1995) Property, planning and European progress, in Berry, J. and McGreal, S. (eds) *European Cities, Planning Systems and Property Markets*, Spon, London, pp. 395–408.

MacLeod, G. (1999) Place, politics, and 'scale dependence': Exploring the structuration of Euro-regionalism, *European Urban and Regional Studies*, **6**, 231–53.

MacLeod, G. and Goodwin, M. (1999a) Reconstructing an urban and regional political economy: on the state, politics, scale and explanation, *Political Geography*, **18**, 697–730.

MacLeod, G. and Goodwin, M. (1999b) Space, scale and strategy: Rethinking urban and regional governance, *Progress in Human Geography*, **23**, 503–27.

MacLeod, G. and Jones, M. (2006) Mapping the geographies of UK devolution: Institutional legacies, territorial fixes and network typologies, in Tewdwr-Jones, M. and Allmendinger, P. (eds) *Territory, Identity and Spatial Planning: Spatial Governance in a Fragmented Nation*, Routledge, London, pp. 335–52.

MacMillan, T. (2009) The politics of farming carbon, *Food Ethics*, 4(4), 3.

Maier, K. (2010) The pursuit of balanced territorial development: The realities and complexities of the cohesion agenda, in Adams, N., Cotella, G. and Nunes, R. (eds) *Territorial Development, Cohesion and Spatial Planning: Building on EU Enlargement,* Routledge, London.

Majone, G. (1997) From the positive to the regulatory state: Causes and consequences of changes in the mode of governance, *Journal of Public Policy,* **17**(2), 139–67.

Mandelbaum, S. (1996) The talk of the community, in Mandelbaum, S., Mazza, L. and Burchell, R. (eds) *Explorations in Planning Theory,* CUPR, New Brunswick, NJ, pp. 3–10.

Marks, G., Hooghe, L. and Blank, K. (1996) European integration in the 1980s: State-centric v. multi-level governance, *Journal of Common Market Studies,* **34**, 341–78.

Markusen, A. (2003) Fuzzy concepts, scanty evidence, policy distance: The case for rigour and policy relevance in critical regional studies, *Regional Studies,* **37**(6/7), 701–18.

Martin, S. (1999) Picking winners or piloting best value? An analysis of English best value bids, *Local Government Studies,* **25**(2), 102–18.

Martin, S. (2003) Local government research: Carers, coroners or collaborators? Paper presented to the ESRC Seminar Series 'Local Government and Local Governance', University of Birmingham.

Martin, D., Scherr, A. and City, A. (2010) Making law, making place: Lawyers and the production of space, *Progress in Human Geography,* **34**(2), 175–92.

Massey, D. (2005) *For Space,* Sage, London.

Mawson, J. (1997) New Labour and the English regions: A missed opportunity?, *Local Economy,* November, 194–203.

Mawson, J. and Spencer, K. (1997a) The Government Offices for the English Regions: Towards regional governance, *Policy and Politics,* **25**, 71–84.

Mawson, J. and Spencer, K. (1997b The origins and operations of the Government Offices for the Regions, in Bradbury, J. and Mawson, J. (eds) *British Regionalism and Devolution: The Challenges of State Reform and European Integration,* Jessica Kingsley, London, pp. 158–79.

Mayor of London and GLA (2004) *The London Plan: The Spatial Development Strategy for London,* GLA, London.

McCormick, J. (1991) *British Politics and the Environment,* Earthscan, London.

McKinnon, A. (2009) The present and future land requirements of logistical activities, *Land Use Policy,* **26**(1), S293–301.

McKinsey Institute (1998) *Driving Productivity and Growth in the UK Economy,* McKinsey Institute, London.

Meijers, E.J., Waterhout, B. and Zonneveld, W.A.M. (2007) Closing the GAP: Territorial cohesion through polycentric development, *European Journal of Spatial Development,* **24**, October, 1–25.

Molle, W. (2002) Globalization, regionalism and labour markets: Should we recast the foundations of the EU regime in matters of regional (rural and urban) development?, *Regional Studies,* **36**, 161–72.

Monbiot, G. (2011a) How the proposed planning reforms make a mockery of us, *Guardian,* 8 September, accessed online 14 October 2011.

Monbiot, G. (2011b) Our planning system is authorized blackmail – and it's about to get worse, *Guardian*, 26 September, accessed online 14 October 2011.

Monbiot, G. (2011c) This wrecking ball is Osborne's version of sustainable development, *Guardian*, 5 September, accessed online 14 October 2011.

Moniz, A. (1994) *The automobile sector and the organisation of the industrial space: The case of Setubal Region (Portugal)*, Munich Personal RePEc Archive, Paper No. 7503, posted 6 March 2008, available at http://mpra.ub.uni-muenchen.de/7503/ accessed July 2009.

Morgan, K. (1997) The regional animateur: Taking stock of the Welsh Development Agency, *Regional and Federal Studies*, 7(2), 70–94.

Morgan, K. and Nauwelaers, C. (eds) (1999) *Regional Innovation Strategies: The Challenge for Less-Favoured Regions*, Routledge, London.

Morphet, J. (2006) The new localism, in Tewdwr-Jones, M. and Allmendinger, P. (eds) *Territory, Identity and Spatial Planning*, Routledge, London.

Morphet, J. (2007) *Modernising Local Government*, London: Sage.

Morphet, J. (2010) *Effective Spatial Planning in Practice*, Routledge, London.

Morphet, J. et al. (2007) *Shaping and Delivering Tomorrow's Places: Effective Spatial Planning in Practice*, RTPI/CLG, London.

Mulgan, G. (2004) Connexity revisited, in McCarthy, H., Miller, P. and Skidmore, P. (eds) *Britishness: Towards a progressive citizenship*, Smith Institute, London.

Murdoch, J. and Abram, S. (2002) *Rationalities of Planning: Development versus Environment in Planning for Housing*, Ashgate, Aldershot.

Murdoch, J. and Lowe, P. (2003) The preservationist paradox: Modernism, environmentalism and the politics of spatial division, *Transactions of the Institute of British Geographers*, **28**, 318–32.

Murdoch, J. and Tewdwr-Jones, M. (1999) Planning and the English regions: Conflict and convergence amongst the institutions of regional governance, *Environment and Planning C: Government and Policy*, **17**(6), 715–29.

Nadin, V. (2007) The emergence of the spatial planning approach in England, *Planning Practice and Research*, **22**(1), 43–62.

Nadin, V. and Stead, D. (2008) European planning systems, social models and learning, *disP*, **172** (1/2008), 35–47.

Nairn, I. (1955) Outrage: On the disfigurement of town and countryside, special issue, *Architectural Review*.

Needham, B. (2000) Spatial planning as a design discipline: A paradigm for Western Europe?, *Environment and Planning B: Planning and Design*, **27**(3), 437–53.

Newman, J. (2001) *Modernising Governance: New Labour, Policy and Society*, Sage, London.

Newman, P. and Thornley, A. (1996), *Urban Planning in Europe*, Routledge, London.

Newman, P. and Thornley, A. (1997) Fragmentation and centralisation in the governance of London: Influencing the policy and planning agenda, *Urban Studies*, **34**, 967–88.

NOMIS (2011) *Labour Market Statistics*, Office of National Statistics, London.

Nugent, N. (1999) *The Government and Politics of the European Union*, Macmillan, Basingstoke.

Oatley, N. (1995) Competitive urban policy and the regeneration game, *Town Planning Review*, 66(1), 1–14.

ODPM (2002a) *Plans Rationalisation Study, Report by Portico*, ODPM, London.

ODPM (2002b) *Your Region, Your Choice: Revitalising the English Regions*, White Paper, Stationery Office, London.

ODPM (2003a) *Community Involvement in Planning: The Government's Objectives*, ODPM, London.

ODPM (2003b) *Planning, Competitiveness and Productivity. Select Committee on Office of the Deputy Prime Minister: Housing, Planning, Local Government and the Regions. Fourth Report.* Stationery Office, London. HC 114–I.

ODPM (2005) *Planning Policy Statement 1: Delivering Sustainable Development.* Stationery Office, London.

ODPM (2006) *Household projections to 2026*, ODPM, London.

ODPM/Arup (2003) *Creating Local Development Frameworks: Consultation Draft on the Process of Preparing Local Development Frameworks*, ODPM, London.

Office of Rail Regulation (2009) *National rail trends*, available at www.rail-reg.gov.uk

Ohmae, K. (1997) *The End of the Nation State*, HarperCollins, London.

Ohmae, K. (2005) *The Borderless World: Power and Strategy in an Interdependent Economy*, Harper Business, New York.

Olsen, J. (2002) The many faces of Europeanization, *Journal of Common Market Studies*, 40(5), 921–52.

ONS (2008) *Population Projections*, ONS, London, available at http://www.statistics.gov.uk/downloads/theme_population/NPP2008/NatPopProj2008.pdf

ONS (2011) *Population Trends 145*, ONS, London.

O'Riordan, T. (2004) Environmental science, sustainability and politics, *Transactions of British Geographers*, 29, 234–47.

Osborne, G. (2011) The Budget Statement 2011, Stationery Office, London.

Osborne, D. and Gaebler, T. (1993) *Reinventing Government: How the Entrepreneurial Spirit is Transforming the Public Sector*, Penguin, New York.

Owens, S. and Cowell, R. (2010) *Land and Limits: Interpreting Sustainability in the Planning Process*, Routledge, London.

Paddison, R. (1997) The restructuring of local government in Scotland, in Bradbury, J. and Mawson, J. (eds) *British Regionalism and Devolution: The Challenge of State Reform and European Integration*, Jessica Kingsley, London.

Painter, J. and Goodwin, M. (1996) Local governance, the crises of Fordism and the changing geographies of regulation, *Transaction of the Institute of British Geographers*, 21, 635–48.

Parkinson, M. et al. (1992) *Urbanisation and the Function of Cities in the European Community*, European Institute of Urban Affairs, Liverpool John Moores University, Liverpool.

Paterson, L. (1998) Scottish Home Rule: Radical break or pragmatic adjustment?, in Elcock, H. and Keating, M. (eds) *Remaking the Union. Devolution and British Politics in the 1990s*, Frank Cass, London

Pearce, G. and Ayres, S. (2006) New patterns of governance in the English region: Assessing their implications for spatial planning, *Environment and Planning C: Government and Policy*, 24(6), 909–27.

Peck, J. (1995) Moving and shaking: Business elites, state localism, and urban privatism, *Progress in Human Geography*, **19**, 16–46.

Peck, J. and Tickell (1994) Too many partners: The future for regeneration partnerships, *Local Economy*, **9**(3), 251–65.

Peck, J. and Tickell, A. (1995) The social regulation of uneven development: 'Regulatory deficit', England's South East, and the collapse of Thatcherism, *Environment and Planning A*, **27**, 15–40.

Peters, D. (2003) Cohesion, polycentricity, missing links and bottlenecks: Conflicting spatial storylines for pan-European transport investments, *European Planning Studies*, **11**(3).

Phelps, N.A. and Raines, P. (eds) (2003) *The New Competition for Inward Investment: Firms, Institutions and Territorial Development*. Edward Elgar, Cheltenham.

Phelps, N.A. and Tewdwr-Jones, M. (1998) Institutional capacity building in a strategic policy vacuum: The case of the Korean firm LG in South Wales, *Environment and Planning C, Government & Policy*, **16**(6): 735–55.

Phelps, N.A. and Tewdwr-Jones, M. (2000) Scratching the surface of collaborative and associative governance: The diversity of social action in institutional capacity building, *Environment and Planning A 32*, **32**(1), 111–30.

Phelps, N.A. and Tewdwr-Jones, M. (2001) Globalisation, regions and the state: Exploring the limits of economic modernisation through inward investment, *Urban Studies*, 38(8), 1253–72.

Phelps, N.A. and Tewdwr-Jones, M. (2004) Institutions, collaborative governance and the diversity of social action, in Wood, A. and Valler, D. (eds) *Governing Local and Regional Economies: Institutions, Politics and Economic Development*, Ashgate, Aldershot, pp. 93–120.

Pratchett, L. (2004) Local autonomy, local democracy and the 'New Localism', *Political Studies*, **52**, 358–75.

Putnam, R. (2000) *Bowling Alone*, Simon & Schuster, London.

Raco, M. (1998) Assessing 'institutional thickness' in the local context: A comparison of Cardiff and Sheffield, *Environment and Planning A*, **30**, 975–96.

Raco, M. (2000) Assessing community participation in local economic development: Lessons for the new urban policy, *Political Geography*, **19**, 573–99.

Raco, M. (2006) Building new subjectivities: Regional identities and the re-scaling of politics, in Tewdwr-Jones, M. and Allmendinger, P. (eds) *Territory, Identity and Spatial Planning: Spatial Governance in a Fragmented Nation*, Routledge, London, pp. 320–34.

Raco, M., Parker, G. and Doak, J. (2006) Reshaping spaces of local governance? Community strategies and the modernization of local government in England, *Environment and Planning C: Government and Policy*, **24**, 475–96.

Radaelli, C.M. (2003) The Europeanization of public policy, in Featherstone, K. and Radaelli, C.M. (eds) *The Politics of Europeanization*, Oxford University Press, Oxford, pp. 27–56.

Radaelli, C.M. (2004) Europeanization: Solution or problem?, *European Integration Online Papers*, 8(16), available at http://eiop.or.at/eiop/texte/2004–016a.htm

Ray, L. (1999) Measuring party orientations towards European integration: Results from an expert survey, *European Journal of Political Research*, 36(2), 283–306.

Reade, E. (1987) *British Town and Country Planning*, Open University Press, Milton Keynes.

Rhodes, M. and van Appeldoorn, B. (1998) Capital unbound? The transformation of European corporate governance, *Journal of European Public Policy*, 5, 406–27.

Rhodes, R.A.W. (1995) *The New Governance: Governing Without Government*, ESRC, Swindon.

Rhodes, R.A.W. (1997) *Understanding Governance: Policy Networks, Governance, Reflexivity and* Accountability, Open University Press, Buckingham and Philadelphia.

Richards, D. and Smith, M.J. (2002) *Governance and Public Policy in the UK*, Oxford University Press, Oxford.

Rittel, H. and Webber, M. (1973) Dilemmas in a general theory of planning, *Policy Sciences*, 4, 155–9.

Roberts, P. (1996) Regional planning guidance in England and Wales: Back to the future?, *Town Planning Review*, 67(1), 97–109.

Roberts, P. and Lloyd, M.G. (1999) Institutional aspects of regional planning, management and development: Models and lessons from the English experience, *Environment and Planning B: Planning and Design*, 26, 517–31.

Roberts, P., Thomas, K. and Williams, G. (eds) (1999) *Metropolitan Planning in Britain: A Comparative Study*, Jessica Kingsley, London.

Rodriguez-Pose, A. (2008) The rise of the 'city-region' concept and its development policy implications, *European Planning Studies*, 16(8), 1025–46.

Rodriguez-Pose, A. and Fratesi, U. (2004) Between development and social policies: The impact of European Structural Funds in Objective 1 regions, *Regional Studies*, 38(1), 97–113.

Rowan-Robinson, J., Lloyd, M.G. and Elliot, R.G. (1987) National planning guidelines and strategic planning, *Town Planning Review*, 58(4), 369–81.

RTPI (2003) *A New Vision for Planning*, RTPI, London.

Rydin, Y. (1999) Public participation in planning, in Cullingworth, B., *British Planning: 50 Years of Urban and Regional Policy*, Athlone, London and New Brunswick, NJ.

Rydin, Y. (2003) *Conflict, Consensus, and Rationality in Environmental Planning: An Institutional Discourse Approach*. Oxford University Press, Oxford.

Rydin, Y., Thornley, A., Scanlon, K. and West, K. (2004) The Greater London Authority: A clash of organizational cultures, *Environment and Planning C: Government and Policy*, 22, 55–76.

Sager T. (1994) *Communicative Planning Theory*, Avebury, Aldershot.

Sandercock, L. (2003) *Cosmopolis II: Mongrel Cities in the Twenty-First Century*, Continuum, London.

SCETR (Select Committee on Environment, Transport and Regional Affairs) (1998) Regional *Development Agencies – First Report*, HM Stationery Office, London.

Scharpf, F.W. (1999) *Governing in Europe: Effective and Democratic?*, Oxford University Press, Oxford.

Schmidt, V.A. (2002) Does discourse matter in the politics of welfare adjustment?, *Comparative Political Studies*, **35**(2), 168–93.

Scott, A.J. (1983) Industrial organisation and the logic of intra-metropolitan location, I: Theoretical considerations, *Economic Geography*, **59**, 233–50.

Scott, A.J. (1986) Industrial organisation and location: Division of labour, the firm and spatial process, *Economic Geography*, **62**, 215–31.

Scott, A.J. (1996) Regional motors of the global economy, *Futures*, **28**(5), 391–411.

Scott, A.J. (1998) *Regions and the World Economy: The Coming Shape of Global Production, Competition and Political Order*, Oxford University Press, Oxford.

Scottish Executive (2004) *National Planning Framework for Scotland*, Scottish Executive, Edinburgh.

Scottish Government (2008) *National Spatial Planning Framework*, Scottish Government, Edinburgh.

Scottish Government (2011) *Land Use Strategy*, Scottish Government, Edinburgh.

Scottish Office (1997) *Scotland's Parliament, White Paper*, Stationery Office, London.

Scottish Office (1999) *Land Use Planning Under a Scottish Parliament*, Scottish Office, Edinburgh.

Selman, P. (2006) *Planning at the Landscape Scale*, Routledge, London.

Sharp, T. (1940) *Town Planning*, Penguin, Harmondsworth.

Shaw, K. and Greenhalgh, P. (2011) Revisiting the 'missing middle' in English sub national governance, *Local Economy*, **25**(5/6), 457–75.

Shaw, D. and Sykes, O. (2005) Addressing connectivity in spatial planning: The case of the English regions, *Planning Theory and Practice*, **6**(1), 11–33.

Shutt, J. and Colwell (1998) Towards 2006: European Union regional policy and UK local government: A new regional agenda, *European Planning Studies*, **6**(6), 709–29.

Smith, N. (1995) Remaking scale: Competition and cooperation in prenational and postnational Europe, in Eskelinen, H. and Snickars, F. (eds) *Competitive European Peripheries*, Springer, Berlin, pp. 59–74.

South African Presidency (2006) *National Spatial Development Perspective for South Africa*, CSIR Project Team, Policy Unit, South African Government.

Spanou, C. (1998) European integration in administrative terms: A framework for analysis and the Greek case, *Journal of European Public Policy*, **5**(3), 467–84.

Stamp, L.D. (1948) *The Land of Britain, Its Use and Misuse*, Longmans, Green, London.

Starkie, D. (1982), *The Motorway Age*, Pergamon, Oxford.

Stern, N.H. (2006) *The Economics of Climate Change*, Stationery Office, London.

Stoker, G. (1990) Regulation theory, local government and transition from Fordism, in King, D. and Pierre, J. (eds) *Challenges to Local Government*, Sage, London, pp. 242–64.

Stoker, G. (ed) (2000) *The New Politics of British Local Governance*, Macmillan, London.

Stoker, G. (2004a) New localism, progressive politics and democracy, *Political Quarterly*, 75(1), 117–29.

Stoker, G. (2004b) *Transforming Local Governance: From Thatcher to New Labour*, Palgrave Macmillan, Basingstoke.

Stoker, G. and Young, S. (1993) *Cities in the 1990s*, Longman, Harlow.

Storper, M. (1997) *The Regional World: Territorial Development in a Global Economy*, Guilford, London.

Swanwick, C. (2009) Society's attitudes to and preferences for land and landscape, *Land Use Policy*, 26(1), S62–75.

Switzer, J.F.Q. (1984) The significance of circulars in the planning process, *Journal of Planning and Environment Law*, 46, 106–16.

Swyngedouw, E. (2005) 'Glocalization' and the contested politics of scale: Scalar reconfiguration, autocratic governance and contested citizenship, in Delladetsima, P., Hadjimichalis, C., Hastoaoglou, V., Matouvalou, M. and Vaiou, D. (eds) *Rethinking Radical Spatial Approaches: 20 Years of the Aegean*, Harokopio University, Thessaloniki.

Swyngedouw, E. and Baeten, G. (2001) Scaling the city: The political economy of 'glocal' development – Brussels' conundrum, *European Planning Studies*, 9(7), 827–49.

Taussik, J. and Smalley, J. (1998) Partnerships in the 1990s: Derby's successful City Challenge bid, *Planning Practice and Research*, 13(3), 283–97.

Taylor, N. (2003) More or less meaningful concepts in planning theory (and how to make them more meaningful): A plea for conceptual analysis and precision, *Planning Theory* 2(2), 91–100.

Taylor, N. (2010) What is this thing called spatial planning? An analysis of the British government's view, *Town Planning Review*, 81(2), 193–208.

TCPA (1997) *Regional Development Agencies: Ensuring Sustainable Regional Planning and Development*, Town and Country Planning Association, London.

TEC National Council (1997) *Regional Development Principles*, TEC National Council, London.

Tewdwr-Jones, M. (ed.) (1996) *British Planning Policy in Transition: Planning in the 1990s*, UCL Press, London.

Tewdwr-Jones, M. (1999) Discretion, certainty, and flexibility in British planning: Emerging political tensions and inherent ideological conflicts, *Journal of Planning Education and Research*, 18(2), 244–56.

Tewdwr-Jones, M. (2002) *The Planning Policy: Planning, Government and the Policy Process*, Routledge, London.

Tewdwr-Jones, M. (2004) Spatial planning: principles, practice and culture, *Journal of Planning and Environment Law*, 57(5), 560–9.

Tewdwr-Jones, M. (2008) The complexity of planning reform: A search for the spirit and purpose of planning, *Town Planning Review*, 79(6), 673–88.

Tewdwr-Jones, M. (2011a) A delicate balance: Localism and planning, *Town and Country Planning*, 80(1), 29–32.

Tewdwr-Jones, M. (2011b) *Urban Reflections: Narratives of Place, Planning and Change*, Policy Press, Bristol.

Tewdwr-Jones, M. and Allmendinger, P. (1998) Deconstructing communicative rationality: A critique of Habermasian collaborative planning, *Environment and Planning A*, 30, 1975–90 .

Tewdwr-Jones, M. and Allmendinger, P. (eds) (2006) *Territory, Identity and Spatial Planning: Spatial Governance in a Fragmented Nation*, Routledge, London.

Tewdwr-Jones, M., Bishop, K. and Wilkinson, D. (2000) 'Euroscepticism', political agendas and spatial planning: British national and regional planning policy in uncertain times, *European Planning Studies* 8(5), 655–72.

Tewdwr-Jones, M., Gallent, N. and Morphet, J. (2010) An anatomy of spatial planning: Coming to terms with the spatial element in UK planning, *European Planning Studies*, 18, 239–57.

Tewdwr-Jones, M. and Lloyd, M.G. (1997) Unfinished business, *Town and Country Planning*, November, 302–4.

Tewdwr-Jones, M. and McNeill, D. (2000) The politics of city–region planning and governance: Reconciling the national, regional and urban in the competing voices of institutional restructuring, *European Urban and Regional Studies*, 7(2), 119–34.

Tewdwr-Jones, M., Morphet, J. and Allmendinger, P. (2006) The contested strategies of local governance: Community strategies, development plans, and local government modernization, *Environment and Planning A*, 38(3), 533–51.

Tewdwr-Jones, M. and Phelps, N.A. (2000) Levelling the uneven playing field: Inward investment, inter-regional rivalry and the planning system, *Regional Studies*, 34(5), 429–40.

Tewdwr-Jones, M. and Thomas, H. (1998) Collaborative action in local plan making: Planners' perceptions of 'planning through debate', *Environment and Planning B, Planning and Design*, 25, 127–44.

Tewdwr-Jones, M. and Williams, R.H. (2001) *The European Dimension of British Planning*, Spon, London.

Thomas, K. (1999) The metropolitan planning experience, in Roberts, P., Thomas, K. and Williams, G. (eds.) *Metropolitan Planning in Britain: A Comparative Study*, Jessica Kingsley, London, pp. 213–34.

Thomas, K.P. (2000) *Competing for Capital: Europe and North America in a Global Era*, University of Georgetown Press, Washington, DC.

Thornley, A. (1991) *Urban Planning Under Thatcherism*, Routledge, London.

Tilson, B. et al. (1997) Partnerships for regeneration: The Single Regeneration Budget Challenge Fund round one, *Local Government Studies*, 23(1), 1–15.

Tomaney, J. (2000) End of the empire state? New Labour and devolution in the United Kingdom, *International Journal of Urban and Regional Research*, 24(3), 677–90.

Tomaney, J. (2002) The evolution of regionalism in England, *Regional Studies*, 36(7), 721–31.

Travers, T. (2003) *The Politics of London: Governing and Ungovernable City*, Palgrave Macmillan, Basingstoke.

Upham, P. et al. (2009) *Public Attitudes to Environmental Change: A Selective Review of Theory and Practice. Research Synthesis for the Living with Environmental Change Programme*. NERC, Swindon.

Vigar, G., Healey, P., Hull, A. and Davoudi, S. (2000) *Planning, Governance and Spatial Strategy in Britain: An Institutionalist Analysis*, Macmillan, London.

Vogel, S. (1996) *Freer Markets, More Rules: Regulatory Reform in Advanced Industrial Countries.* Cornell University Press, Ithaca, NY.

WAG (2005) *People, Places, Futures: The Wales Spatial Plan*, Welsh Assembly Government, Cardiff.

Wannop, U.A. (1995) *The Regional Imperative: Regional Planning and Governance in Britain, Europe and the United States*, Jessica Kingsley, London.

Ward, K. (1997) The Single Regeneration Budget and the issue of local flexibility' *Regional Studies*, 31, 78–81.

Waterhout, B. (2008) *The Institutionalization of European Spatial Planning*, IOS, Delft.

Welsh Office (1997) *A Voice for Wales, White Paper*, Stationery Office, London.

While, A. (1999) Looking for regional politics: the logics of institution-building in two English regions, mimeo, copy available from author, CUDEM, Leeds Metropolitan University, Brunswick Building, Leeds LS2 8BU.

While, A., Jonas, A. and Gibbs, D. (2004) Unblocking the city? Growth pressures, collective provision and the search for new spaces of governance in Greater Cambridge, England, *Environment & Planning A*, 36, 279–304.

Wilkinson, D. and Applebee, E. (1999) *Implementing Holistic Government*, Policy Press, Bristol.

Wilkinson, R. (2000) New labour and the global economy, in Coates, D. and Lawler, P. (eds) *New Labour in Power*, Manchester University Press, Manchester.

Williams, G. (1999) Metropolitan governance and strategic planning: A review of experience in Manchester, Melbourne and Toronto, *Progress in Planning*, 52(1), 1–100.

Williams, R.H. (1996) *European Union Spatial Policy and Planning*, Paul Chapman, London.

Wilson, D. and Game, C. (2002) *Local Government in the United Kingdom*. Palgrave Macmillan, Basingstoke.

Wong, C., Baker, M. and Kidd, S. (2006) Monitoring spatial strategies: The case of local development documents in England, *Environment and Planning C: Government and Policy*, 24(4), 533–52.

Wong, C., Ravetz, J. and Turner, J. (2000) *The United Kingdom Spatial Planning Framework: A Discussion*, RTPI, London.

Xu, J. and Yeh, A. (2005) City repositioning and competitiveness building in regional development: New development strategies of Guangzhou, China, *International Journal of Urban and Regional Research*, 29(2), 283–308.

Yeung, H.W.C. (1998) Capital, state and space: Contesting the borderless world, *Transactions of the Institute of British Geographers*, 23, 291–309.

Zetter, J. (2001) Spatial planning in the European Union, in Faludi, A. (ed.) *European Spatial Planning*, Lincoln Institute of Land Policy, Cambridge, MA, pp. 179–91.

Zonnenveld, W. and Faludi, A. (1996) Cohesion versus competitive position: A new direction for European spatial planning, paper presented at the ACSP-AESOP Joint International Congress, Toronto, 24–28 July.

Index

Lightning Source UK Ltd.
Milton Keynes UK
UKHW02f1822220718

326107UK00012B/278/P